DATE DUE		
MAR 1 1 1993		
NOV 0 6 2003		
DEC 04 11		

GAYLORD 234   PRINTED IN U.S.A.

MARGARET SANGER:
PIONEER OF THE FUTURE

By the same author | REMEMBER THE LADIES

EMILY TAFT DOUGLAS

Margaret Sanger: Pioneer of the Future

HOLT, RINEHART AND WINSTON
New York · Chicago · San Francisco

Published simultaneously in Canada by Holt, Rinehart
and Winston of Canada, Limited.

Library of Congress Catalog Card Number: 72-80339

First Edition

Designer: Golda Fishbein
SBN:03-081844-3
Printed in the United States of America

Acknowledgments

For nearly three years I have lived in the exhilarating if incorporeal company of Margaret Sanger. Because I had no former acquaintance, my comrade was admittedly the product of her writing, the views of others and the tons of material, including intimate correspondence, divided between the Library of Congress and Smith College.

Since documentation on this much publicized woman is vast and since she lived until the fall of 1966, I had assumed that all important facts were known, but was dismayed to find no firm skeletal framework. The three official biographies, all out of print and two of which she wrote, are almost devoid of dates. Contemporary accounts, such as *Who's Who,* either give no dates or wrong ones. Her obituaries agree that she was born in 1883, but this turns out to be the birth year of her younger sister.

Some of the uncertainties arose because Margaret Sanger was a natural storyteller who stressed vivid impressions, not chronology. Most of the omissions were deliberate. As the leader of a cause widely thought to be obscene, if not subversive, she simply avoided some items which might have helped her enemies. Furthermore, always looking much younger than her years, she encouraged the illusion by suppressing telltale dates. Without the help of her relatives, I might never have established even the starting point.

Of those whom I consulted, I am most grateful to her family who answered my questions with candor and patience. Dr. Grant Sanger interrupted a busy schedule to give me several hours and cheerfully replied to later queries. Olive Byrne Richard, Mrs. Sanger's niece, and Margaret Sanger Marston, her granddaughter, not only shared their memories, but their scrapbooks of personal letters and clippings. Dr. Stuart Sanger answered my written questions from Mexico, and Robert Higgins, the one surviving brother, received me in his home at College Park, Pennsylvania, a few months before he died.

For the untold story of the famous "pill," I am indebted to Dr. John Rock, Dr. Hudson Hoagland and William H. Bemis, Mrs. Stanley McCormick's lawyer. For special insights, I thank Morris Ernst, who won the notable "One Package" court victory, Anna Lifshiz, the secretary with unique memories, and several long time friends: Senator Ernest Gruening, Dr. Stuart Mudd, Dorothy Gordon, Florence Stephenson Mahoney, Mrs. Max Freedman and Mrs. William Benton. Florence Rose, Mrs. Sanger's aide for thirteen years, loaned me her cherished collection of papers shortly before her death. The film and recordings that the Planned Parenthood of America made available supplied useful background.

At the Library of Congress, where I worked for more than a year, I owe special thanks to Legare H. B. Obear and to the Legislative Reference Service and the Japanese Section of the Orientalia Division which tracked down elusive points. To no one am I more indebted than to Elizabeth S. Duvall, Bibliographer of the Sophia Smith Collection at Smith College. Her aid was constant, many-sided, and resourceful.

Contents

Sixteen pages of black and white photographs follow page 116.

MARGARET SANGER:
PIONEER OF THE FUTURE

Retrospect

On her good days when her mind was clear, Margaret Sanger read the letters and clippings that still poured in to her. Although bedridden, she could not complain, since she was eighty-six years old. Propped up on her pillows at the nursing home, she tried to ignore her infirmities, as she had often done in the past, but now, instead of forcing herself on to new efforts, she indulged in memories of the enormous victory, the triumph of her cause.

What was it H. G. had said? That Margaret Sanger was the greatest woman in the world? Extravagant, of course, but there was something else, less personal, more significant. Wells was always talking of the future and he had predicted. . . . Yes, that was it. He had predicted that within a hundred years the movement that she had started would be the most influential of all time in controlling man's destiny on earth. Already in 1966, less than half a century later, the changes had begun to equal her titanic hopes.

When she started her crusade, in 1914, federal, state and local laws were all arraigned against her. She was jailed eight times. The medical profession denounced her, the churches excoriated her, the press condemned her and even liberal reformers shunned her. She entered the fight alone, a frail young woman without much education, with no social or financial backing, with nothing but conviction. Yet step by step, she made her points and eventually won her battles.

At first even her friends opposed her tactics. Those who approved her goal said that she must change the laws as reformers did in other fields. But at that period, legislative relief at any government level was as remote as the chance for Negroes in the Deep South to gain their civil rights by state action. Indeed, for all the later efforts of many people, including herself, most of the laws still remain on the books exactly as they were when she began her fight.

Her winning strategy was to secure new interpretations of existing laws. After challenging the restraints, she appealed the judgments of the lower courts and was upheld by the broader views of the upper courts. Thus she won *de facto* repeal of restrictions long before the civil rights leaders followed the same course.

And what had these legal changes accomplished? Margaret Sanger, immobile though she was in the nursing home, once more zestfully reviewed the milestones of her career. Birth control instruction, which she had introduced at the Brownsville clinic, had spread across the nation to countless clinics, hospitals, and health services. That was not all, for she had carried her message around the globe on mammoth lecture tours. Five times she had campaigned in Japan, and today that country offers triumphant proof that planning can halt a runaway population.

In the twenties, she conceived and set up the first World Population Conference at Geneva. After World War II, when she was seventy-three, she organized the International Planned Parenthood Federation, and as its president for six years, she built its strength. Today with fifty member nations, the federation gives birth control instruction to twice that number of countries.

Hers was the steady, driving force in the development of modern contraceptives. At home, she had to start by educating the hostile medical profession, which she did through instructional clinics and by financing a full-time lecturer to speak before the state and local associations. The most persuasive argument came from her own Medical Research Bureau, whose unprecedented body of case histories not only confirmed the need of child spacing, but assessed the value of current techniques. This pioneer body of statistics inspired the first studies in birth control and family living.

At Zurich, in 1930, she mounted an international conference

where doctors and scientists considered physiological problems. In the next decades, channeling funds into promising studies, she became the catalyst for biochemical research. Just as the American Polio Foundation gave the impetus for the development of vaccines, her efforts led to cheap, safe, and effective ways to turn the rich lady's privilege into protection for the poor. She democratized the movement.

But the test of her work, as Margaret Sanger always insisted, was not measured in abstractions, but in the reduction of human tragedies. Today birth control not only saves the lives of countless mothers, but enhances the health and happiness of many times that number. Where it is used, it ends the nightmare of constant pregnancy and of bearing more children than the parents can support. It introduces the spacing of babies for optimum welfare and gives mothers the basic right of determining their maternity.

Perhaps above all, her influence was in teaching people to accept sex as it is, a part of life that needs a rational response. When she was young, the very word was outlawed in polite society. Nice girls grew up in ignorance of their own anatomy, while, on the other hand, boys were encouraged to face the facts of life with guffaws, in brothels and accommodated by a white slave traffic. Before she started her campaign, the law had suppressed her article, *What Every Girl Should Know*. Today public schools teach the physiological facts for which she was once censored.

And how did all these changes come about? She used to say, in Victor Hugo's words, that there was no force so great as an idea whose hour had struck. A technological age had created the hour and she was the alarm that aroused the lethargic world. Some thought her leadership as unlikely as that of the fifteenth-century peasant girl to whom she was so often compared, the girl who led the King's defeated army to victory. Again extravagant! But at least they shared the same devotion to their cause. They let nothing stand in their way, not health, money, security, family or friends. Her friends? She made them work, starting with that brilliant galaxy of English authors who first espoused her views. Early in life she had closed her heart to every other need so that she might fulfill this one.

People smiled at her Celtic mysticism, but she saw a unifying force, like a thread of destiny, determining her career. In her mother's early death she had glimpsed the results of birth by chance, not choice. In her own tuberculosis, twice activated by pregnancy, and in the sufferings of her patients, she had learned the ravages of the old way. Her life was of one piece, all fashioned to her task.

From her window in the nursing home, Margaret Sanger watched the sun go down and the world grow dark. In just one night, by tomorrow's sunrise, there would be 160,000 more babies on the earth. This quickening growth put her achievements in agonizing perspective. At this rate, world population would double before the next century and triple not long after and so advance with ever-increasing speed. Technology had postponed the old restraints—famines and plagues—but had brought new evils. Man was overloading the once clean air, water supplies, even the earth itself, as well as all utilities and cultural institutions. Sheer proliferation was lowering standards to meet the needs of quantity. Experts agreed that her program now offered the only hope of progress with peace and rational solutions, but the will to promote it was still lacking.

In the darkening room Margaret Sanger closed her eyes. As a last legacy, she longed to leave her sense of urgency in coping with mankind's supreme challenge.

As the Twig Was Bent

1

It was eleven o'clock, dark and cold, when Michael Hennessy Higgins, the red-headed sculptor of tombstone angels—yet a free-thinker himself—placed a bag of plaster and some tools in a wheel-barrow, signaled to his ten-year-old daughter, Margaret, and started to the graveyard. A few hours earlier, taking her hand, he had told her that he would need help and so she had proudly sat up, wondering what more she could do.

That day they had buried her four-year-old brother, Henry George Higgins. Since he had not responded to his father's home-made croup remedies, death had called for the first time at his home which had known only birth.

Margaret herself was the sixth child, born in Corning, New York, 1879, and since then babies had come so fast that they created no more excitement than a litter of kittens. Two years earlier Margaret had helped wash a fourteen-pound boy who had given her mother a difficult time. As usual, her father had pulled his wife through with the help of his favorite prescription, "good whiskey." He had not lost any of their eleven large babies, although his wife was weaker after each birth and coughed more. Today her grief deepened as she realized that there was not even a snapshot of her boy's darling face.

Just outside the graveyard Michael Higgins hid the lantern un-der a bush, telling Margaret to swing the light if anyone ap-proached. Her heart jumped at the sight of a white figure, but she stifled her scream when she realized that it was only one of her father's marble angels. Since he was treating her like an adult, she tried to act like one and was soon reassured when she heard the nearby sound of his shovel and then a thud when it struck the casket.

In her several accounts of that night, Margaret later wrote that she had not known that it was against the law to dig up the dead, but had she known, it would not have mattered, since she had complete faith in her father who set her standards of right. Nevertheless, this was the longest hour that she had lived through.

For two evenings Margaret helped in the workshop while her father broke the death mask made in the graveyard, poured the mould and finished the cast. Then he led his family into the studio to unveil the head. To the brokenhearted mother it was a wonderful comfort, as well as a unique tribute of love from a husband who often failed in his role of breadwinner.

He would have failed less often had he been more single-minded. This graveyard sculptor, with his rich Irish brogue, had once been a soldier-hero, then a medical student and a member of the Noble Order of the Knights of Labor, but above all, he was a philosopher. Human freedom was his passion and to him that meant freedom of thought and religion, free trade, free schools, textbooks and libraries. At this time he was absorbed in Henry George, whose *Progress and Poverty* stood in his meager library along with the *Bible,* a world history, *Aesop's Fables* and a book on phrenology. Although the small boy who had died was the author's namesake, the choice of names could not have pleased his mother, since Henry George had been the cause of one of the couple's few conflicts.

Michael Higgins had conceived a bold educational project for his town. He had ensured the presence of Corning's fifty leading citizens at a lecture by Henry George by inviting them all to a hotel banquet. No one recalled much about the speech, but for the Higgins family, it was a long cold winter. Michael had paid for the dinner from the joint funds saved up for fuel. During the winter months, his wife could not forget that the children of the gentlemen who had enjoyed the feast were always warm, well-fed, and pampered.

The Higgins children were never pampered. Dressed in hand-me-downs, thriftily fed, and without any spending money, they went to work as soon as possible. The older ones, who had already left home, helped with the family finances.

Since Margaret came in the middle, she was the big sister of the younger four. She had her mother's wide-set eyes and erect carriage and like her sisters, was small-boned and slender. The boys took after their brawny father and all of the young Higginses had a touch of red in their hair, running from Margaret's chestnut to the bright carrot of a younger brother.

Enterprising, as well as poor, the youngsters developed great resourcefulness. The girls could do anything about a home: cook, sew, launder, take care of babies, upholster the furniture, and fix the plumbing. There was not much time for play, but on holidays the boys and girls went swimming, skating, or rabbit hunting in the woods. On Saturdays, they often staged theatricals in the barn, where Margaret showed a flair for recitation.

Lack of pocket money inspired Margaret's own views on the progress and poverty of the early eighteen-nineties. She saw that the rich lived on the pleasant hillsides of Corning in large houses with well-tended lawns where they played croquet or tennis. Even the adults played or strolled hand in hand with their children. The mothers looked young and stylish, and their little girls skipped about in brand-new dresses. Watching them, Margaret noticed that the rich had few children.

Down by the river flats sprawled the glass factories, whose belching smokestacks dirtied the neighborhood. A dozen shrieking children swarmed around each of the ugly little houses, convincing Margaret that large families went with poverty, noise and violence. Small families meant wealth, leisure and fun with parents.

As a craftsman with a monopoly on graveyard sculpture, Michael Higgins's future should have been assured, but as his family grew, his income dropped. This was the result of another attempt to edify his city. Hearing that the famous social crusader, Colonel Robert Ingersoll, was booked for a nearby lecture, Higgins hastened to secure him for Corning. This time he promised his wife that the feast would be purely intellectual and paid for by advance subscriptions. The only hall in town was managed by the Catholic priest, Father Coughlan, a kindly man who, enjoying arguments with the best talker in town, was glad to accommodate him.

But reports about Ingersoll finally reached Father Coughlan also. He heard that the man was a blasphemer. He had once challenged God—"if there was such a one"—to smite him there on the platform. In spite of his agreement and advance payment, Father Coughlan could not risk such a scandal.

Margaret was with her father when he escorted Colonel Ingersoll, this other tall, red-headed, and kindly looking man, to the hall. From a distance they saw a good crowd waiting, but when they arrived, they found the door locked. Boys started booing and throwing tomatoes, while their once friendly townsmen had turned into an angry, snarling mob. Michael Higgins glared around at those trying to suppress free speech. He brushed a squashed tomato from his cheek and then on the spur of the moment, announced that the talk would be given within the hour in the wood-clearing near his home on the outskirts of town.

Down the street he set off with his red head very high, leading the Colonel, whose red head was also high. Clutching her father's hand, and her posture as proud as she could manage, Margaret trotted at his side. Those who had come to hear and not to stop the speaking, fell in behind them and were soon seated under fragrant pine trees. The sun set in a blaze of glory, making a proper setting for the fiery orator. But again, the results of the meeting were more memorable than what was said.

Next morning, when Margaret led the younger Higginses past the parochial school on their daily three-mile hike to the public school, they were greeted by shrieks of "Devil's children! Heathens!" In the future, there was a rift between the Higgins youngsters and their neighbors. Increasingly the family depended on itself and lived apart from the community. Far worse for the children than the social ostracism was the economic boycott of their father. There were no more local orders for tombstone angels, and he had to go far afield for commissions.

Michael Higgins used to boast that while he could not give his children riches, he left them "unchained from dogmas." Some of his children grew up resentful of his trouble-making independence.

More than the others, Margaret patterned herself on him, learning to make up her own mind and hold steadfast, in spite of public opinion. In later years she felt that her childhood had been hard, but had prepared her for the future. Vaguely she saw that her father's independence was related to his physical courage, on which were based the many stories of his youth.

As a lad of thirteen, newly arrived from Ireland, Michael had answered Lincoln's call for volunteers by trying to enlist. He had to wait for his fifteenth birthday before the Twelfth New York Cavalry accepted him as drummer boy. Once, single-handedly, he had captured a Confederate captain on his mule and he always insisted that the latter was more valued than the former. General Sherman had cited the boy for bravery, but by mid-life Michael Higgins was more concerned with intellectual than with physical courage.

As though foreseeing from her father's example that courage must be her chief resource, the shy Margaret set out to conquer her own fears. She learned to go to bed without a candle and to jump, like her big brothers, from the rafters in the barn to the hayloft thirty feet below. Then she faced her worst test, an ordeal that she thought important enough to repeat at some length in her two autobiographical accounts.

In Corning, the Erie Railroad crossed the Chemung River on a narrow iron span which men used as a short cut. Margaret's father had once helped her across by lifting her over the wide gaps, but the experience had terrified her. For that very reason, and in spite of the fact that it was forbidden, she decided that she must cross the bridge alone.

Halfway over she heard the dreaded hum of an oncoming train, and she stumbled. Perhaps that saved her life. She fell between the iron ties, over which she instinctively curled her arms. Unable to pull herself up again, she dangled there over the deep, rapid river. In a moment, the cars rushed down upon her and the wheels crashed over her head. Numbed and helpless, she hung there as the train thundered across the bridge. Providentially, a fisherman below saw the child and rescued her. He gave her two smacks on the rear, faced her toward home and went back down to his line.

Margaret turned around again. Since the trip was as long one way as the other, she decided to fulfill, not fail, her test and in a few minutes she arrived triumphant on the other side. Although she took the long, safe way home, and her arms were bruised and bleeding, she had not learned to be cautious. Inwardly, she was excited by a new self-confidence. She began to feel that Margaret Higgins could achieve what she set out to do. In her Corning days, she had no idea what she wanted to achieve, but her father said that everyone should leave the world better for having lived in it and she meant to leave it very much better.

Michael Higgins stretched his daughter's thoughts toward general welfare, but her mother was the practical guardian of the family welfare. While he was enjoying a book which he sometimes shared with his children, she was usually ironing those white starched shirts on which he prided himself. Rarely did she find an hour to sit down. Yet for all her cares and gentle nature, she too had an independent spirit. She banned corporal punishment and said that scoldings should be given in private. She was the peacemaker, as well as the champion of any child who suffered injustice. When a teacher beat her young son Joe, she walked miles to give that teacher a tongue lashing. Afterward, she made her reluctant husband report the matter to the Board of Education, which, after inquiry, fired the offender.

If Joe was bruised by a teacher who beat her pupils, his sister was bruised by one who humiliated them. Margaret had almost finished eighth grade when she arrived a few minutes late one morning and was greeted by a tirade of sarcasm from the teacher. Some of the boys, welcoming a distraction from their lesson, prolonged the scolding with appreciative guffaws. On and on went both the abuse and the laughter until Margaret decided that she had had enough. She stacked up her books and marched out of the room.

Back home, she announced that she would never return to that school. Her horrified parents protested that there were only two more weeks before graduation. What would become of her, a dropout from eighth grade? When she set her chin in what they called her Rock of Gibraltar look, her father summoned a family council, the first of many to consider Margaret's future. Her two older sisters took the initiative.

These were unusual women, as indeed, would be all four of the Higgins daughters. Feminine and charming, not one followed the traditional role of wife and mother. It was as though Anne Higgins's everlasting burdens had instilled a deep rejection of that part. Yet each of the sisters was endowed with her mother's gift for self-sacrifice.

Mary Higgins was said to have given up marriage because the family needed her earnings. While still young, she had become the paid companion of the daughter of a wealthy Corning couple and she remained with that daughter for the rest of her life. Nan became a stenographer and together these sisters prevented their parents' economic plight from becoming desperate. They also offered special opportunities, such as helping the younger brothers through college.

These older sisters now resolved that Margaret should have more education. They finally arranged with a Methodist school in the Catskills for her to earn her board by waiting on table and washing dishes. They guaranteed the other expenses. Claverack, they persuaded Margaret, would be a step toward Cornell, on which she had set her heart.

School and Romance

2

Claverack was one of the first coeducational schools in the East. Besides the innovation of teaching young men and women together, it fostered a humane spirit that awakened Margaret's zest for both studies and people. There she made enduring friends such as Amelia Stuart, whose last name she would give as a first name to her elder son.

Saturday morning chapel was exciting because students were then allowed to present their own concerns. For most girls, participation in this hour was torture, but for Michael Higgins's daughter, it was a golden opportunity. With the help of her father's long-range advice and before a staunchly Republican audience, she was soon championing free silver. Echoing the Boy Orator, William Jennings Bryan, she warned: "You shall not press down upon the brow of labor this crown of thorns; you shall not crucify mankind upon a cross of gold."

More characteristic was her talk on women's rights, although again she was abetted by her father. He relayed Susan B. Anthony's arguments and cited potent ladies of the past, such as Helen of Troy and Cleopatra. Still under his influence, she went out to the nearby cemetery to practice her oratory. At last, with the same feeling at the pit of her stomach that she had known in her graveyard vigil at Corning, she delivered her talk at the chapel.

Her preannounced subject created much hilarity because some young men passed around cartoons of trousered females smoking huge cigars. Margaret did not make many converts that day, but she did impress the elocution teacher who encouraged her to recite dramatic bits. She had shown unusual poise under harassment and had a pleasant voice that carried to the back of the hall with some eloquence. Years later Amelia Stuart, then Mrs. Michell, recalled that her friend played the lead in most of Claverack's dramatic productions. In her *Autobiography,* Margaret said that for a season she considered going on the stage.

She must have been a picture on the platform with her slender, erect carriage and the bronze halo of her hair. From a host of photographs, we see her posing and preening, sometimes vain and callow looking, but always pretty. If the young men had disapproved of her chapel talks, they now found her a very feminine feminist. In the Hersey biography, Mrs. Michell says that Margaret had great appeal for both sexes. "Anything she touched, she glorified in some mysterious way." Margaret's natural reserve, Mrs. Michell also reported, sometimes gave way to gales of laughter. The shy but purposeful girl who had entered Claverack, was developing the lighthearted gaiety which would remain one facet of her nature.

With her growing popularity, Margaret's enthusiasm for reform speeches shifted to escapades at an off-limits dance hall. This phase ended with a memorable talk with the principal. He could have expelled her for breaking the rules, but instead, he spoke of her gift for leadership. Would she learn to use it constructively or would she always stir up mischief for herself and her followers? Because he neither scolded nor threatened, but spoke of her potential, Margaret was deeply moved.

After three happy years at Claverack, her father called her home to nurse her mother. As far back as the Higgins children could remember, their mother had been plagued by a formidable cough. No one had guessed that there could be anything seriously wrong with this indispensable member of the family, but now she was bedridden, spitting blood and with strange Harlequin red spots on her cheeks. Her husband finally put her in the hands of a doctor who called often.

In Margaret's eagerness to speed her mother's recovery, she borrowed several medical books that fired her own ambition to become a doctor. Unfortunately the obsolescent texts did not warn about infection. The untrained nurse conscientiously closed the windows so that no draft or fresh air ever reached the sick room. There was an old Irish saying that if a consumptive survived the month of March, he would live until fall. Anne Higgins died on March 31, 1896, and with her went the happiness of the home.

On Margaret's young shoulders fell her mother's cares—the cooking, washing, scrubbing, mending, ironing, and the losing struggle to make ends meet. What was worse, her father became a changed man. In his lonely grief and sense of inadequacy, he turned into a petty tyrant, especially with Margaret, perhaps because she was his favorite. Ethel, the youngest daughter, was in high school and in love with a fellow student. Naturally her father thought she was too young, but he was even more upset because Margaret went out with a variety of beaux. When she was a child, he had trusted her as an adult, but now that she was almost grown up, he treated her as a child. Since he disliked everyone who called, she stopped seeing anyone. Yet he was never pleased.

One night, when she and Ethel arrived home a few minutes late after a band concert, he locked them out. Then he opened the door for Ethel who, he said, was not responsible for the tardiness, but slammed the door in Margaret's face. She was stunned and since she had worn no coat, she was also very cold. Finally, she left to spend the night with a friend. The punishment boomeranged on her angry father who had only meant to teach her a lesson. He tramped the streets for hours looking for her. Father and daughter were soon partly reconciled, but after three years away from home, Margaret knew that she could not remain there. Neither could she start medical school, for lack of funds, but she made the crucial decision to take nurses' training. Toward the close of the century the mother of one of her Claverack friends arranged for her to enroll at a new nursing school at White Plains, New York.

The great challenge of her training was maternity work. In her third year she was called out on night cases, miles away from the hospital. Her first duty was to boil the water over the woodfire stove in the kitchen and sterilize the forceps. Meanwhile, the doctor was supposedly scrubbing himself, but sometimes he was late.

It was an awesome responsibility for a girl not yet through nurses' training, to take charge, but Margaret had to deliver many babies.

More than a half century later a Mrs. O'Connor, born at White Plains early in 1902, claimed to be Margaret Sanger's first delivery. According to the parents, it had been a complicated birth, but the courage and skill of the student nurse had saved the child from suffocation. To the end of her life, Margaret felt that witnessing a birth was the most momentous human experience. Holding a newborn infant with its tiny perfection made her want to pray.

Some patients, who had already had several children and miscarriages, begged Margaret to tell them how to prevent another pregnancy. She had no idea. When she asked the doctors, they were indignant that anyone would raise the question with a nice girl.

Margaret's apprenticeship was rugged, largely because of the long hours and the primitive working conditions. The hospital at which she trained had been an old manor house with many steps and no conveniences, not even electricity or adequate washrooms. Margaret was soon running a temperature and suffering from what was called tubercular glands. With decreasing strength, she could hardly get through her long days and to relieve the glandular infection, she was twice operated upon.

Her final assignment was in New York at the Manhattan Eye and Ear Hospital. There the equipment was modern and the work lighter, but an extracurricular event overshadowed everything else. At a hospital dance, a small dark man interrupted a waltz to show her partner some blueprints. While the doctor examined his building plans, the intense eyes of the architect never left Margaret's face. The next morning at seven-thirty, when she went for her early walk, she found this man waiting for her at the foot of the hospital steps. For her, this was romantic. For him, it was love at first sight. The man's name was William Sanger.

Waiting for Margaret at the hospital steps became Sanger's habit as he started a whirlwind courtship. Since he was eight years her senior and already making a good living, he was the most impressive suitor she had known. He had more social status than she and was acquainted with interesting people in New York. Already an expert architectural draftsman, he meant to abandon this work to become a great painter. Like her father, of whom he often reminded her, Bill seemed to have an unconquerable spirit.

Soon they were talking of marriage, with a long honeymoon in Paris where Bill would study. The stumbling block, on which they could never agree, was when they would marry. Margaret insisted on receiving her degree, and really wanted to work a year, although trainees were not allowed to marry and Bill did not want to wait. At last he cut the Gordian knot. On an August afternoon in 1902, when they met during her two hours off duty, he gave her an ultimatum. It must be then or never. He had arranged everything, ring, minister, witnesses, and even a boy to hold the horse of his hired carriage.

Margaret was always reticent about personal matters, but her unpublished family letters describe that afternoon. To her sister Mary she wrote: "That beast of a man William took me away for a drive last Monday and drove me to a minister's residence and married me. I wept with anger and wouldn't look at him for it was so unexpected. . . . I had on an old blue dress and looked horrid. . . . He was afraid this precious article [herself] would be lost to him. . . . I'm very sorry to have the thing occur, but yet I am very, very happy." To her sister Nan she wrote much the same, but added that Bill was jealous, "beastly, insanely jealous." That too may have seemed romantic.

Why did such an independent girl acquiesce in an elopement that made her cry with anger? First love, about which she later warned, was, no doubt, the chief reason, but at this time both she and her younger sister Ethel were vulnerable because they had lost their security with the death of their mother, followed by estrangement from their father. While still in high school, Ethel had secretly married John Byrne. Margaret had not meant to follow her sister's example, but on that August afternoon the risk of losing forever the man she hoped one day to marry was simply too great.

To his new sisters-in-law, Bill Sanger explained his demand. Margaret had many admirers, several serious ones who made him feel that he must act at once. She was "a treasure and the very embodiment of sunshine," who would make almost any man happy. This would always be his view.

3

Bill Sanger, who had pushed through his own desires, could not control his wife's destiny, not even at the start. Her glandular operations had been palliatives and when she became pregnant six months after her marriage, the tubercular symptoms burst out with new virulence. Doctors advised her to settle permanently somewhere at a high altitude out west, but instead, because of Bill's work, she went to a sanitarium in the Adirondacks.

Since home delivery was the custom, in November she returned to their flat on 149th Street, but again she had bad luck. When her early morning labor pains began, Bill could not reach her obstetrician and had to settle on a young general practitioner. Margaret always felt that her prolonged, agonizing labor was a decisive factor in her future. Apparently the doctor agreed. Years later he wrote that he had often wondered what effect his "ignorance of obstetrics" had on her career. It had been "a hard night" for both of them.

The baby, Stuart, was born strong and healthy, but the ordeal nearly finished his mother. She was shipped back to the Adirondacks, along with the infant and a nurse who lived next door in the same cottage. At this place tubercular treatment involved large doses of creosote, which took away her appetite, and vast amounts of milk and eggs which nauseated her. The days and the weeks slipped by while the patient who answered to the name of Margaret Sanger, existing in almost a comatose state, felt nothing in common with the vital girl who had become pregnant. In the outer world there was a presidential election, with Teddy Roosevelt urging a "life of strenuous endeavor." Endeavor! Margaret could not even down her breakfast! She felt remote from the world, her husband, and even the baby next door.

At the end of eight months she was physically weaker and emotionally past caring about anything. After conferring with her family, two doctors came to question her. What would she like to do, they asked. Where would she like to go? To whom would she like the baby sent? To every question she answered, "I don't care." They finally left, baffled by her negative attitude.

On an impulse, the younger doctor returned. His patient was still sitting exactly as he had left her when he dropped his hand on her shoulder and said with emphasis, "Don't be like this. Do something. Want something. You'll never get well if you keep on this way."

His words cut through her lethargy. They sank deep into her consciousness to awaken that spirit that used to believe that she could achieve whatever she set out to do. It occurred to her that she did not have to sit there day after day. Even if she died—as they seemed to expect—it would be better to do so at home than in this alien place. She did not sleep that night, but before the next dawn she, the startled nurse, and the baby were on their way back to New York.

Bill met them at the station and agreed with all her wishes. She need not force herself to eat. Certainly, he would not let her die. For three weeks Margaret lived mostly on water and then, with a restored appetite, began to gain.

When her convalescence was assured, Bill decided that they should live in the suburbs where she would have clean air, a garden, and a view. They found all these at Hastings-on-Hudson, and also a group of pleasant professional people. Until they could build a house of their own, the Sangers rented one near the lot where they intended to sink their roots. It was a good place for Margaret to recuperate and a fine one for Stuart to toddle from infancy to boyhood. Margaret's days were much the same as other young mothers' and she welcomed the low-keyed tempo of the community. Bill, who was a devoted husband, lightened her tasks by doing er-

rands and chores. With real insight, he encouraged her to channel her returning energy into efforts that might bring permanent
satisfaction, such as writing and composing talks for children on
social hygiene. Years afterward she recalled that he had filled
her days with "loving kindness."

In their leisure together they mulled over blueprints or she read
aloud while he sketched. Bill had not given up his hope of becoming a painter, although Paris constantly receded from possibility.
The scale of the Hastings house that he planned added to its distance. Because he wanted his home to prove his professional quality, he designed a showpiece. It was square, with fireproof, stucco
walls, a great verandah overlooking the Hudson, a studio for himself, a fireplace and bath for each bedroom.

As the building rose, Bill became a perfectionist. At night he
often knocked out what the workmen had done during the day,
insisting that some parts be rebuilt several times. Later both Sangers
took a hand in the finishing. They stained the woodwork and
together built a rose window. For three weeks they toiled over
it, cutting their fingers and fraying their nerves as they leaded
and welded together each glowing petal. This window was to suf-
fuse the central stairway with radiance, symbolizing the beauty and
permanence of the Sanger home.

In this time of joint labor, Margaret saw her husband at his creative best. He spared no pains and was achieving on a more ambitious scale what their neighbors wanted, a physical structure to
represent their family status and aspirations. And the family was
growing. Five years after her first pregnancy, Margaret was pronounced well enough to have another baby and, with restored joy,
she was looking forward to the new life, as well as to the new
home.

In February 1908, although the house was not quite finished
and the weather was stormy, the Sangers could wait no longer, and
they moved in. It was like Christmas, opening the crates which
had long been in storage and choosing the right place for their special treasures. Margaret's enthusiasm outran her strength, but at
last she went to bed. Before following her, Bill stirred up a roaring fire in the furnace.

They were awakened by their maid, banging on the door. Bill's efforts had overheated the new steam pipes, not yet wrapped with asbestos. A great fire had burst out in the basement. Since there was no telephone, Bill raced out in his pajamas to call the Volunteer Fire Department. Seizing Stuart, Margaret rushed over to their neighbors across the street. With her son settled in a new bed, she came out again to find the Fire Department vainly trying to climb the icy hill. Then she turned to watch the gaudy show of her blazing dream house.

As a nurse in training, Margaret had found that she did not panic. During a crisis she saw things clearly with insights that she never forgot. That night she even recognized the beauty of the moonlight on the ice and the strange patterns of the flames. Suddenly a tongue of fire curled up through the rose window and one by one the petals fell. So it was for this that they had slaved! It was for this that they had mangled their hands and lost their tempers! How futile to spend one's efforts on things that perish in an hour. She felt aloof and curiously relieved. She was freed from the temptation of making a fetish out of a physical structure. This was not the way she meant to use her life.

Because the walls were fireproof, Bill salvaged much of the house. He went over it patiently, tearing out scorched parts and saving what he could. That summer they moved in again, but it was never the same. There was always the smell of charred wood.

Yet outwardly the next three years passed much as they had planned. Soon after they were again settled, Margaret bore her second son, Grant. She was happy caring for him, as she had not been able to care for Stuart, and she wanted a third child, hopefully a daughter and close enough to be a companion to Grant. Twenty months later, Peggy arrived, a little girl so satisfying that Margaret did not mind when the doctor forbade any more children. The third pregnancy, coming too soon after the second, had reactivated the old infection.

Once more, and this time with three children in the house, Margaret had to think first about her own health. From her bedroom, where she spent most of Peggy's first year, she saw the world in transition. Revered figures, including Mark Twain and Julia Ward

Howe, who had seemed like permanent institutions, died. The last ties with the nineteenth century were cut in the solemn splendor of the funeral of Britain's King Edward VII. England's most famous lady, Florence Nightingale, also died. She had founded the nursing profession, for which Margaret had trained so arduously and for which she had practiced so little. As Margaret wrote in the *Autobiography*: "I was not able to express my discontent, . . . but after my experience as a nurse with fundamentals this quiet withdrawal into the tame domesticity of the pretty riverside settlement seemed to be bordering on stagnation."

Sharpening her discontent were financial worries. Her sickness had been costly, as had the house. Although it had been insured against fire, the furniture had not been, and Bill had again borrowed heavily to replace it. During the eight years of her marriage, Margaret had learned that Bill himself was the chief obstacle to solvency. He was as improvident as her father. When he had money, he spent it foolishly, often on gifts for her, orchids perhaps or a piece of Oriental silk which she had no occasion to wear and could not enjoy while she owed every tradesman in town.

Bill was as unconcerned as Michael Higgins used to be. After years of bickering over finances, Margaret decided that the only solution was for her to earn and pay for her share of the expenses. If they lived in New York there would be no problem about the children because Bill's mother, whom they all loved, would like nothing better than to run her son's house again.

The idea of returning to the city opened tantalizing prospects, for as she convalesced, she felt that life was passing her by. They had "drifted into a swamp," as she put it, but they must not wait for the tide to set them free. She loved her children, she enjoyed her home and the community, but there were limitations. She knew everything that her neighbors had to say on their three main topics: their families, school, and domestic help. She wanted to hear about the outside world. She wanted to be in the midst of events, helping to shape them, not eternally sitting on the sidelines, dimly watching the performance of her generation. The stronger she grew physically, the more impatient became her spirit.

For a time Margaret hesitated to broach the subject to her husband lest she wound him in suggesting that they leave "Margaret's palace," as he fondly called the house. The fact was, however, that Bill had only come to the suburbs for her sake. His work, his mother, friends, and interests were all in the city. Perpetually riding the New York Central, he was irked at the waste of time. Both of them, as she summed it up in her *Autobiography,* "were feeling what amounted to a world hunger, the pull and haul towards wider horizons."

Bill accepted the first offer for the house. They paid their debts and moved to a large, old-fashioned apartment on 135th Street, over which Mrs. Sanger Sr. presided. Margaret was then free to take occasional cases. Both Sangers emerged from Hastings as from a long hibernation, eager to catch up with contemporary ideas.

Finding Herself

4

The New York into which the Sangers plunged was ebullient with ideas which would soon create a cultural divide. Muckrakers had stripped the glamour from the nation's tycoons by exposing their ties with racketeers, boodlers, and the vice ring. Labor was in a fighting mood, with a new eloquence gained through the support of writers and artists in whom social and aesthetic radicalism merged. This group helped plan the Armory Show of Modern Art, whose daring dissonances and distortions staggered most of its viewers, but intoxicated Greenwich Village. Down in the Village, young Will Durant was lecturing on the heretofore undiscussed topic, sex psychology, inspired by Havelock Ellis and Krafft-Ebing.

Even politics was in for a change when Teddy Roosevelt came home from big-game hunting in Africa, and broke with his hand-picked successor, President Taft. In New Jersey, the scholarly Governor Woodrow Wilson was talking about the New Freedom, but in Manhattan that phrase meant more than moderate reforms. It meant a social revolution that would trample on the old gentilities and the very ethos of American Puritanism.

Bill Sanger had always called himself a Socialist, but like his father-in-law, politics to him meant talk. Still, Local 5, the party headquarters, was only a few blocks away and both Sangers joined, making their flat a meeting place for members. As Margaret said, "They came to see Bill; I made the cocoa." Later they drank beer and came increasingly to see her.

Bill, a friend of Eugene V. Debs, the beloved party leader, upheld the official view that the good society must be won by ballots, not bullets. Some of his guests defended violence; some talked casually about class war, while anarchists and members of the International Workers of the World—the Wobblies—argued that in a showdown, they must rely on bombs.

These brutal views were created by brutal conditions. American industry was still protected by armed Pinkerton men, as well as by government troops and court injunctions. Labor, mostly unorganized, in some industries still worked a twelve-hour day, with low wages and no social security. The raw injustice of this system had created a ferment of revolt that exploded verbally in the Sanger parlor. In her book *My Fight for Birth Control,* Margaret herself appraised the era:

In those years before the war, a new religion was spreading over the country. It had no definite name and its adherents would have been the first vociferously to deny that they were religious. This new faith was made up of the scoffers, rebels, revolutionists, anarchists, socialists of all shades from the "pink tea" intellectual to the dark purple lawbreaker. The term "radical" was used to cover them all. But while all were freethinkers, agnostics or atheists, they were as fanatical in their faith of the coming revolution as ever any primitive Christian was for the immediate establishment of the Kingdom of God.

Faith is infectious and radicalism . . . made a tremendous appeal to the young, to idealists, to all who were brought face to face with the tragedies of modern society and who were totally disillusioned by the blight of conservative reaction then entrenched in power. Gross injustices were to be witnessed on all sides . . .

Almost without realizing it, you became a "comrade" or "fellow worker," like the primitive Christian, a member of a secret order. The martyr, it has been well said, creates the faith. Well, there were martyrs aplenty in those days—men and women who had served in prison for their beliefs and were honored accordingly. One had hardly any social standing at all in radical circles unless one had "worked for wages," or brushed up against the police or had served at least a few days in jail. As in the early Church, most of the members of this order were of the working classes, though there were eccentric millionaires, editors, lawyers and rich women who had experienced "conversions" and were active in the "movement."

Three who often came together in the Sanger parlor were examples of these disparate elements—John Reed, son of Portland's leading family, in his mid-twenties was a first-rate journalist. His western speech, overlaid with a Harvard accent, contrasted oddly with that of his associate, Bill Haywood, leader of the Wobblies. Margaret found a gentle and discerning side to this uncouth giant as did Jessie Ashley, Haywood's usual companion. She was a wealthy blue blood and, thanks to the training of her brother, dean of the New York School of Law, the city's first woman lawyer.

The Sanger parlor became a microcosm of New York's left wing, but the full spectrum was soon on display at the famous Evenings of Mabel Dodge. Lincoln Steffens, king of the muckrakers, had suggested a salon for the radical left and Mrs. Dodge, trying to fill a vacuum in her own life, agreed to start such a group.

This literate and clever Buffalo heiress grew up with a sense of everlasting emptiness. From early childhood, her unloving and eccentric parents had planned their days so that all three of them separately lived out their "different modes of loneliness." Now in her early thirties, disenchanted with her second husband and before her stupendous affair with John Reed and his successors, Mrs. Dodge presided over her drawing room off Washington Square.

In her autobiographical volume, *Movers and Shakers,* Mrs. Dodge told how she entertained trade unionists, anarchists, suffragists, poets, lawyers, murderers, and Wobblies. The last, sitting cross-legged on the floor, were as hirsute as latter-day Hippies, although inside, they were men of steel. Apparently Big Bill Haywood did not look so, for Mrs. Dodge once described him as "a large, soft, overripe Buddha with one eye." He was stretched out that evening on her yellow damask chaise longue with a bevy of maidens at his feet.

On that occasion stocky Emma Goldman, the anarchist, harangued. Present also were two recent and disparate Harvard graduates, Walter Lippman, self-assured and precise of speech, earnestly trying to achieve a meeting of minds, and John Reed, who poured out his breathless and boyish enthusiasm.

Margaret Sanger sat serene and quiet, "the Madonna type of woman with soft brown hair parted over a quiet brow." This was early in the salon's history before Margaret became what Mrs. Dodge called the "arbitrarily chosen . . . voice of a new gospel."

By curious chance Margaret described Mabel Dodge that evening: "brown bangs, outlining a white face, simply gowned in velvet, beautifully arched foot, beating the air." For two hours she watched that "silken ankle in its violent agitation." These two young women both gifted, attractive, ambitious, and moving in the same circle, noted in the other a trait that seemed significant in their divergent lives. Margaret's outer repose sprang from her inner strength, while Mrs. Dodge's foot expressed her rudderless dilettantism.

Although Margaret was not ideologically inclined, she accepted various assignments from Local 5, hoping to find some worthwhile part to play. For a time she recruited working women for the Socialist Party and wrote for its paper, *The Call*. Her first assignment was an article on the laundry strike. To gather material, she went into the homes of the poorest-paid union members. Some of them rose at five, had ten minutes off for lunch, another ten minutes for supper, and reached home at eleven o'clock. This was one of the few strikes in which men and women picketed together, but Margaret found their attitudes different. The women, also wanting shorter hours and higher wages, nevertheless, were skeptical. After all, a few more pennies would not care for another baby. What the men fought for was not as important as what they refused even to discuss with their wives, family limitation.

One day Margaret reluctantly agreed to pinch-hit as a speaker to a small group of women. When she felt the old alarm at the pit of her stomach, she realized that this was her first speech since school days. Although she switched the subject from labor to her own specialty, health, she wrote afterward that she was too nervous to eat any dinner. Still, the subject was such a welcome change that the group asked for a series of talks, which she prepared while on an obstetrical case as her patient slept. As the series of talks progressed, she was rewarded by a constantly growing audience.

Because of the unusual interest, *The Call* asked for some health articles to be run Sundays in its Women's Section. These columns, named "What Every Mother Should Know," were later published as a pamphlet. They included some thoughts that Margaret had developed in her Hastings days.

When her son Stuart and his little friends had begun to ask about babies, she had called them together. If she did not specifically mention the birds and the bees, nevertheless, she approved the traditional approach. By starting the explanation with other forms of life and moving up the evolutionary ladder from plants and insects to fish, frogs, and mammals, sex was depersonalized, the mother lost her self-consciousness, and the child learned his place in nature.

The column was so popular that *The Call* asked for more and Margaret agreed on a second series, "What Every Girl Should Know," an introduction for adolescents to the subject of sex. Everyone seemed pleased until one Sunday she turned to the Women's Section with its familiar heading, "What Every Girl Should Know," and read in large black type "Nothing!" Underneath were the words "By order of the Post Office Department."

It was no joke, no accident. Into Margaret's mind flashed the well-known likeness of Anthony Comstock, bull-necked, white side whiskers, and bald pate. For forty years he had been the special agent of the Postmaster General, enforcing the obscenity laws that he himself had drafted and almost single-handedly put through Congress.

Comstock was known satirically as the nation's Guardian of Purity, but in this article, which dealt with venereal disease, Margaret felt that her motives were the same as his, the protection of the young. The censorship seemed the more baffling since the city itself had lately opened a Bureau of Social Hygiene to fight the "social evils." In her article, Margaret, as a nurse, had treated the subject explicitly. That, she was informed, was just the trouble. She had used the words "gonorrhea" and "syphilis," instead of generalities which her readers would not have understood.

This first brush with Comstock was characteristic of the man who could not distinguish between education and obscenity. He, more than any other individual, would obstruct her way and in so doing, assure her future.

. . . . .

It was in the cause of labor and again as a nurse that Margaret first attracted national attention. At Lawrence, Massachusetts, 25,000 low-paid and unorganized textile workers staged a walk-out. Fourteen hundred soldiers were rushed there, but instead of keeping the peace, one of them accidentally shot a girl picket. With this as an odd excuse, the labor leaders were arrested, whereupon Big Bill Haywood appeared on the scene to direct a spectacular show with parades, songs, speeches, and pickets endlessly circling the plants.

The question was the staying power of labor, for parents usually gave up as soon as they heard their children's hunger cries. Since the strikers were mostly Italian, New York's Italian colony borrowed an Old World practice and offered temporary adoption of the strikers' children. Probably it was Haywood who suggested that the nurse, Margaret Sanger, should head a committee to bring the children to New York.

On Margaret's insistence, the youngsters had a physical examination before leaving town. She sent one child home with diphtheria, several with chicken pox. All of them were in bad condition, undernourished and dressed in rags in spite of the bitter weather. Six weeks later when the young visitors came back to Lawrence, she had the pleasure of seeing them transformed into healthy, happy, and warmly dressed children. Between times, playing a small part in the successful outcome of the strike, she stepped for a moment into national prominence.

In answer to a charge that the children's exodus was a publicity stunt, Milwaukee's Victor Berger, the Socialist congressman, started an investigation of the workers' conditions. Among those whom he called to testify was the nurse, Margaret Sanger. For the first of many times she took the train to Washington and appeared in the crowded chamber of the Rules Committee.

The strikers' testimony had made a poor impression with too few facts and too much emotion before Berger called Margaret to the stand. Although a few months back she had flinched at speaking to a handful of working women, now she had the outward calm of a veteran as she addressed an audience of congressmen and industrial and labor leaders, as well as a barrage of blinding, clicking cameras.

Her nurse's training had taught Margaret to classify significant details and so, with the help of her notes, she could answer questions about the children's ages, weight, and physical condition. She reported that they were all undernourished, and that most had enlarged tonsils and adenoids. Only 4 out of 119 wore overcoats, none had woolen clothes, and few had underwear.

Next morning many people across the country admired the photograph of the slim young nurse who had testified so ably.

The Die Is Cast

5

As a nurse, Margaret specialized in obstetrical cases, in part so that she might plan her schedule and be back home in the usual two weeks. At that time most women still had their babies in their bedrooms and Margaret's calls ranged from the professional and clerical classes down to the very poor.

Sometimes she went to prosperous homes where the long hoped for child was a cause of celebration. Here the mothers were treated like heroines who had just performed their highest service. Friends showered them with flowers, gifts, and tender solicitude. Even before his birth, the baby had been endowed with a layette of charming clothes and equipment for every need. These young mothers were eager to learn all about infant care so that their precious progeny would start with every asset.

Some of the poor also saved money for doctors and nurses. They had painfully scraped it together over the months by sacrifice and with the help of donations from relatives. But among the poor, Margaret seldom attended a first baby. Often, in addition to older children, there had been many miscarriages and abortions. The shocking fact was that in such families a baby born dead was a reprieve from deeper misery. Margaret saw, firsthand, that all babies were not created equal, since the wanted ones had a vast headstart over those whose coming spelled disaster. Unless the mother was physically fit and the father could support him, a child might be handicapped for life.

Some of her calls came from the lower East Side of New York, from cold water flats where sunshine never entered the rooms which opened on dark courts reeking with refuse. As the ultimate in desolation, she recalled once plodding up five flights of stairs to find the baby had arrived ahead of time. A ten-year-old-boy, helping his mother, had cleaned up by dropping the placenta out of the window.

In this district, the women, who were worn out at the age of thirty, were all obsessed by their need to prevent another pregnancy. When word spread that there was a nurse in the building, neighbors appeared one by one with gifts of homemade delicacies. The real reason for the calls came out in their questions as they lingered at the door.

At first Margaret tried to explain the two ways on which the middle class relied: the condom and withdrawal. The women hooted at the notion that their men would ever use either method. Margaret began to see that since sex was the poor man's only luxury, he would not mar his instant pleasure with prudence for the future. What the women wanted was some protection that they could use themselves. They wanted "the secret" which they were certain rich ladies possessed.

Occasionally, after an interval, Margaret returned to the same street, where she learned the tragic end of some of her visitors. Mrs. Cohen had been taken to the hospital and never came home. Mrs. Kelly had sent her children to her sister's and then put her head in the gas oven.

What did the others do about unwanted children? They tried everything, from herb tea to turpentine and patent medicines. They rolled downstairs or inserted button hooks and knitting needles into their bodies. When all this failed, they collected their nickels and dimes and queued up on Saturdays, sometimes a hundred, at the office of the $5 abortionist. He performed a quick curettage and sent the patient home, where she might bleed to death. There were few complaints, since the whole business was illegal.

Saints might like to help the poor, thought Margaret, but she preferred to work with the clean and happy middle class. It was not just the physical hardships from which she shrank, but the fact that she was inadequate. She could neither give the women what they needed, nor convince them that she had no secret.

In mid-July 1912, Margaret took on a case of a woman near death from blood poisoning caused by a self-induced abortion. Jake Sachs, a truck driver, had come home one evening to find his three small children in tears on the floor huddled about his unconscious wife. He called a doctor; the doctor called Margaret and together they started a frantic, uphill fight to save the woman. Sachs took the children to relatives and did what he could to help Margaret. Since his home had no conveniences, every morning before leaving for work, he lugged up the water supply and in the evening, took down the slops and refuse. Neighbors brought groceries and carried up heavy squares of ice.

A fierce heat wave hit the city, turning the little flat into an inferno with no respite even at sundown. It was an incredible heat that went on day after day, night after night while Margaret, with few breaks for sleep, performed her round-the-clock chores as if herself in a fever. Never had she worked so hard and continuously, but at the end of two weeks the doctor said that the crisis was past. They had won a victory.

Still in her twenties, Sadie Sachs had a gentle gravity even in the days of rejoicing when her husband and children hugged her. She managed only a wan smile when the neighbors brought in their custards and congratulations. During the third week she seemed brooding, aloof from everyone until Margaret was about to leave. Then she voiced her fears.

"Another child will finish me, I suppose?"

Margaret, evading the question, turned it over to the doctor on his last call. He nodded emphatically and stepping over to the bed, warned,

"Any more such capers, young woman, and there will be no need to send for me."

For a moment Mrs. Sachs stared back at him and then, as though summoning all of her courage, asked, "But how can I prevent it?"

Now it was the doctor's turn to hesitate, although he had no intention of becoming involved in that subject. "You want to have your cake and eat it too," he chuckled. Just before leaving, he added another jocular word. "Tell Jake to sleep on the roof!"

As the door closed Margaret saw a look of desolation on Mrs. Sachs's face. Clasping together her thin, blue-veined hands, she pleaded with her nurse to tell the secret. She was so desperate that Margaret dared not admit her ignorance. Instead, she promised to return soon for a talk. She made her patient as comfortable as possible and when she fell asleep, Margaret guiltily hurried off.

All the way home on the subway and for many nights after, Sadie Sachs's face haunted her. She meant to return, but in the next days she was busy with her own family and with writing her columns for *The Call*. Later she took other cases. Yet, her real reason for not going back was that she had nothing to tell Mrs. Sachs.

Jake telephoned in October. His wife was sick again and in the same way. Now it was Margaret who felt desperate. She wanted to say that she could not come. She thought of sending someone else, but in a few minutes she was back on the subway, heading south.

Once more she found Sadie Sachs near death; this time she was gone in a few minutes. Jake sobbed like a maniac. "My God! My God!" he wailed. Margaret folded the thin, blue-veined hands that had vainly pleaded with her. She pulled the sheet over the white face and left.

That night, during hours that she later recalled as the most momentous in her life, she walked and walked, hardly conscious of her surroundings or aware of the heavy nurse's bag that she carried. She was acutely aware of a great change. Something within her had gone with Sadie Sachs's life. It was her reluctance to face a forbidden truth. This was a turning point. Because of this night, tomorrow and forever would be different. She knew the future. She would close her heart to every other cause to give herself to one great goal.

At three o'clock, when she reached home, everyone was asleep. She looked down from her window at the hushed city. As she wrote in the *Autobiography*, she saw "with photographic clearness women writhing in travail to bring forth little babies; the babies themselves naked and hungry, wrapped in newspapers to keep them from the cold; six-year-old children with pinched, pale, wrinkled faces, old in concentrated wretchedness, pushed into gray and fetid cellars, crouching on stone floors, their small scrawny hands scuttling through rags, making lamp shades, artificial flowers; white coffins, black coffins, coffins, coffins interminably passing in never-ending succession. The scenes piled one upon another." She could bear it no longer.

The Search

6

Although Margaret Sanger had made a decision that would alter her future, she awoke with no plan of action. She knew in which direction she meant to go, but being a practical woman in a technological age, she also knew that she must have careful guidelines. As she saw it, her task was to liberate the masses of poor women from their age-old sexual servitude. She would no longer patch them up to repeat their pitiful ordeals and never again did she take a nursing assignment. That decision was easy, but before she could plan her strategy, she must educate herself.

Again she turned to her doctor friends, asking, as so many women had asked her, if there were not some way for a wife to protect herself against an unwanted pregnancy. No one gave her a definite answer, and she began to suspect that most of the medical profession were as ignorant as she. Beyond that, physicians feared to discuss a subject that was banned by both state and federal laws. That was the crux of the matter; they salved their consciences by saying that since the poor enjoyed breeding like rabbits, they would never use contraceptives. They always closed their remarks by warning that the bogy Comstock would get her if she didn't watch out!

Margaret's next hope was the libraries. She tried many, including that of the American Academy of Medicine, but neither private nor public collections helped her. The Comstock laws had insured a vacuum of information.

During her search, she did discover Krafft-Ebing's recent study of homosexuality and Havelock Ellis's seven volumes on *The Psychology of Sex,* which she "swallowed in one gulp." Later, suffering from psychic indigestion, she wondered why there should be so much material on abnormalities but nothing on the needs of normal married people.

In this winter of frustration she failed to find any support for her cause. She had thought that all feminists would be her allies, but those she talked with said that they could do nothing until they had won the vote. To her this was the wrong priority because millions of women would remain politically indifferent until freed from the burden of excess children. From their standpoint, the suffragists were indubitably right. They had been inching along, state by state, for three generations until they had almost enough congressional support to insure a national victory. It would have been absurd to endanger the outcome by embracing a new and explosive issue. Furthermore, once women had the vote, they could take the lead in support of the needed changes.

Her labor and Socialist friends were also cool. "Wait until we win our economic rights," they told her. "Wait until a million more Sadie Sachses die," she sputtered. Bill Sanger began to think she was obsessed. After all, it was not her problem; she had wanted three children. Sometimes she doubted that any man would understand this feminine tragedy. Yet it was a man and a labor leader who finally suggested her first practical step.

By spring she was a dispirited crusader. Not for a moment did she abandon her cause, but since she had reached an impasse, she decided to remove the children from New York's oncoming heat and retire to some cool, quiet place, where she might gain a perspective. Whatever the future, about which she had forebodings, she and the children would have this time together.

She had heard of a lovely isolated spot on Cape Cod, near a fishing village called Provincetown, unknown as yet except to a few artists and writers. There she rented a cottage with a porch on the Bay. Sitting on the steps of the house, the children could dabble their toes in the rising water, while at low tide they had a two-mile beach for play. Stuart, nine years old and active in all sports, was the leader, after whom the younger ones, hand in hand, tagged behind. Grant, with his father's dark hair, was the protector of blond, mischievous Peggy.

More than a half century later the brothers, who had both become doctors, agreed that Peggy at some time contracted an unrecognized case of poliomyelitis, leaving one leg with a slight muscular atrophy. Grant believed that this had occurred during the 1912 epidemic. He also thought that the illness, inflicting a permanent limp, was a source of dissension between his parents. However unjustly, Bill Sanger felt that his wife's deep preoccupation with her new concern had made her deficient in caring for Peggy. The fact that Margaret never mentioned the affliction, in spite of all that she wrote about this beloved daughter, may testify to the poignancy of her feelings.

Bill had joined the family for a long vacation in order to paint. He was now in his forties; he still disliked his profession and had never had a chance to go to Paris. Furthermore, he and Margaret were drifting apart. He had been very patient during her illnesses. In fact, he had been at his best when caring for her, but her new commitment seemed to threaten their relationship and made him irritable. Meanwhile, her absorption in ending the needless tragedy of mothers may have lessened her interest in his personal ambition to be a painter.

Into the small summer colony lumbered Bill Haywood, guest of Jessie Ashley, who had brought him to recover from the collapse of the silk workers' strike at Paterson, New Jersey. During long walks with him on the beach, Margaret became fascinated by his belief that he belonged so fully to the oppressed workers of the world that he would make no binding, personal ties. Perhaps that was the price for successful leadership. Out of his one good eye, Big Bill watched the young Sangers at play and then offered some surprising advice. Margaret should never sacrifice the happiness of her children. She had no thought of sacrificing anyone, but she always recalled his idea of belonging to the world.

Sympathetic to her cause, although to him it was a secondary issue, Big Bill one day made a fruitful suggestion. There was a country, he reminded her, where, for three generations the birth rate had been declining and where most families practiced some kind of contraception. Why not go to France for a spot investigation? He would be there in the fall and could introduce her to the Syndicalist workers who had fraternal relations with his own Wobblies.

The idea struck the Sangers as an inspiration. Paris was what they both needed. At last Bill would have his chance to study modern trends, while she gathered information. To finance the trip, they would use the last of the Hastings house payment and savings which they had made for the children's education. Someday they would replace this. Meanwhile, they would start their trip with a Scottish detour so that Margaret might add to their funds by writing a series of articles for *The Call*.

In October 1913, the five Sangers set out together for the last time. Their two-week stopover in Glasgow proved a surprisingly useful contrast to Paris. For twenty-five years this Socialist government had run all of its institutions, banks, schools, markets, hospitals, laundries, and even tenements. *The Call* thought Margaret might appraise and extol this record. Margaret appraised, but could not extol. Instead, Glasgow corroborated her views that neither socialism nor any political system would solve the problems of the poor.

She had been enthusiastic about what she saw until she learned that there were two Glasgows. There was the municipal showpiece and there were the unspeakable slums. The scientifically planned tenements were fine for small families, but where did the larger families live? "Not here!" insisted the building superintendents. Large families were shunted to ghettos on the city's outskirts, where they squatted in filthy hovels in the shipyard areas, out of bounds of the much vaunted city utilities. In these teeming suburbs, every woman carried a baby, while the older children begged for a halfpenny for bread. Socialist Glasgow catered only to small families, the city's aristocrats!

The Sangers saw Paris at the end of an epoch, as it would never be again. Everyone talked of the coming war, but Margaret and Bill, discounting such archaic nonsense, followed their personal concerns. Plunging into his long-delayed studies, he was enchanted when he met Matisse, whose work he had recently seen in the New York Armory Show of Modern Art.

Among Margaret's letters of introduction was one to the editor of *L'Humanité,* the organ of the French Federation of Labor. His English wife was doubly helpful, not only acting as interpreter, but arranging meetings with key people. When Bill Haywood arrived, he further broadened Margaret's contacts by taking her into the homes of Syndicalist workers. Since there were neither Comstock laws, nor Puritan traditions, the French wives spoke as a matter of course with no embarrassment. After a few moments of casual chat, a stranger might explain the mysteries for which Margaret had vainly sought for years in the United States.

At this period "the secret" consisted of tampons, suppositories, and douches, used according to individual choice. "And where did you learn your system?" Margaret would ask. "My mother taught me," was the usual answer. "And where did she learn?" "From grandmama." For generations French women had been experimenting with homemade devices, the formulas for which they prized as they did their recipes for pot-au-feu.

Although French wives had created their own protection, they had not greatly affected the birth rate until their husbands saw an economic motive for doing so. Napoleon, paradoxically, was given credit for stabilizing the population, although, like all warriors, he urged large families. But he had come to power championing the goals of the French Revolution, and his legal code provided that a man's children share equally in his "estate." This was a reversal of the old laws, favoring the oldest son.

The Napoleonic Code stirred up unforeseen resentment among a new class of property owners, the once landless peasants. They had just gained their coveted plots of earth and had no mind to dissipate it among numerous children. The solution was a small family. For the first time men saw an advantage in contraception and insisted on its use. From now on a wife's duty was to regulate the numbers in the household, as well as to manage the work. If her system failed, she might have an abortion, which in France was relatively safe because it was performed by reputable surgeons.

This point of view was shared not only by the peasants and the well-to-do, but by at least one group of industrial workers, the Syndicalists. "Conscious Generation" was a part of their platform, and the results showed in their living standards. Their wage scale was close to that of the Glasgow workers, but since it covered only one or two children, by contrast, their homes looked affluent. The gain was not just material, but spiritual. Because parents had the leisure and vitality to be companions to their children, whole families strolled in the parks together or visited the Louvre and other historical places. This way of life encouraged quality instead of quantity.

Although individualism had developed Conscious Generation, it also accounted for some failures. Since neither the medical profession nor any health agency was responsible, there were no standards, which resulted in needless errors and suffering. Too often family limitation was achieved by abortion and so the French system, which was no system at all, did not please Margaret. Nevertheless, she had finally learned what she had so long sought and felt as though she would explode with the illicit information which she wanted to bootleg back home. From then on she was impatient to leave.

Bill, on the other hand, was just starting his long postponed year of study and needed peace and quiet. As he put it in a letter, the winter had been hard, "storm-tossed by the din and roar of children and no studio." He knew that he was irritable, and at last agreed that the solution was a temporary parting of the ways.

On New Year's Eve 1913, the family, minus Bill, sailed from Cherbourg. When the children were asleep, their mother went back to pace the deck. Again her thoughts were racing as on the night of Sadie Sachs's death and again this woman whom she had failed, represented the millions whom she meant to save.

In her unpublished diary, Margaret wrote that the next day would start her new life, as well as the New Year. After fourteen months of hunting, she had found what she was looking for, but how could she use it? Of course someday she would describe all that she had learned and her work would doubtless be the first American one on contraception. But if she released the material now, it would be banned and her usefulness ended before she had achieved anything.

First she must create a following. Her articles for *The Call* had appealed to the lower income women whose cause she championed. Perhaps she could fire their interest by a journal planned especially for them. She would announce that there were safe ways for women to prevent excess pregnancies and that in France those ways were freely used. She would teach wives to insist on their own rights. She would publish a paper to make the meek revolt. The journal's name would be *The Woman Rebel*.

The Comstock Walls

7

In the months of spiritual gestation, Margaret saw her battle as against one individual, Anthony Comstock. Almost single-handedly he had built the legal walls which in her view preserved a medieval ethos. They not only barred scientific knowledge, but maintained the old taboos of ignorance and superstition.

Since sex, according to Comstock, was a subject neither discussed nor thought of by nice people, he relegated it to the gutter, where it continued to flourish in the form of brothels, prostitution, and the white slave traffic in young girls. In 1912 America's foremost woman, Jane Addams of Hull House, had shown the link between these institutions and poverty in her book, *A New Conscience and an Ancient Evil*. Organized vice always depended for its recruits on the daughters of the poor. Comstock attacked neither the guilty institutions nor their backwash—venereal disease, defective children, and crime. Instead, he vented his wrath on the crusaders against them for using frank words, such as "syphilis."

Margaret saw her mission as breaching the Comstock walls and letting in the twentieth century. To her it was self-evident that she spoke for the future, for reason, and for mute, helpless mothers. Comstock spoke for the past and for the persecutors who harried the weak.

Certainly Comstock spoke for the past, but Margaret vastly oversimplified his character. A displaced Puritan, he embodied both the worst and best of seventeenth-century New England. He was irreproachably devout, hard-working, chaste, and incorruptible. His enemies tried to discredit his honesty, but they never could. Probably he was as dedicated to his cause as Margaret Sanger was to hers.

They had another bond, the impact of their mothers' untimely deaths upon their respective careers. Both women came from long-lived stock, but were worn out by constant pregnancies and drudgery. Mrs. Comstock, a farmer's wife, bore ten children and died when Anthony was ten years old. Mrs. Higgins had eleven and died in her forties. Because Margaret was a girl and went at once into nurses' training, she soon connected her mother's many pregnancies with her frail health. Had the boy Anthony, more than three decades earlier, possessed such insight, he would never have made war on a policy that might have saved his mother's life.

Anthony Comstock was born in 1844, in New Canaan, Connecticut, of Anglo-Saxon, Protestant stock. He sucked in Bible stories with his mother's milk, and a half century after her death, he claimed that the whole purpose of his life was to honor her. He also said that he was in the service of the Lord.

At twenty he enlisted in the Union Army to take the place of his brother, killed at Gettysburg. Although he saw little of the war, his journal shows that he waged many battles with the Devil. Indeed, young Anthony seldom compromised and in spite of the anger of his fellow soldiers, he always poured his whiskey rations on the ground. Apparently the only time that he tasted liquor, except for medicinal purposes, was as a boy when he drank some of his neighbor's homemade wine, for which his father beat him.

After the war he found both work and a wife in New York. The bride's father was a Presbyterian elder, which in the eyes of his son-in-law no doubt outweighed his business failure. Certainly there was no worldly reason for marrying Maggie, who was "a little wisp of a woman," ten years his senior and already a bit worn out. Perhaps he was still thinking of his mother. In any case, he was always loyal to Maggie, even when her bedridden sister moved in with them.

Since Maggie's only child soon died, he adopted a little orphan, whom he had found on one of his raids. Unfortunately, she was feeble-minded, although her father never seemed to notice it. From all reports, he was both patient and kind to the three rather dilapidated females who made up his household. Anthony Comstock, the large man with the Atlas shoulders, the bull neck, and the choleric temper, found savor in an otherwise drab life by battling the sins of others.

As a boy, he had started battling when he broke into an unlicensed shop to destroy the liquor. After marriage, in the same spirit, he resolved to be a good citizen by personally enforcing the law in Brooklyn, where he was living. Tersely he noted in his journal that "crimes stalked the streets, while the police winked." As in his youth, the illicit traffic in liquor was his main concern until he recognized a greater evil.

Long aware that young businessmen took pleasure in lewd picture cards, he finally identified them as the cause of youth's growing depravity. This led to his true vocation. One day, professing a taste for "French cards," he bought some and then within the hour returned to the shop with a policeman to arrest the owner and seize his stock. This was Comstock's debut, and over the next decades he merely enriched his technique with decoy letters, false signatures, impersonations, and an army of spies. To the end of his days he loved sleuthing, relishing above all personal encounters and the arrest of the enemy.

To understand Comstock's drive, one must return to his Civil War journal. His battles with the Devil had largely concerned masturbation and lascivious fancies. Taking the Bible literally, he believed that "whosoever looketh on a woman to lust after her, has committed adultery with her already in his heart," and that the Lord hated "A heart that deviseth wicked imaginings." By equating a lustful thought with the deed, Comstock vastly increased the importance of pornography.

Comstock's authorized biographer, C. G. Trumbull, delves even deeper into his hero's past. His mother had once discovered that some farm hands—"vicious fellows"—had introduced Anthony to "lines of temptation" that proved harder for him to overcome than anything he learned later. Her grief so impressed her son that forever after he wanted to battle vicious fellows who polluted other boys' minds and habits. The memory of his mother inspired his books, *Traps for the Young,* and his crusade against pornography. He brought to the crusade his juvenile pugnacity and an arrested development.

There were many people in the eighteen-sixties equally appalled by the "French cards," which the recently incorporated New York Y.M.C.A. called "feeders for brothels." This organization took the lead, in 1868, in securing passage of a state law that banned lewd materials. When Comstock conceived a new plan of attack, he turned as a matter of course to the Y.M.C.A., whose president saw eye to eye with him. The latter appointed a committee for the suppression of vice, which for a while financed Comstock's work, although not quite openly. Few wanted to stand with Comstock in all of his slugging campaigns, and in the end the Comstock fundraising committee became autonomous.

Up to this time the churches had usually served as censors, a function which to some extent the courts later assumed. However, in 1842 Congress had barred the importation of foreign pornography. After the Civil War it took a second step, banning all obscenity from the mails. Nevertheless, pornography continued as a growing, profitable business.

Comstock resolved to close the legal loopholes. Although no one openly defended commercialized obscenity, large interests, including the press, which carried covert advertisements, had a stake in it. But the great hurdle for Comstock was to secure a hearing in a short session of Congress while the spotlight was on the financing of the Union Pacific Railway—the notorious Credit Mobilier affair, in which many congressional members were involved. Comstock's problem was to make the post card scandal seem as important as the national political scandal. With his rudiments of genius, he decided to show them, not tell them.

He spent weeks lobbying key persons, senators, committee chairmen, and the Vice President, but relied mainly on visual aids. Since his bill had been referred to the House Committee on Post Offices and Post Roads, he persuaded the chairman to set up a full display. This exhibit was either so convincing or so titillating that it was taken to the very floor of the House where it remained through-

out one memorable day. In the Senate, the Vice President obligingly opened his office for the show. To some whose probity was
being questioned, it was a welcome chance to join in a pious rejection of obvious filth. In any case, the bill passed the Senate in February, and on March 1 the House suspended the rules to pass it
without a roll call.

Most of the bill dealt with the material displayed, which was described in Section 211 as "obscene, lewd, lascivious, filthy and indecent." All of this was barred from the United States mail and from
express and common carriers. Advertising, which had been the
main sales channel, was prohibited. So disgusting was most of the
display that few members objected to a blanket suppression, although later some questioned it.

What was not commonly understood was the addition to the bill
of the phrase "prevention of conception," which included information as well as contraceptive devices also termed "obscene, lewd,
lascivious, filthy and indecent." The original bill had exempted
physicians, but the senator in charge offered an amendment to
strike out the exemption. On the Senate floor, when questioned
about his amendment, he evaded the matter. In neither house was
there any discussion whatsoever of this section, which would govern
American policy on contraception. To this day Congress has not
changed it.

President Grant signed the bill on March 3, 1873. In the next
years there was some dismay over the law, and shortly before Margaret Sanger's birth, her father's hero, Colonel Ingersoll, presented
a petition calling for its repeal. "Mental, moral and physical health
and safety," he urged, "are better secured and preserved by virtue
resting upon liberty and knowledge than upon ignorance enforced
by government supervision." But the law remained.

Comstock's legislative triumph was followed the next day by a
more personal one when he was named special agent, later inspector, for the Postmaster General. This gave him authority to make
arrests and confiscate illegal material. In itself, his law was a major
victory, but it also led to twenty-two little Comstock or state laws,
modeled on the federal act. This was not all. To the previously
passed New York obscenity law, he secured an amendment to cover

contraceptive materials. Eighteen other states then passed laws based on New York's.

Comstock followed up his legislation by organizing cooperative groups to suppress vice, such as the famous New England Watch and Ward Society and others with headquarters in Chicago, St. Louis, and Cincinnati. Now he had a network of vigilantes to crack down on evildoers. Toward the close of his life, summing up his achievements, he claimed to have caused the conviction of enough persons to fill a passenger train of sixty-one coaches, sixty of which contained sixty passengers each with the sixty-first almost full. Furthermore, he had destroyed 160 tons of obscene material. Earlier he had boasted of driving fifteen persons to suicide.

Comstock's assessment was not applauded by some of the public. His zeal for retribution sounded sadistic. A decreasingly Puritan people were shocked at the inspector's power to invoke final earthly judgment on his fellow citizens. Granted that most of the material that he destroyed was revolting, as were most of the careers that he ended, nevertheless, it had become obvious that Anthony Comstock could not distinguish between pornographic, medical, sociological and aesthetic works. He could not draw the line between artists, educators, humanitarians and the lowest smut-purveyors. Among the 3,760 persons whom he bragged of convicting, were many who should not have been there.

A tragic case was that of the Midwesterner, Dr. Elliott, who had publicly denounced the ban on contraception, before receiving two letters. Allegedly these were both from married women, one of whom had a syphilitic husband and the other, two children. Dr. Elliott granted their pleas and sent them contraceptive information. For this Comstock got him sentenced to six years at Leavenworth. When he emerged, Dr. Elliott was a broken old man.

For himself, Comstock's most costly fumbles were in art censorship, as in the case of "September Morn." Since this painting had won the medal of honor in the Paris Spring Salon of 1912, the American firm that reproduced it put a copy in its New York display window. Comstock always maintained that the most sacred thing in the world was "a maiden woman's body," but that it must not be "denuded." When he chanced to view this chilly but demure young girl in the window, he ordered the picture removed, as one unfit for the eyes of passing school children. The press seized on his quaint ban, which became the more droll when he volunteered that the picture had hung in "the saloons of Paris."

George Bernard Shaw had an early altercation with Comstock, whom he mistakenly blamed for removing his play *Man and Superman* from the public library. "Comstockery," he quipped, "is the world's standing joke at the expense of the United States." The inspector, who had never before heard of Shaw, rejoined by calling him a smut dealer, and later tried to suppress *Mrs. Warren's Profession,* a very serious play. All his life, Shaw told the press, he had been trying to awaken the public conscience, while Comstock had been examining and destroying tons of indecent post cards. Still, he could not fight Comstock "with the American nation at his back and the New York police in his van." Yet fighting Comstock, with the American public at his back and the New York police in his van, was precisely what an unknown young American woman aimed to do.

Comstock's mother had taught her boy a verse that always inspired him. It went:

> Build it well, whate'er ye do.
> Build it straight and strong and true.
> Build it high and clean and broad.
> Build it for the eye of God.

So he had built the Comstock walls. Margaret Sanger's mission was to demolish those high, strong walls to let in the light. She did not underestimate her task, nor want to be a martyr, but she was ready to do what was needed. She believed that her cause was that of human freedom. If she could make a breach, she would not quarrel with her punishment.

The Woman Rebel

8

After renting a cheap little flat in uptown New York, and entering the children in a local school, Margaret started work on her magazine. She still cherished the hope that some labor union or wealthy feminist would back her. Years later she admitted that it would have been strange indeed if anyone had risked much on a relatively unknown young woman who had no experience as an editor and whose purpose was to advance an illicit cause.

But aside from her courage, she did have the asset of warm if impecunious friends, a few of whom offered publicity in labor and left-wing publications. Their advance notices of her paper brought in several hundred paid subscriptions at a dollar a year. Some unions also offered free distribution and the use of their mailing lists.

Another group of cooperators donated their spare time. Some wrote or did research in the libraries, and most of them addressed envelopes and typed letters in the Sanger dining room, which was the office for the forthcoming *Woman Rebel*. Margaret herself, as editor, manager, circulating department, and bookkeeper, was solely responsible for the publication.

One evening a few of these hard-working friends helped make an epochal decision. Since she was starting a movement, it needed a name. The terms then in use, such as Conscious Generation in France and Neo-Malthusianism in England, were too long, obscure, and lacking in appeal. She had mulled over the matter a long while before trying out on her friends certain possibilities, including "population control," "race control," "birth rate control."

"Drop the 'rate,'" someone suggested. At once everyone recognized that "birth control" was the name of her movement. The name would soon travel around the world.

Behind a movement should be an organization, and so they founded the National Birth Control League. Just when this occurred is not clear, and certainly the growth and maintenance of a national society was not a major objective.

The first issue of *The Woman Rebel* appeared in March 1914. Its lead article declared that the aim of the paper was to "stimulate working women to think for themselves and to build up a conscious, fighting character." Relying on shock treatment to teach downtrodden wives, the editor jolted them with slogans, such as, "No Gods, No Masters!" She told them to "look the world in the face with a go-to-hell look in the eyes; to have an idea; to speak and act in defiance of convention."

In its eight issues the magazine hammered away at such topics as child labor, women and children in industry, health, social hygiene, and above all, the results of having too many children. One article began, "Can you afford a large family?" Another explained the assets of a small one, starting with better living standards and going on to health and cultural opportunities. The provocative refrain was that a woman must be "mistress of her own body" and must determine her maternity. This was the most precious freedom.

At this period Margaret saw her fight in terms of the First Amendment to the Constitution, freedom of the press. For this reason she accepted some contributions that were irrelevant to birth control. After all, freedom of the press included even an anarchist defense of assassination in times of despotism. Later she dismissed this particular piece as "vague, inane and innocuous," but it was never innocuous. It was immediately hurtful and years later opponents still attacked Margaret's judgment on the basis of this article.

Her conscious policy was to harpoon Anthony Comstock. Waving a red rag at him, she tried to make him both so angry and ludicrous that he would strike out blindly on some unconstitutional ground. Max Eastman, of *The Masses,* ably appraised her efforts:

"We must thank Margaret Sanger for speaking out clearly and quietly for popular education in the means of preventing conception. . . . There is no more important stand, and no stand that requires more bravery and purity of heart. . . . And if the virtue that holds heroes up to these sticking points must be united with the fault of rather unconvincing excitedness and intolerance—all right, we will hail the virtue and call it a bargain at the price."

For the editor, fringe benefits brought introductions to the world's leading feminists, from whom she quoted profusely. Her correspondence with English Mrs. Emmeline Pankhurst, Swedish Ellen Key and South African Olive Schreiner later ripened into warm friendships.

In response to *The Woman Rebel,* many thousands of letters proved that labor wives were interested, although most of them wanted contraceptive information at once, and this she could not give. In spite of the fact that she never broke the law, in April she received an official, unstamped envelope from the New York postmaster. He wrote that the March issue of *The Woman Rebel*—the first—was unmailable. Since no specific article was mentioned, Margaret was puzzled and asked for particulars for future guidance. The reply was a copy of the first statement. In the next months she and the postmaster repeated this routine when the May and July issues were also banned.

Reports soon proved that the only copies of the March number that had been seized were those mailed from her local post office. After that, Margaret and her friends dropped the next issues into downtown mail boxes.

Meanwhile, Bill had sent cartoons for the first number, telling her not to use them unless she liked them. She did not, and he was deeply hurt. The overage student was working hard without much encouragement. He missed Margaret badly and was full of misgivings. Once he had to cable for money from her share of their rapidly dwindling funds, but in compensation, he sent some of his paintings to be sold. They were unsalable.

Bill planned to stay abroad for another year with a tour of Spain, Italy, and Germany, but instead, he would come back if she wished. She advised him to remain abroad, since it was his chance of self-fulfillment. Besides, she had found herself much freer for her work in his absence. Increasingly, she felt remote from his aspirations, in which she had lost faith. Finally, she wrote him what he called an "epoch-making" letter, asking to be released from every tie. She wanted no personal relationship with any man, for in Bill Haywood's words, she was giving herself to the world.

About that time, the world intruded on her personal problems with the news of the assassination of an Austrian archduke in a Balkan town with the unpronounceable name of Sarajevo. There were headlines of possible war which Margaret, pacifist that she was, dismissed. In any case, she had enough troubles of her own to consider, and with this her friends heartily agreed.

Once more the Higgins family was conferring about Margaret. She was obviously ill again, this time with her mind affected. Some feared a complete nervous breakdown and insisted that Michael Higgins, the patriarch, must go to the big city which he had not visited in forty years, to take counsel with his distraught daughter. No longer sympathetic to rebels and despising talk about sex, he blamed the nursing profession for having disclosed to his little girl "all of the secrets of the human body."

In New York father and daughter entered at once into a marathon argument which was interrupted one morning by the doorbell. Two agents of the Department of Justice greeted the editor of *The Woman Rebel* with a warrant. She had been indicted by the grand jury on nine counts for alleged violations of the federal statutes. If found guilty, she would be liable to forty-five years in the penitentiary.

When Margaret grasped the message, she asked the men to come in and sit down. As they stumbled over a pile of woolly animals and a misplaced velocipede, it was their turn for surprise, which continued to mount as she explained about birth control. She must have made one of the best presentations of her life, for three hours later the federal agents agreed that there should be no such laws as those she had violated. Still, the laws existed and she must go to court.

After the door closed, her father came out from the adjoining room where he had been pretending to read the paper. Deeply moved, he took her in his arms as though she were again his favorite little girl. She was a "brave, clean warrior," he assured her and would win her case. Had he known before what he had just learned, her mother would still be alive. For the first time since Anne Higgins's death, father and daughter were united in spirit. When he returned to Corning, he tried again to collaborate with clippings and advice.

In Europe, the guns of August were in full blast when Margaret was arraigned in her personal war with her government. Nevertheless, her first session in court was so reassuring that she guessed that the federal agents had said a good word for her. Not only did Judge John Hazel postpone the case until fall, but the assistant district attorney volunteered that if this was not enough time, he would grant more. It seemed to her that these reasonable men would surely accept her story, as had the federal agents and her father.

Nevertheless, with an uncertain future, she must make new plans for the children. Bill's mother had died, but luckily they were used to being cared for by others. At the moment ten-year-old Stuart, wholly engrossed in sports, was enjoying summer camp in Maine. At her sister Nan's suggestion, she enrolled him for the next year at Winnwood, a Long Island boarding school. If need be, Nan herself would look after the younger ones who were spending August with friends in the Catskills. Margaret felt easier about Peggy because Grant remained her cherished guardian.

With the care of her children settled, Margaret turned to her long delayed task of writing up all that she had learned in France. She still had no idea when she might release it, but if she were to be locked up for life, the pamphlet, which she would call *Family Limitation,* must be ready as a last will and testament. "It is the big battalions of unwanted babies," she wrote, "that make life so hard for the working woman and keep her in poverty and stress from generation to generation. Every mother feels the wrong that the State imposes upon her when it deprives her of information to prevent bringing into the world children she cannot feed or clothe or care for." After a brief introduction, she set down in simple, straightforward language the forbidden knowledge, describing the condom, tampon, suppositories, and douches.

Friends and family were now bombarding her with pleas for caution. Margaret was blind and deaf to them as she poured out on paper what she had been longing to tell the Sadie Sachses of the nation. Later, in writing of this period, she said that it was a wonderful sensation to live through weeks of apparent fanaticism. Her single-minded vision obscured the possibility of defeat. When she had finished writing, she began to look for a printer. She interviewed specially recommended ones, twenty of whom turned her down before a Russian linotype setter agreed to do the illegal work after hours when the shop was supposedly closed.

She had thought in terms of printing 10,000 copies, but after testing union demands, she wanted a million. For lack of funds, she compromised on 100,000, most of which would go to leaders in the West Virginia coal mines, the Montana copper mines, and to the New England wool and New Jersey cotton workers. She still did not know when to release them, although friends were already addressing the bundles. It would have been exhilarating to have known that over the years they would sell 10 million copies of this pamphlet, that it would be translated into thirteen languages and that for a time in the Yucatan, Mexico, it would be given to each couple along with the marriage license.

With her task done, Margaret felt singularly at peace. Short of funds, she had not consulted a lawyer, nor had time to consider her defense plea when she learned one day in October that her case had been called and that she must be in court the next morning. Still relying on the promise of whatever time she needed, she asked for a deferral.

But the world had changed since August. Belgium was overrun, the French lines had broken, and the Battle of the Marne was raging. That was not all, thought Margaret, when the clerk trumpeted the words "The People versus Margaret Sanger." Her country was really at war with her. In her mind flashed a huge map of the United States, which came alive like a prehistoric monster ready to trample on her, so small and helpless. It was then she realized that with a European war on, no one would care about her little freedom-of-the-press battle.

Judge Hazel's attitude had certainly changed. He advised her to get an attorney at once, for the trial would start that afternoon. She found a labor lawyer who promised to secure a month's delay, but he failed. The utmost concession was a postponement until the next morning. The lawyer, by now convinced that her conviction had been decided on, insisted that she plead guilty, in which case he might be able to get her off with only a fine. Horrified, she said that she would call him later and went home.

She had eighteen hours to determine her fate. Somehow she had fallen into the one intolerable position—defeat with no effective protest. Unprepared as she was, she would be convicted by what had become a hostile court. Certainly she would not plead guilty because that would repudiate all that she stood for; furthermore, her children would have a mother known as a peddler of obscenity. On the other hand, if she served a long term, she might be broken in prison, which would hurt her cause, as well as herself.

Interrupting her thoughts came friends and relatives, most upsetting of all, Bill Sanger, just back with the last wave of refugees from France. He had taken a studio on Fifteenth Street, and now came to urge her to give up the fight. She must plead guilty and do what her lawyer said. Her mind stopped functioning. Then she asked everyone, including Bill, to leave while she made her decision. Alone at last, but surrounded with reminders of her children, she was still distracted. Finally, she packed a bag, went downtown and locked herself into an anonymous hotel room.

Her watch kept ticking off the seconds, devouring her period of freedom. Had she been indicted for *Family Limitation,* instead of *The Woman Rebel,* she could have projected her message to make the ordeal significant. Finally her course became clear. She must arrange the timing of the trial to favor her cause. By removing herself from the country, she could prepare an adequate defense. Meanwhile, she would release her blast on birth control.

Hastily she wrote letters to the judge and district attorney, explaining her plans. Because they had refused time for adequate preparation, she was leaving home, but she would inform them when she returned. To make her commitment clear, she added to each letter one of her illegal pamphlets.

All alone she made the tactical decision of her life. Then after calling a friend, she reached Grand Central Station shortly before midnight. There were a few to see her off, bringing money and promises to raise more for her needs abroad. With no passport and leaving behind all that she loved—her three children—Margaret Sanger boarded the train for Montreal, en route for England in the midst of war.

Exile

9

Reckless and immoral as her decision to leave seemed to many, it was, nevertheless, an inspiration. It proclaimed to millions not only that there were safe ways to limit the size of a family, but that discussion of the subject was a crime. Overnight the name Margaret Sanger became synonymous with a challenge to the law.

From her own standpoint, Margaret was simply buying time. Since she had been trapped in a position where defense was impossible, she had forced a postponement of her trial. Unexpectedly, her tactics achieved what Comstock and the Post Office most wanted to avoid, vast publicity on the censorship of birth control.

While on the train, to avoid extradition, Margaret changed her name. Later she regretted her ugly choice, but unconsciously she may have been attracted by the phonetics of the first name. For the next year she answered to Bertha Watson.

Friends who met her at Montreal volunteered to join with the New York group in raising money for her months in exile. Then, as soon as she was at sea, Margaret cabled her labor associates to release the 100,000 copies of *Family Limitation*. With that achieved, she felt completely drained, and for the next weeks suffered only an aching loneliness for her children, especially for little Peggy. Someday she hoped that her daughter would understand, perhaps would find life easier, because of her mother's crusade.

The ship on which she sailed was loaded with munitions and with men returning for home duty. All through Margaret's life well-wishers would appear when she faced emergencies. This time one passenger was indispensable because on reaching Liverpool, she was told that she might not debark without a passport. England was at war. Although she never disclosed what happened, someone's personal intervention made it possible for her to land.

A prolonged fog and then a cheerless London lodging house increased Margaret's sense of desolation. Her flight had severed her life like a self-inflicted amputation. Here she was, thousands of miles from her family, with nothing to do in an alien land. In her unpublished journal she wrote: "How lonely it all is. . . . Could any prison be more isolated . . . ? Could one be more alone . . . in solitary than wandering about the world separated from the little ones you love, from their childish prattle, caresses, whisperings and quarrels . . ." As planned the previous summer, Stuart was at boarding school, but the care of the younger children had been hastily improvised. Margaret had been relying on Nan, but for once this most conventional of the sisters had been too shocked to help. Margaret had been forced to leave the younger ones with Bill's neighbors on Fifteenth Street.

To enlist the moral support of her sister Mary, now living in Buffalo, Margaret wrote a long letter, trying to explain what she had done and why. She also confided that Bill's year in Paris had "sort of prepared us both for a parting of the ways." Then, since her great concern was the younger children, whom Mary did not know, she described them, "beautiful dears, Grant dark with brown eyes and Peggy light with blue eyes . . . just my romantic dream come true." Would Mary please keep in touch with Bill Sanger, who had promised to supervise the children? Of course various friends were also looking after them.

In these first London days she also noted in her journal that she had been so impressed by a lecture on the German philosopher, Friedrich Nietzsche, that she meant to study his works with a view to preparing her own talk. This was more than a passing impulse, for a quarter of a century later she closed her *Autobiography* with his words, "Build thou beyond thyself."

Since compassion had inspired her career, Margaret never accepted the simplistic view that Nietzsche exalted ruthless power. On the other hand, she, too, disliked weakness in herself and in others, and agreed that so-called morality was often merely conformity. She found downright unhealthy the priestly rejection of physical joys, while approving Nietzsche's "Overman" who affirmed all phases of life and used the full powers of a trained mind, with passions controlled, but not deadened. It was better, she wrote, to develop the God within oneself than to worship "at the shrine of other egos."

Most earlier women crusaders had found their support in religion, but Margaret Sanger, alienated from orthodox churches, turned in her loneliness to this famous anti-clerical writer. Her study of Nietzsche probably toughened some of the fibers of her complex nature, helping her to stand alone, even to the point of relinquishing her husband. Interspersed among comments on Nietzsche, she wrote, "I have this day cast the die. I have written Bill a letter ending a relationship of over twelve years." Later she added that Bill would not be surprised, for she had prepared him: "Only I am very slow in my decisions. I cannot separate myself from my past emotions quickly, all breaches must come gradually to me."

One day she screwed up courage to write to the C. V. Drysdales, with whom she had been in touch as editor of *The Woman Rebel*. Dr. Drysdale was the current head of a family which for two-thirds of a century had headed the British movement for population control—the portentous-sounding Neo-Malthusian Association.

On a dark November afternoon Margaret swashed through drizzle to find her homesick despair dissolve in the cheery comfort of a fire, tea with scones, and the warmest welcome she had ever known. Several persons were present; they all knew her story and accepted her stand. More than that, they exulted in it.

It was as though she had met some close but hitherto unknown relations. These were her people. Their purposes were hers and, indeed, they had long been struggling for similar goals. They received her as an ally from the United States, a country just entering the first stage of a campaign which they had won decades earlier. So with her first London contacts, she found that she was not alone.

True, the English group had worked in quieter ways, because their goal had been to educate the educators. In British tradition, they believed that if the upper classes supported family limitation, the masses would follow. But forty years of meager results had created so much dissatisfaction with their tactics that no one wanted to rebuff the brave young American; instead, they offered her their resources, helped to publicize her story, and later booked her for their meetings.

With the Drysdales' encouragement, Margaret began a course of self-directed study in the reading room of the British Museum. There she was given her own desk where she spent most of her waking hours. One December afternoon she shortened her usual schedule to accept another invitation to tea, this time with the author Havelock Ellis.

Contemporaries sometimes placed Ellis beside Darwin and Freud as a genius who had opened up a new science. This overstated his contribution, since he offered no new scientific system, but he did help to raise sex from the gutter and purify it in the sunlight of reason. A prodigious, wide-ranging writer, his unique contribution was *The Psychology of Sex,* whose seven volumes Margaret had read the preceding winter. While it did not give her the answers for which she was looking, she revered its author as the authority in the field from which her crusade stemmed.

Diffidently she had let the brass knocker drop and then was overwhelmed when her host himself opened the door. At fifty-five, he seemed a slender giant with the outdoor glow of a Viking, but combined with the snowy hair, beard, and brooding eyes of a prophet. He smiled a beautiful welcome as he led her into a small room cluttered with books and only slightly warmed by the gas fire on the hearth.

Margaret groped to fill a long silence, stuttering banalities, to which he hardly responded. Gradually it occurred to her that he was saying little because he was as shy as she. She relaxed and within the hour they had established real communication which they would maintain as long as he lived. On that first day they discovered profound similarities, including a single-minded sense of destiny which had come suddenly to each.

At the age of twenty, Ellis had settled his future by deciding to explore the field of sex. He made the choice not because he was a highly sexed youth, for the fact was the reverse, but because the subject was a vast unknown territory, which, for the welfare of man, he thought should be examined. For him, it opened a unique career, starting with fifteen years of study, followed by fifteen years in which he poured out his erudition on paper. When he had fulfilled his plan, he wrote, "The work that I was born to do, is done."

Margaret understood his commitment, which strengthened her own. But there was another bond between them, their conflicts with archaic laws. Sixteen years before *The Woman Rebel* was banned, the first volume of Ellis's sex studies was condemned in London as "lewd, wicked, bawdy, scandalous and obscene." A promoter of the book had pleaded guilty when arrested, and Ellis had not intervened. Having a thin, reedy voice, he never spoke in public and feared that contention would reduce his scholarly creativity. The whole trial was bungled and the author so wounded that he never published any more books in England.

Ellis had relied on time to win his victories, and it had vindicated his faith. Soon after the trial, in the nineties, the controversial volume was issued in Germany and then in the United States by a medical publishing house. In the next years the series was translated into many languages. Avoiding disputes, the author had quietly pursued his work and although his books seldom made money, his prestige steadily mounted.

Havelock Ellis did not exult, as had the Drysdales, at his new friend's defiance of the law. Although deeply sympathetic and admiring her courage, he always urged caution. Had she followed his tactical advice, probably she would not be known today. On the other hand, she needed precisely the traits which he encouraged, a deeper understanding of her subject, moderation in statement, and an improved style.

As she studied his works, her first impulse was to burn all of her own. There was no reason for that, he assured her. While he was not certain she had a gift for writing, he liked *The Woman Rebel* because it was direct and sincere. Years later the great stylist cheered her progress with his enthusiasm for *My Fight for Birth Control*.

His immediate influence was to guide her daily reading. Since no one was more knowledgeable in her field, he became her counselor. His own habit was to spend two days a week in the library, and on those days they lunched together. Under his guidance, she developed an intellectual background that gave depth to her leadership.

But Ellis's impact was more than that of academic guide. To her, he was Olympian and when he stretched out his hand in friendship, she clasped that hand, never to let it drop. Years later in describing their first meeting in the *Autobiography,* she said that her emotion was too deep to be called excitement. She felt as though she had been "exalted into a hitherto undreamed of world." Their response to one another was such that they called each other "Twin."

The Background of the Movement
10

In the library Margaret began her task like a genealogist tracking down ancestors, although she was looking for spiritual forebears. It had been easy to recognize her kinship with the Drysdales; now she wanted to find the roots of her family tree. Who had first challenged the rights of church and state to force people to multiply with no curbs on their fertility?

Even before she began her studies, Margaret realized that throughout most of man's existence, survival had been the problem, and that required the proliferation of vast numbers of expendables. And yet, as Margaret found, from the very dawn of history there was evidence that man had tried to limit his own fertility. Whenever there were too many mouths to feed, infanticide had been the answer. This practice had continued right into modern times, not only among primitive peoples, but in the case of girl babies, throughout the sophisticated Orient, as well as illegally in every land. As a means of race improvement, Plato and Aristotle had endorsed it. They had also suggested it for family limitation, to be used under a council of elders to insure a proper balance between the state's population and its food supply.

But as far back as one can go, there had also been experiments in the prevention of birth. Four thousand years ago, among the first medical reports, the Chinese included instructions for abortion. A thousand years later the Egyptian Petri Papyrus gave advice for suppositories made of honey and alligator's dung, which may have been as effective as the "antiseptic pastes" sold in later times. The Hebrews, Hindus, and Persians all left prescriptions for suppositories, some using alum or olive oil.

Yet for all the urgency in helping special cases of privileged ladies, few, except the Greek philosophers, had worried about the overall birth rate until the great upsurge in population following the Industrial Revolution. This expansive age inspired wide-ranging speculation, much of it too sanguine, which in turn started a reaction. Enthusiasts of the early phase of the French Revolution believed that people's governments, with the help of modern machinery to create material abundance, would not only end poverty, ignorance, and disease, but raise up ideal societies.

To Thomas R. Malthus, English pastor and later professor of history and political science, this was utopian nonsense. When his own father argued that way at the breakfast table, his son was goaded into rebuttal. He claimed that the chief cause of human strife and misery was man's constant tendency to increase beyond his means of subsistence. Malthus built his thesis on wide reading, including evidence presented three decades earlier by Benjamin Franklin in his *Notes* on the then British Colonies.

Franklin had observed that the population of his country had doubled in twenty-five years. He had also predicted that for some time it would go on doubling every quarter of a century. The cause of this growth was the New World's vast, unpeopled land, which encouraged early marriage and large families, averaging eight children. As Dr. Franklin saw it, the chief restraint on the spread of any species, plant or animal, was overcrowding. In the Old World, mutual interference on a limited food supply had kept the population stable. Without such interference, any species would proliferate until it finally covered the earth. These points from Dr. Franklin helped trigger the ideological bomb which Malthus exploded in 1792.

For Margaret Sanger, Malthus was only a name when she began to read at the British Museum, but the name to which all references led. She studied the famous *Essay on Population,* and then secured her own copy to keep on hand for her life work. She was amazed, however, to find nothing about the problem which had launched her own career. Nowhere did the author so much as hint that women had a special stake in his subject.

With lofty scholarship Professor Malthus set forth his postulates: (1) Food is necessary to the existence of man. (2) The passion of the sexes is necessary and will remain in its present state. (3) The power of population is infinitely greater than the power of the earth to produce subsistence because population, if unchecked, increases in geometric ratio, e.g., 1, 2, 4, 8, 16, etc., while subsistence increases only in arithmetic ratio, e.g., 1, 2, 3, 4, 5, etc. In other words, the seeds of life are profuse, while the room to raise food is restricted. Under this curb all species, fauna as well as flora, shrink, as must the race of man. Nature keeps a last dreadful resource to enforce its law, famine. But man himself helps maintain the balance through his vices, which constantly reduce the population. Therefore political reforms to end poverty and disease would merely increase the numbers and hasten famine.

As a cleric, Malthus recognized only one way to check nature's harsh laws. Man alone of all species is endowed with reason and a conscience. If he chooses, he can restrain his sexual passion. A policy of late marriage and abstinence could control the birth rate.

To the nurse who had worked in New York's tenements, this solution was as utopian as the instant reform plans at which Malthus had scoffed. Because his contemporaries were also skeptical, some of them groped for alternatives, but the most practical suggestion had been made even before Malthus published his essay.

Jeremy Bentham, the philosopher, had thrown out a curious observation when he wrote on *The Situation and Relief of the Poor*. He said that French women relied on a sponge to stop conception. Thirty years later the benign old bachelor again referred to the sponge, this time in writing to the man who is today called the father of family limitation.

Francis Place was a master tailor of Charing Cross, London, when he received Bentham's letter. He had become not only prosperous but well read through self-imposed exertion and a small library. Slowly, painfully, he had lifted himself out of poverty and squalor. Married at the age of nineteen, he had at once begun to sire the first of his fifteen children, five of whom he buried as infants. He seemed the archetype of all the sexual recklessness that Malthus had condemned and he might have remained just that, had it not been for his wife. For all her burdens, it was she, he insisted, who had inspired him to rise in the world through intellectual effort.

As though to atone for his own concupiscence, he gave much of his later life to family limitation. Like the American nurse who read about him a hundred years later, he, alone of those concerned, was motivated by personal experience. Since to him the problem was not an abstraction, he launched an activist campaign.

Convinced by his own failure that Malthus's hope of moral restraint would never succeed, Francis Place called attention to realistic remedies. As he saw it, the task was not to preach to the poor, but to teach them how to avoid excess children. He advised them to follow their better nature by marrying early and remaining chaste, but at the same time to limit their families in "hygienic ways."

He explained all this in a broadside to *Married Working People,* currently known as the "diabolical handbill." For the use of the poor, and for the first time in history, Francis Place listed three types of contraception: (1) withdrawal, known from Biblical times as "coitus interruptus" and later called "male prudence." (2) the sheath for the male, made of sheer cloth or animal guts. (3) a sponge, tampon, douche and suppositories for the female.

Aware of the risks in his undertaking, he printed the handbills anonymously and had them placed in bundles under market stalls to use for likely customers as wrappers for candles and other merchandise. In some places the leaflets were passed out at factory gates or among crowds of workers. One of those who did the passing and got caught was Bentham's foremost protégé, seventeen-year-old John Stuart Mill, who was readied for the task by two gruesome experiences in one fateful hour.

Strolling through St. James's Park one morning, young Mill had come upon a bundle, half-hidden under a tree. He prodded the wrapping until he recognized a blue-faced, strangled, newborn baby. Still shaken by the sight when he passed Old Bailey prison, he faced a group of freshly hanged prisoners, dangling grotesquely by the neck.

Shortly afterward, meeting Francis Place, he blurted out what he had seen. The older man then explained to him the tragedy of unwanted children and their train of misery and vice. Place also confided his own project for reform. Soon young Mill and a friend were hurrying about London with the tracts. They were especially eager to help those most needing help, young married women. But the boys were arrested and spent at least one night in jail on the soon to become familiar charge of distributing obscene literature. In later years, the philosopher-economist wrote cautiously about population pressures, but his activist career had closed the day after it began.

Closely in touch with the Bentham-Place circle was Robert Owen, the venturesome Scottish industrial reformer who founded a cooperative colony at New Harmony, Indiana. Owen began with the highest hopes, but not much staying power. When he left his dreary and primitive Utopia, his son, Robert Dale, took over and tried to carry on his father's ideas, which included curbing human fertility. He wrote an essay, *Moral Philosophy,* expounding the reasons for and the nature of the known methods of contraception. This was the first American book to touch the subject, and it inspired a second, whose impact was historic and international.

A copy of Owen's book came into the hands of Dr. Charles Knowlton of Taunton, Massachusetts, a graduate of Dartmouth Medical College. As a physician, his practice had brought him in touch with many women who needed contraception, but he had never heard of it. By himself, he quietly made a few experiments which convinced him that a douche with some chemical base was a preventive. His preference was for alum, a favorite among the ancients. After reading Owen's book, Knowlton wrote his own from the medical standpoint. In 1832 he published it anonymously under the discreet title, *The Fruits of Philosophy,* relying, as had Owen, on a lofty title to shield the subject; only the subtitle, *The Private Companion of Young Married People,* suggested something more.

Since the book was written by a doctor in a temperate style, it was for many decades the most impressive work in its field. To this day there are no better answers than Knowlton's to such perennial charges as that family limitation is an unnatural act. To this he readily agreed. It is as unnatural as cutting one's hair or fingernails or shaving. Civilization is a constant war against nature. "The high prerogative of man consists in his power to counteract or to control nature."

Although writing in Puritan Massachusetts, Dr. Knowlton did not share Malthus's views on abstinence, for he saw no virtue in thwarting the normal sex instinct. Instead, he advised married couples to enjoy their pleasures, but using proper safeguards, which he forthwith explained.

Unfortunately Massachusetts was still Puritan. When the authorities tracked down the author of this "lewd" book, they arrested him and after due process of law, sentenced Dr. Knowlton to three months at hard labor. This savage punishment served its purpose. No other doctors risked their careers to tell mothers about contraception, even in cases where another birth might be fatal.

In England, Dr. Knowlton's book continued to sell for forty years, after which it again became a cause célèbre. Hoping to profit from a new concern in the subject, a printer brought out another edition of *Fruits of Philosophy* in the eighteen-seventies, this time with charts and illustrations. Perhaps the graphic aids brought the change of tactics, for the police arrested the printer and persuaded him to plead guilty to the obscenity charges in exchange for a suspended sentence. This satisfied the printer, but not the Malthusian League, recently founded by the Drysdale family of doctors.

In a direct test of the legitimacy of the cause of fertility control, Annie Besant, famous later as a theosophist lecturer, joined with a publisher, Charles Bradlaugh, in bringing out still another edition of the American book. They too were arrested and, in conducting their own defense, became the talk of London. At her trial, Annie Besant declared that she was not the defendant, but the counsel for the poor. "I find my clients amongst the mothers worn-out with over-frequent child-bearing. . . . mothers who beg me to persist in the course on which I am entered."

Nevertheless, they were both sentenced to six months in jail. By appealing their sentences, they achieved their purpose. The Upper Court dismissed the case on a technicality. This decision rendered in 1876 settled for all time in England that contraception was not an obscenity.

To Margaret Sanger, studying in the British Museum, most of this history was news. She had searched the American libraries from Washington to Boston, where the *Fruits of Philosophy* was first published, but she had found no mention of it. She had to cross the ocean to learn the part played by her fellow countryman, Dr. Knowlton, in the genesis of what had become her struggle. Beyond that, she had found in the Bradlaugh-Besant precedent the strategy on which she would build her movement. She too would rely on the higher courts.

In her studies Margaret had gained a second curious insight which would help her in New York. She had found that the best-known article of contraception had always been immune from attack. Back in the eighteenth century, an English Colonel Cundom had developed and advertised without molestation, a sheath made from sheep guts. The condom, as it became known, was apparently legal because its purpose was to protect the male from venereal disease and not to protect the female from conception.

Margaret had established her spiritual forebears and found useful precedents, but that was only a fraction of what she learned that year. Havelock Ellis broadened her vision of the potentials of birth control not only as a means for protecting mothers, but as the key to race improvement and the adjustment of population to world resources. From henceforth her emotional commitment was reinforced by a vast fund of exact information in related fields.

"The Sage of Sex"

11

By the winter of 1914 Margaret had reached a turning point in her personal as well as her public life. Separated for a year, the Sangers had been drifting apart for much longer. In both of her autobiographies she said that her marriage had failed not "because of lack of love, romance, wealth, respect or any of those qualities which were supposed to cause marital rifts, but because the interests of each had widened beyond those of the other. Development had proceeded so fast that our lives had diverged, due to the very growth which we sought for each other." From her standpoint this was true, although Bill would not have agreed.

From Paris he had written that ever since their first meeting her personality had set the die deep across his soul and he did not want to erase it. He had "basked in the sunshine of her mind, revelled in her vivacity and womanliness" and beyond that, had seen what she might become. Her "ways of thought would flash to the very skies" and there was no intellectual height she could not reach. Of course she must be relieved of family cares—although he did not suggest how—but he would rather accomplish less himself so that he might have "the priceless privilege to sit beside her spiritually while she expressed the best within her."

Margaret did not want to live with anyone "conscious that her necessities were thwarting or dwarfing his progress." Furthermore, in her new, demanding role she had neither time nor inclination to cherish a struggling painter in whom she had lost faith. Like a runner stripping off nonessentials, she wanted to be free of

Bill Sanger. In spite of his devotion, he seemed to Margaret jealous, blundering, overbearing, insensitive, and always improvident. Probably the truth was that she had never loved him as he loved her. Some of his traits which had at first attracted her, because they were so like her father's, she no longer admired. Her instinct had been sound in trying to delay the marriage, just as he had been right in thinking it must be then or never. His insistence had won his young bride, but now his beloved wife wanted her freedom.

In England that winter there seemed a parallel in the personal lives of Margaret Sanger and Havelock Ellis. He too was married in what his wife called a "semi-detached" way, which included living apart. Currently she was on an American lecture tour, but the real separation had grown over the years through a series of complicated relationships. By this time Ellis had concluded that his wife was "congenitally unfit" for marriage.

Ellis's own unusual traits emerge from his posthumous *My Life,* as well as several biographies. After the shy, precocious youth had decided to make sex his specialty, he studied medicine, taking a certificate of honor in midwifery, which he practiced for a year in London's slums. This background gave some authority for his later writing. He then retired to his studies. Karl Marx, he once observed, "a student seated in the library of the British Museum," was consumed with zeal in behalf of the proletariat whom he did not know. He might have added that Havelock Ellis, a student seated in the same library, became an authority on sex, with which he had slight personal acquaintance.

His pseudo-introduction to the subject came in the eighteen-eighties with his friendship for Olive Schreiner, the South African feminist who was visiting England. For four years they were spiritually inseparable. Affectionately she called him her "other self" and more picturesquely, "a cross between a satyr and Jesus Christ." Since neither type appealed as a husband, they did not marry. He frankly said that she realized that he was not fitted to play the part which her "elementary, primitive nature craved." To him, she remained a wonderful preview of future women, freed from the taboos imposed upon them by possessive males. So he became the champion of Woman.

In 1891 he married Edith Lees, another dynamic feminist. Before the wedding, he made clear that his work would always come first and since it was not remunerative, Edith must care for herself and have no children. He would continue in his quiet bachelor quarters, but they would vacation and later spend their old age together. She accepted these rules partly because she too was independent, having revolted against a harsh father and stepmother, partly because she had a small income and faith in her own creative powers, but mostly because she loved him. After the wedding she found another barrier to conventional marriage. They were physically incompatible and after much frustration, they agreed to forget about sex. Both of them doubted his virility and they never again tested it.

Their letters, with which *My Life* is replete, show that they remained remarkably affectionate, although there was a change. Perhaps because of her unhappy childhood, Edith began to invest her husband with the maternal qualities that she had never known. He responded and always said that she had the spirit of a young boy. Meanwhile, in nonpsychiatric terms, a recluse had married a very active and sociable woman. To occupy herself, as well as to increase her income, Edith undertook many projects, including writing, and had some success. These activities filled the days of a wife who had no children nor husband to care for.

To fill the emotional void, she turned to those who wanted her company and over the years developed a series of intense friendships with other women, most of which Ellis said were like schoolgirl crushes. Edith yearned, he explained, for someone on whom to lavish her attentions and to "expend a love which was like passion, even if an ethereal one." So etherealized was her greatest love that she conceived a posthumous, mystic cult around the memory of this woman.

Being forthright, Edith confided her feelings to her husband, although in the first instance she seemed to plead for his understanding and attention. According to *My Life,* which is largely an account of his marriage and ends with Edith's death, only this one attachment shocked him. He had not yet diagnosed Edith's case and had he done so, he would not have blamed her. He explicitly said that her acts were in good taste and she could not be reproved for errant feelings. What jolted him was that the new love proved that she was less absorbed in him. After subduing his hurt pride, Ellis wrote reassuringly and sent his "sweetest love" to her lady friend. In retrospect, some critics thought that had he tried to meet her emotional needs at this time, he might have ended such incidents, but perhaps deep down he was relieved that she also was vulnerable.

In the first weeks of their marriage Ellis had been bored by her social demands on him. He wrote bluntly that he was not dependent on her for friends and did not want her to depend on him. Privately he admitted that her exuberance exhausted him. He recalled the old saying that a writer should marry a feather bed, but far from being a reposeful bed, Edith was more like a porcupine. To preserve his tranquillity and to ward off her pricks and proddings, he threw up an insulating wall around himself.

There may have been another reason why he did not oppose Edith's ardent friendships. Although he always maintained that his marriage was an ideal comradeship of the spirit—which was the best type of union—Ellis later found that he craved certain feminine traits that Edith did not have, but which were embodied in Amy Smith, a young girl whom he had long known. He kissed her once and then, as candid as Edith, he told his wife. She was furious, which he thought unjust, in light of his own self-imposed tolerance. Later he argued that Edith's double standard, conflicting with his own belief in mutualism, drove him into his first liaison. Still forthright, he gave her a play-by-play account of his affair and to please her, once temporarily broke with Amy.

Edith then proposed that they should both drop their extramarital attachments and be self-sufficient again. Since he would not discuss this proposal, nothing changed. While they had failed in their first concept of devotion, he came to believe that having faced their problem honestly, they had achieved a new harmony with greater depths of love. As he finally convinced Edith, it was easy to imagine a more or less sexual relationship with some other person, but the spiritual passion of their marriage was unique.

During this period Ellis brought out his first volume of the sex studies, on inversion, a theme which Edith disliked. Meanwhile, she wrote a novel, *Kit's Woman,* on the spiritual love that sustained a marriage after an accident had rendered the husband impotent. He thought it her best work and for many years did not connect it with their relationship.

Meanwhile, Edith developed nervous afflictions, as well as suffering bouts of pneumonia and heart trouble. By 1913, her doctor diagnosed diabetes, which was serious in pre-insulin days. Nevertheless, at the age of fifty, she seemed in fair health when she launched her most daring plan, an American lecture tour. With a beautiful voice and good platform presence, Edith had always enjoyed public appearances and now, billed as Mrs. Havelock Ellis, she hoped to boost their fortunes. She would speak not only on her famous husband, but on his contemporaries and the new outlook on sex and marriage, with special stress on spiritual passion. Ellis, being a shy man who never made a speech in his life, winced at the public exposure, but since the tour would stimulate book sales, which he needed, he agreed. The preliminaries had all gone well in the fall of 1914.

In her *Autobiography,* Margaret says that Ellis often left notes for suggested reading at her library desk; sometimes they went to a concert or had tea in his apartment. Forty years later she threw a sidelight on this period in an unpublished letter to Françoise de Lisle, Ellis's last close friend. To her, Margaret wrote that Ellis had confided that his wife was a "congenital homosexual," whom he had tried to shield from gossip through marriage. By this time he believed that she was also a manic depressive.

In *My Life,* speaking of the young American woman, Ellis said that he had never known a more charming and congenial companion, nor found one so swiftly. Their moods synchronized perfectly, which had never been the case with Edith. "The relationship was one of calm friendship, even though there was a sweet touch of intimacy about it." The unpublished letters at the Library of Congress, as well as other evidence, suggest more than a calm friendship brightened by an occasional cup of tea.

One of Ellis's biographers, Calder Marshall, noted that it was months before Ellis kissed Olive Schreiner, years before he kissed Amy, but only a few days before he kissed Margaret Sanger. In *Impressions and Omens,* which Ellis published a decade later, he celebrated that New Year's kiss: "I cannot tell in what lurid gloom mixed with what radiant halo this year will stand out from all the years in the eyes of men alive on the earth before us. Yet we two are still living and for all living things hope springs afresh from despair. So it is that I have begun this new year at the stroke of midnight with a kiss." Down through the years, as he once wrote Margaret, "this holiday is forever associated with the memory of your dear presence."

After this they were in daily communication. "Dear Woman Rebel," began an early note and then dropping the "Rebel," his salutation became generic—"Dear Woman," or "Pearl of a Woman," or "You Darling Woman." He usually signed himself, "Lovingly, H." as he did to Edith. They exchanged photographs, and she cherished a clip of white hair, which to this day is kept with his letters. He treasured a twist of brown hair with a golden glint.

On January thirteenth he wrote:

I think we should agree, dear Twin, on the subject of love. I think that passion is mostly a disastrous thing and certainly ruinous to work, for it makes all work seem of less than no account. And then too, it's always felt for the wrong person. Indeed, its very intensity seems due to a sort of vague realization that *there's nothing there.* But I cannot say that I think love is anything but good, and good for everything including work. I mean by love something that is based on a true relationship and that has succeeded in avoiding the blind volcano of passion (or has continued to pass safely through that stage). To secure the peaceful, joyous and consoling and inspiring elements of love—and to escape the other—seems to me a very desirable and precious thing indeed and by no means a common thing.

In *My Fight for Birth Control,* Margaret wrote that "as we talked, we wove into our lives an intangible web of mutual interests, and speaking for myself, I developed a reverence, an affection, and a love which have strengthened with the years." In her 1939 *Autobiography* she said, "I have never felt about any other person as I do about Havelock Ellis." It may have been the supreme relationship of her life, although later she declared that she had not been interested in marriage, since she was not divorced, had three children, and a cause to which she had dedicated herself.

In *My Life,* Ellis explains rather awkwardly the long silence about Margaret in his letters to his wife. It was not his habit to practice deceit, but in this case he felt no need for secrecy, since he had no sense of guilt. He had failed to mention Margaret only because he was usually slow in becoming acquainted and wanted to be sure that this swift friendship was genuine.

Meanwhile, Edith's tour was prospering beyond all hopes. Her first lecture on her husband was at a crowded theater in New York. People were turned away when she talked on "The Loves of Tomorrow," in which she stressed spiritual passion. Off the cuff, in an interview, she volunteered that an enlightened wife should even love the woman her husband loved (just as she had learned to love Amy!). Because of her lectures, the book stores sold out their Havelock Ellis stocks and were ordering more.

For two months the Ellises corresponded about the climax of her tour, which would be at Chicago's Orchestra Hall. A group of women doctors was sponsoring a meeting on "Sex and Social Hygiene," and as a special feature, she wanted him to write a message for her to read. Obligingly, he wrote it, then forgot the meeting, the strain of the tour, Edith's excitable nature and apparently everything except Margaret Sanger.

Convinced at last that the friendship was authentic, he poured out the good news in a paean of praise to the nobility, charm, and intelligence of the woman with whom he had joined in a new spiritual comradeship. He sent the letter to Chicago where Edith received it on the eve of what she thought the greatest day of her public life. That night she drank a cocktail, toasting her husband and his latest love. Somehow, she managed the lecture, but afterward she only wanted to die.

Because of wartime delays it was three weeks before Ellis learned of her reaction and could soothe her. Meanwhile, he had written five more letters, all about Margaret. He later suggested that the strain of the tour had shattered Edith's health and brought on one of her illogical depressions. It was the letters that had prostrated her, Edith always insisted, but since she destroyed them, neither could prove his point.

Certainly the tone of her letters changed overnight from confidence to grim despair. She wrote of loneliness and death, and while denying jealousy, said that she was weary of everlasting crucifixion. The well-balanced Havelock Ellis, always serene and rational, mostly ignored this melodrama.

Yet she had a point. For twenty years Edith had schooled herself to accept Amy. Her husband had convinced her that a "more or less sexual relationship" with another woman was unimportant compared to her unique spiritual comradeship. So she had triumphed over her early jealousy and learned to send her love to the other woman in her husband's affections. Although not sure of herself in the conventional role of wife, on this tour, dedicated to the exaltation of Havelock Ellis, she had tried to embody the happy modern, married woman. She was in this exposed public posture when her husband announced that he had a new spiritual comrade. This one was a heroine, young enough to be Edith's daughter. She was famous too and the New York *Call* soon linked her name with that of Ellis. Gossips even reported that Edith was not really married anyhow.

If her husband were, indeed, "merged" with another being, Edith lamented from across the ocean, then her own foundations were gone. She apologized that her pride and pain could not always bear all things. She would rally herself to smile with a broken heart, and, in Ellis tradition, she sent affectionate greetings to "M." If she herself died, she wryly suggested, her possessions could furnish an apartment large enough to share with both "M" and "A."

Then she collapsed with fever, throat ulcers, and a heart attack. Canceling the rest of her tour, she miserably began to consume her hard-earned profits. At this point a kindly woman doctor took her into her own home for treatment and convalescence. She wrote Ellis suggesting that he come to America to escort his sick wife home. He thought the letter a mere formality and failed to answer it.

Just after the *Lusitania* sank, Edith crossed the dreadnaught-studded Atlantic in a crowded, filthy ship. Still weak as she landed, she was badly upset when a newspaper woman asked if Mrs. Sanger would be waiting at the dock with Mr. Ellis. "Are you alone?" was her anguished and mysterious greeting to her husband.

She stayed a few nights at his London flat, but one day, after Amy called, Edith took morphia tablets. Ellis rescued her, but seemed to miss the link between the visit and the tablets. From her letters to him, published in *My Life,* it is clear that Edith's two desires were for her husband's presence and the assurance of his love. During the last terrible year he found it hard to grant either. She suggested divorce so that he might marry Margaret, and she finally drew up a strange "deed of separation."

Actually, Edith's return hastened the end of the first phase of the Ellis-Sanger relationship. They saw each other only rarely before Margaret returned to the United States, when their correspondence slackened to a weekly rate. She had been home for a year when he wrote, "Your birthday was a sad, sad day for me. On that early morning Edith died peacefully [A diabetic attack following a chill] . . . I wished that I had been more with her of late, as she always wished, but I know it was wiser as it was. . . . She was always a child, although a very lovable child . . ." Neither suggested anything symbolic about Edith's leaving the world on the anniversary of Margaret's birth.

Along with some of Ellis's erudition, Margaret took home with her his attitude toward sex. One of the first to view the subject in a scientific way, he thought that he had slain the dragon of guilt and that the world would be sweeter for his work. While not going as far as Freud in judging sex the one cause of great emotion, he knew that it was part of the deepest and most volcanic human feelings, but unlike the hunger drive, it could be transmuted into creative outlets. Theoretically, he approved unlimited sexual freedom and for women too. Men had always indulged their lusts, but Ellis insisted on a single standard of morality, as well as a new concern for women's erotic needs. He thought that if all relations were guided by love, they would be pure; the only remaining monster would be jealousy.

Visit to the Future

12

While Margaret was studying the history of her movement in London, Anthony Comstock made Sanger history in New York. He did so with his usual routine. One day a man introduced himself at Bill's studio as an old friend of Margaret's. Telling a pitiful tale of too many children and his wife's poor health, he asked for a copy of *Family Limitation*. Bill regretfully explained that he had none. Since the pamphlet had been written in his absence, he had nothing to do with it. The man seemed so disappointed that Bill rummaged through a desk and came up with his one personal copy.

A few days later the decoy returned with his familiar side-whiskered, massive-framed boss. Flourishing a warrant for Bill's arrest for circulating obscene literature, Comstock told him to come along quietly, presumably to the police station, but instead, with Bill protesting that he must see a lawyer, they went to a restaurant. Comstock assured Bill that he would advise him as a brother; lawyers would only aggravate the case. Growing affable as he enjoyed his dinner, the Inspector volunteered that once Bill had pleaded guilty, he would receive a suspended sentence. Bill rejected the idea on the grounds that the pamphlet was not obscene.

"Young man," declared Anthony Comstock between mouthfuls, "I have been in this work for twenty years and that leaflet is the worst thing I ever saw."

At one point in their talk, which Comstock was prolonging, he hinted that Bill would be acquitted if he told where his wife was. When Bill flared up about hell freezing over first, they finally adjourned to the police station. As planned, they arrived too late for Bill to reach a lawyer, and Comstock informed the press that Sanger could not secure bail. His victim spent the night in a filthy cell.

Bill sent word to Margaret to remain away until after the trial, which the court kept postponing. He was acting admirably, although for Margaret it was the ultimate irony that he should be harassed for her work, which had helped to alienate them. When the court deferred his case until the fall of 1915, she decided to remain abroad, in part because her research had reached a point involving another trip.

Poring over vital statistics in the British Museum, she had become enthralled by what looked like a benign force working exclusively in behalf of the Netherlands. In the last third of a century that little country had not only cut its overall death rate in half, but had achieved the lowest maternal death rate in the world, as well as the lowest urban death rate for babies. In grim contrast, the rich United States had the highest maternal death rate of any nation that kept statistics—three times that of Holland.

The Drysdales happily identified the benign force as a chain of birth control clinics. For three decades Holland had acted as a pilot project, showing the effects of contraception on race health. This work had originated through the efforts of Aletta Jacobs, the heroic Dutch woman doctor who had opened a free clinic, offering contraceptive counsel for the first time in history. Within a few years and within the radius of a few miles, the results were so striking that other people asked for clinics. Most of the subsequent ones were organized and supervised by Dr. J. Rutgers of The Hague. When Margaret learned that both of these innovators were still vigorously at work, she could hardly wait to see them.

From every prudent standpoint it was reckless to travel, for not only was Europe at war, but her false name might be discovered. Her fears were somewhat quieted when she asked for a visa at the Dutch consulate and the official merely said, "Eighty cents." Later she found that a letter from the flamboyant Bernarr McFadden of *Physical Culture* was her best passport. Before embarking on the channel boat, she nervously faced a battery of British inspectors who wanted to know if she was on an American joyride. Had she any good reason for going? She answered with McFadden's request for articles on population growth and the problem of the unfit. With new respect, the official let her through.

Sighting neither submarines nor bombs, the channel boat arrived early one morning in Holland, an oasis of tranquillity in the war-torn continent. The Hague had embodied man's hopes for international arbitration, and even at this time its Peace Palace was being prepared for a Women's Peace Conference, to be presided over by America's Jane Addams. Margaret, also a pacifist, would have felt at home there, especially as she believed that her cause must be the cornerstone to world peace. However, with a false name and passport, she had to remain anonymous.

It was not yet nine o'clock when, quite unheralded, Margaret presented herself at Dr. Rutgers's home. The ringing bell started a chain reaction, with the opening of a tiny upstairs window, out of which darted a wizened head, like a cuckoo clock. It was the doctor himself, not yet dressed or breakfasted. He had deficient English but a welcoming spirit and was soon plying her with good Dutch coffee and brioches, while he commiserated over her story and answered her questions.

Margaret had been baffled by a major aspect of the Netherlands' program. The population had continued to grow. Dr. Rutgers set her right about the purposes of the clinics, which had nothing to do with either an increase or decrease in the numbers of Dutchmen. Instead, the aim was to ensure a good life for each individual. Basic to this was proper child spacing. After every birth, the mother was discouraged from another pregnancy until her own health and economic conditions assured a welcome for a new baby. Under this policy, infant mortality had dropped far more rapidly than the birth rate.

Since Dr. Rutgers was currently training two midwives for a new clinic, he obligingly enrolled Margaret in the class. Her apprenticeship in the Dutch system completely changed her views on contraceptive methods. She also learned that the issue was not just free speech, but trained instruction.

Of all the known techniques, the Dutch had found one vastly

superior. It was a diaphragm pessary developed by Dr. Jacobs in cooperation with a Dr. Mensigna, whose name it bore. Margaret had never heard of the device, but for several decades it would surpass all others and would be used around the world. The diaphragm's chief drawback was that there were fourteen sizes so that the skill of the fitter was as important as that of an optician picking the right lenses. With her professional knowledge of anatomy, Margaret found the task simple, and she personally fitted seventy-five women. After years of frustration, she was exhilarated.

At the Central Bureau of Statistics in off hours, she discovered how effective the program was.

In London she had learned about the low Dutch mortality rates, but at The Hague the army records showed that the nation's improved health was reflected in the increased stature of their men. Among the other social changes was the closing of all houses of prostitution. Few prostitutes were left and almost no native ones. Venereal disease in Holland had decreased, as had illegitimacy. The rate for the latter was the lowest in the world, a fourth that of its neighbor Belgium and less than half of England's. Most illegitimacy was found among Catholics, who did not use the clinics. Without fear of large families, other young people married early, and their children's educational achievements rose. In a land of small families, child labor was rare which, in turn, improved the position of labor.

In Holland, voluntary parenthood had, indeed, meant quality breeding and race improvement. Instead of condemning contraception as immoral, Dutchmen applauded it as a constructive force. Queen Wilhelmina had recently presented a medal of honor, along with a charter, to the Neo-Malthusian League. Margaret had the reassuring sense that she had looked into the future and it worked.

After her first exultation, she learned that the admirable start suggested many unfulfilled possibilities. In the American sense, the clinics really were not clinics at all. At their best, they were perfunctory fitting rooms, where the person in charge had neither the time nor inclination to answer his patient's questions. Furthermore, for want of personnel, no records, except for names and

addresses, were kept. This was the reason why the Dutch innovation was so little known and had made no impact on the rest of the
world. Had the Dutch centers written up case histories and maintained some follow-up, they would have had a treasure house of
information for all nations. On her return to England, Margaret
meant to publicize the activities.

A London lodging house might be a necessity in winter, but
Margaret's friends thought it so intolerable for spring that Dr.
Drysdale's mother found a room next door to her own ivy-covered
home in Hampstead Gardens. There, under the appleblossoms,
she and Margaret enjoyed tea and talk at four o'clock. The hostess was no ordinary person but the grande dame of the Malthusian movement.

In mid-nineteenth century the Drysdales had all been united on
the subject of fertility control, but the two doctor brothers had
been rivals for the hand of another doctor, brave Alice Vickery, the first English woman physician. Dr. George won scholas-
tic honors with a pioneer study of eugenics, which was translated
into fifteen languages, but Dr. Charles won the lady. Together they
launched and successively headed what they then called the Malthusian League. Now, fifty years later, Dr. Vickery, a leader of
the nineteenth century, shared her insights, enlivened with clippings and photographs from the attic, with the new leader of
the twentieth century.

Although in her eighties, Dr. Vickery lived chiefly in the present. Nearly every day, stick in hand, she boarded the tram for some
suffrage or eugenics meeting, where she would rise, calm but determined, to set the speakers right on controversial points. One day
she rounded up her friends, all modern-minded like herself, to
hear about the Dutch clinics and Margaret's personal story.

Some of those at Dr. Vickery's tea decided that Margaret deserved a larger audience, which they provided by booking her for
a lecture in Fabian Hall, to which came many important civic
leaders. On this occasion she met Dr. Marie Stopes, a young and
striking looking paleontologist. They immediately struck up a

warm friendship which at first was mutually helpful and made a great impact on each of their careers.

Dr. Stopes wanted to hear more about the clinics and the subject of contraception, with which she was unfamiliar. Beyond that, she needed help with a manuscript called *Married Love*. Because of its forthright nature, she had been unable to find an English publisher and Margaret undertook the dubious task of finding an American one.

The Fabian lecture increased the number of Margaret's influential friends, who in the long run were a major asset. In the short run, however, with her funds almost gone, she was for the only time in her life tempted to abandon her cause. A publishing house had offered such a congenial and well-paid position that she longed to send for the children and settle down in a tolerant and friendly country. Instead, in September, bad news about Bill's trial brought her home.

Comstock had struck the keynote to the hearing when he told the press that the incriminating pamphlet was by "a heinous criminal [the defendant's wife] who sought to turn every home into a brothel." Presiding Judge McInerney apparently agreed, for he denounced *Family Limitation* as indecent, immoral, and a menace to society. Gratuitously, he added that men would not get into such trouble if they married decent wives who concentrated on having babies.

Bill was not allowed to read his carefully prepared defense, based on the rights of free speech, which the judge dismissed as "rigmarole." When offered the choice of a $150 fine or thirty days in jail, Bill chose the latter, shouting to the judge, "I would rather be in jail with my self-respect than in your place without it," which, according to *The New York Times,* set off a volley of handclapping. This was the bright spot of the day, along with what Bill described as a sudden "apoplectic look of fury on the face of Anthony Comstock." The effect on Comstock was, indeed, the chief result of the trial.

Margaret felt sure that Bill had chosen jail in the hope not only of softening her penalty, but also of securing reconciliation with her. Thwarting that hope, as she must, made the return harder. People had predicted that as Bill's trial went, so hers would go, but Comstock had announced that the author deserved five years at hard labor for every copy of her pamphlet. It took more courage to sail back to her children than it had taken to leave them.

Homecoming

13

In fog and darkness, for all lights were dimmed, the ship steamed across the Atlantic. The future, as well as the trip, were filled with foreboding. Margaret felt a weight at the pit of her stomach; at night she woke in a cold sweat. Sometimes she heard Peggy's voice trying to reach her, as she had often heard it in London. Once in a dream she was straining to move forward against an onrushing mob which suddenly turned into mice, so realistic that on waking she had to open the porthole to clear the musty stench.

On landing, her mood swung to exuberance when her over-wrought nerves seized on several good omens. As she passed a newsstand, she read the headline, "What's to be done about birth control?" *The Pictorial Review* was taking a poll and had greeted her with the phrase that she had coined, "birth control." More startling, Anthony Comstock was dead! With him gone, perhaps after all, her obstacles would shrink into mice. The Sanger friends boasted that Bill's trial had finished Comstock, for at that time he did catch the cold that prostrated him some time later after exertions at a Purity League Conference.

Margaret's hopes began to soar. She had fled from her native land in bitterness, but it was good to be home! In those first hours she liked everything. Even the faces in the streets shone with vigor and honesty. When she saw her children, it was pure joy. In spite of her worries, the reports had been right, for they were in excellent health. Stuart had changed the most and was now a broad-shouldered boy, completely engrossed in sports and in his hero,

Uncle Bob Higgins, former all-American football star and now coach at Pennsylvania State University. The younger ones, still inseparable, were also, thank heavens, still affectionate. Grant was shy and winsome; Peggy, very bright and full of mischief.

The exile, fulfilling her promise to Judge Hazel and the assistant district attorney, Mr. Content, informed them that she was home and asked if the indictments still held. They did. Outwardly she was back where she had been a year before, although now her money was gone and she owed a great deal to Nan; Bill was in prison, and she had to face both the expense of her trial and family maintenance.

Two possibilities seemed to offer at least moral support. In her absence, the New York Academy of Medicine had elected Dr. William Jacoby president. In his acceptance speech, he had supported the principles of contraception and later had appointed the liberal Dr. William J. Robinson to head a study group on the subject. This gave Margaret premature encouragement which was quickly dispelled. Enclosing a check for $10 as his personal contribution, Dr. Robinson warned her to expect nothing more.

Her other hope rested on what looked like a ready-made ally, the new National Birth Control League. The little committee of that name, which she had launched the previous year, had been reorganized by prominent women under the leadership of Mary Ware Dennett, able writer and suffragist. Presumably the goals, as well as the name, remained the same, and since they had taken over the files and mailing list of *The Woman Rebel,* Margaret asked what support they would give. In answer, she was invited to an executive meeting, at which Mrs. Dennett spoke for the group.

In this first encounter, Mrs. Dennett set forth her enduring opposition, which had been fortified by a study of *The Woman Rebel.* As late as 1926 in her book, *Birth Control Laws,* Mrs. Dennett insisted on Margaret's "atmosphere of violence," exemplified by the "wild words" of the 1914 journal. In 1915, Mrs. Dennett told Margaret Sanger that the purpose of the Birth Control League was to change the laws in an orderly, constitutional way. Since the league completely disagreed with her tactics, which they considered lawless, they would not sanction her activities.

Stunned at the rebuff, Margaret stared silently round the group which included a few of the old members. Perhaps to ease the tension, Mrs. Dennett rose and began to walk her to the door. On the way she observed that the league would welcome Margaret's list of distinguished Europeans interested in birth control.

Before she could improvise new plans, Margaret was engulfed in tragedy. Peggy came down with pneumonia. Putting off her appointment with Mr. Content, she became a full-time mother, night and day, first at home and then at the hospital. Everything was done for her child except that which might have helped. It was twenty years too soon for penicillin. The little girl, who Margaret always thought a perfect daughter, wasted away. Once, she opened her eyes to whisper, "Are you back, mother?" Again, as in her dreams in London, the child could not hear her reassurance.

Peggy's death was the most poignant blow that Margaret ever received. As she wrote in her *Autobiography* twenty years later, "The joy in the fullness of life went out of it then and has never quite returned." For a while she was numb and indifferent to the future. She could take no initiative.

But there was no longer any need to act. Although she was unaware of the fact, her tragedy had brought a turning point in public opinion. The story was in the headlines, and from across the country poured letters of condolence. Miners from West Virginia, lumbermen from the West Coast, unknown friends who had read *Family Limitation,* rallied to her support with small donations.

Closer at hand came impressive offers, although some hinged on a change of tactics. Most persuasive was the distinguished lawyer Samuel Untermyer. It was all so clear to him. Mrs. Sanger need only sign a statement saying that she would not break the law again. With that, he could persuade the district attorney to quash the charges and there would be no trial. "But the law would remain the same?" asked Margaret. Of course! But she would not go to jail. Going to jail was not her main concern, she tried to explain. She would not plead guilty, when she had not been obscene. Untermyer, a few minutes earlier, so kind and understanding, lost patience. So did others. By the time Clarence Darrow offered his services, she was convinced that any lawyer would cloud the basic issues.

She had parted with her first attorney on this point and in England had been confirmed in the rightness of her stand. Now she meant her trial to be the equivalent of the historic Bradlaugh-Besant trial of the nineteenth century. By refusing to plead guilty, the English defendants had forced a test and while at first convicted, on appeal, their case had been dismissed on a technicality. Margaret wanted to test the issue in the same way, but lawyers were not concerned with this because their prestige was bound up with keeping their clients out of jail.

All right, she would take another page from the famous trial and defend herself. This was no easy decision for a shy woman with no legal training, but, like Annie Besant, she would use the trial as a public forum to arouse the nation about birth control. She too would explain that she was not the real defendant, but the counsel for the poor mute mothers who were denied their human rights. Having made up her mind, she asked Mr. Content to call the case as soon as possible. It was scheduled for the end of November and then postponed until January.

Meanwhile, the public image of a militant woman rebel had been displaced by that of the mother-nurse who for three weeks had watched day and night over her child. To this new pathos was added a touch of heroism when she announced that she would speak for herself. Finally an appeal from England gave an international dimension to her story.

An open letter to President Wilson urged him to use his influence "not only for the benefit of Mrs. Sanger, but of humanity." This well-publicized message called for an end to criminal prosecution for circulating material which would be allowed in every civilized country except the United States. The letter had originated with Dr. Marie Stopes who had secured the signatures of nine of England's most famous authors, including William Archer, Arnold Bennett, Gilbert Murray and H. G. Wells. Its effect, as Margaret hastened to tell Dr. Stopes, was of the greatest importance on the American public.

To many who had discounted Margaret Sanger as a fanatic, this

English appeal was impressive. Some were eager to ride the band-wagon; others, aroused for the first time to the importance of the issue, offered help. A group of experienced suffragists gave Margaret what she had never had before, support from New York's top social register. Up to this time she had been either unknown or suspect to those whose shining names vouched for all important charity and social events. Her new volunteers organized a Night-Before-Trial dinner at the Brevoort Hotel. There would be just two speakers, Dr. Jacoby and Mrs. Sanger, but the guest list was composed of two hundred personages.

This carefully planned testimonial began with a crisis which Mrs. Stokes, the toastmistress, explained to Margaret as they went into dinner. Her own Cinderella-rise from Rose Pastor, the little cigar maker, to the wealthy Mrs. J. G. Phelps Stokes, had given the lady unusual insights. The crisis that she disclosed was that Dr. Jacoby had perversely decided to blast the guest of honor for meddling in medical matters. To forestall him, Mrs. Stokes would introduce Margaret first, and Margaret must spike his guns. This was a hard assignment for a nervous and inexperienced speaker.

When she arose, disarmingly small, with her tranquil, Madonna look, Margaret Sanger began in a soft voice that made people strain to listen. It was strange, she said, for one as ill equipped as she to address this group in which there were so many from whom she could learn. Some, she knew, wanted to endorse birth control, but disapproved her tactics. She had broken the law and used methods they found sensational. But she had been appealing to overworked and ignorant women who needed contraception and she wondered if academic arguments would reach them. Wise men had known about contraception for centuries, but they had not helped the poor. Even today in New York City, those in the depths of poverty had to limit their families in the old barbaric ways of infanticide and abortion. As a nurse who had worked in the slums, she knew the facts. She was one who saw a house on fire and shouted for help.

When she was done, Dr. Jacoby had been forestalled. He shifted his subject to quality in population, which, as Margaret wryly said, might be construed as a speech in her behalf. But she had scarcely finished her own talk before a dozen persons were on their feet offering special aid. Among them she was surprised to hear the imposing Mrs. Dennett announce that the National Birth Control League was backing Mrs. Sanger in her ordeal. Furthermore, the league needed contributions.

Her social debut at the Brevoort was to be only a prelude for her real test the next day, but since the place swarmed with well-known writers, including Walter Lippman and John Reed, the papers covered it in full. Next morning a record number of reporters appeared in court. Her new friends came en masse, and the *Evening Globe* noted that twenty limousines with liveried chauffeurs clogged the streets around the Federal Building.

The common man and his wife also jostled for room to see the show of the season. The star was a young woman pitting her wits against all of the resources of the state attorney's office. The issue was whether poor women might have the right that the rich already enjoyed, to prevent unwanted pregnancy. The stakes were freedom for the young defendant-mother or up to forty-five years of prison.

Perhaps the crowded court house, as well as the Brevoort dinner, changed proceedings. After a long delay, the judge entered and at once granted the request of the district attorney to adjourn the session. It was a terrible anticlimax. In the streets, the disappointed audience cheered the heroine of the suppressed drama and promised to return. They did—again and again. The *New York Sun* said that the Sanger case presented "the anomaly of a prosecutor loath to prosecute and a defendant anxious to be tried." The *Washington Post* called it one of the most unique trials in the history of the nation.

In February the *Pictorial Review* announced the results of its poll on birth control: 97 per cent favorable. Experts had warned Margaret that in the midst of world events, her trial would be ignored, but it made the front page during the Battle of Verdun. In Tennessee, the *Chattanooga News* saw strong sentiment for Mrs. Sanger, while sympathizers in Los Angeles started a Birth Control League.

On February, 18, 1916, the government entered a nolle prosequi.

"Victory and vindication!" cried the defendant. Certainly the government had retreated and instead of sending her to jail, had raised her to a national figure of protest against an unjust law.

However, on somber second thought, Margaret agreed with the *New York Globe* that the quashing of the indictment settled nothing. The right to discuss birth control was just where it was, subject to the "mutton-headed restrictions of some post office clerk and the complaisant persecution of a federal district attorney." From the district attorney's office came various explanations. They had not wanted to make a martyr of Mrs. Sanger. The indictment was two years old and it had become clear that the defendant was not a "disorderly person" nor in the habit of publishing obscene articles.

Telling Her Story

14

After all of the emotional investment, it was sad that Margaret's case was not the Bradlaugh-Besant equivalent for America. Nevertheless, although it ended ambiguously, it had broken the sound barrier which John Reed reported had formerly kept even the *New York Times* from using the words, "prevention of conception." More than that, it raised birth control from gutter smut to a serious national issue. Meanwhile letters coming from all over the country persuaded Margaret that her next task was a lecture tour.

For one who dreaded public appearance, she seemed to have a strange compulsion about speaking, but the decision followed naturally from her commitment. She had gained a million dollars worth of free advertising and the time to use it was at once. Besides, she might promote birth control leagues and, she hoped, some clinics.

On the other hand, because she dreaded lecturing, Margaret painstakingly mastered the art. She not only thought out a speech, but wrote it out and spoke it out, as she had her first one at Claverack. For lack of a handy graveyard, she gained her privacy in the vertical, Manhattan way. Cilmbing to the roof of her small Lexington Avenue hotel, she recited it to the housetops. In premicrophone days Margaret had to learn to project her voice without seeming to shout but she rehearsed chiefly to familiarize herself so well with her material that her mind would not black out in stagefright. Prematurely she tried her speech on a small suburban audience, but at the last moment she read it. The response was tepid. Back she climbed to the chimney pots where she practiced until it was second nature. When she opened in Pittsburgh early in April, 1916, she laid aside her notes and the audience was hers.

She put a great deal into her basic speech, which she gave 119 times the first year. Although she always remained a nervous speaker, she was never again an inexperienced one. Usually she began in a quiet way while her listeners became used to the fact that this was the notorious Mrs. Sanger. "The first right of every child is to be wanted," she might start. No one could object to that.

Being wanted, she would explain, depended on a father's wages and the spacing and number of other children in a family. For the sake of the unborn child, as well as the human race, birth control should be practiced in at least seven circumstances. Here she paused as people fumbled for their pencils. The circumstances were:

1. When either parent had a transmittible disease, such as epilepsy, insanity, or syphilis.

2. When the wife suffered from a temporary infection of the lungs, heart, or kidneys, the cure of which might be retarded by pregnancy.

3. When parents, although normal themselves, had subnormal children.

4. When either husband or wife was an adolescent. Parenthood should be postponed until the boy was at least twenty-three and the girl twenty-two.

5. When the father's earning capacity was inadequate.

6. Until the passage of two, preferably three, years after the birth of the mother's last child.

7. For at least a year after marriage so that the couple had time for physical, mental, financial, and spiritual adjustment.

In lighter vein Margaret often suggested a bureau of application for the unborn, where a couple might register as for a cook or chauffeur. The child-to-be would want assurances from potential parents as to their health, habits, and state of nerves. In addition, what was the family income and how many other children were there? "Eight living in two rooms? No, thank you," any smart baby would end that interview. "Next applicant, please."

At the close of her Pittsburgh lecture, she met with a group who wanted to form the first state birth control league. Foresightedly, she had outlined the needs of a well-balanced group and the matter of some central liaison. Since she herself had no organization and the National League greatly wanted to assume the role its name. implied, she had decided, with some misgivings, to turn over to Mrs. Dennett whatever groups her trip produced. She began with the Pennsylvania League and soon added others in Cleveland, Milwaukee, and Detroit.

That was beginner's luck, for she shortly faced frustration and even melodrama. Frustration started in Chicago, where she had received overtures from the prestigious Woman's Club. On follow-up, the executive committee prudently withdrew its invitation and an officer imprudently told the press that admirable as Mrs. Sanger might be, she was "a little too strong for Chicago." In response, Margaret was quoted as saying that the "sophisticated club members doubtless knew all that she could tell them" and she really wanted to talk to working women.

She had expected aid from Hull House, which eventually helped launch the second birth control clinic in the nation, but in 1916 Jane Addams was absent and ill. Although Margaret underestimated the hostility of the Catholic power structure, which she had not yet encountered, her Chicago impasse was finally resolved by a young woman, Fania Mindell, who was so inspired by Margaret's presence that she soon moved east as a permanent aide. Before that, she arranged for Margaret to address a large stockyard rally.

A more imposing recruit from this trip was Frederick A. Blossom, head of Cleveland's Associated Charities, who became convinced that birth control was the issue of the age. His first service was to arrange an extracurriculum assembly in Indianapolis during the National Social Workers Conference. Because of its representative nature, Walter Lippman reported that the meeting would "kick the football of birth control straight across to the Pacific." It did. Delegates from the conference helped schedule the western tour.

The fireworks started in St. Louis, where the Victoria Theater had been paid for. To Michael Higgins's daughter the occasion brought a flashback of a Sunday a quarter of a century earlier and some 1,500 miles away. The drama was much the same, but played in an urban setting with herself as speaker. She was escorted to the theater in an open car by two well-known men, Robert Minor, the cartoonist, whom she had known in New York, and Roger Baldwin, later head of the American Civil Liberties Union. As they approached, they found the streets blocked by an angry, churning crowd of some two thousand, who wanted to break down the locked door of the theater. Threatened by a permanent Catholic boycott if Mrs. Sanger spoke, the manager of the building had left town.

Up to this point Margaret's main opponents had been Protestants of Puritan tradition, personified by Anthony Comstock, but from now on, as the Protestant churches had second thoughts on birth control, Catholics took over the opposition. This was the first time that the Church used extralegal steps to silence her.

Minor urged her to stand up in the car and make her speech right there. With her memory of the happy outdoor finish at Corning, she gamely tried to do so, but since she did not have the voice for it, she was relieved when a policeman intervened and the chauffeur started his car.

"To throttle free speech is to give it a megaphone," thundered the *Globe Democrat* next morning. All that her opponents achieved, said the *Post Dispatch,* was to multiply Mrs. Sanger's audience. A cartoon in *Reedy's Mirror* showed the national Capitol topped by a papal crown. The St. Louis Men's City Club, which had never before thought of inviting Mrs. Sanger to address them, held an overflow crowd for her, larger than the recent record one for Teddy Roosevelt. Forty Catholics resigned, but a hundred new members joined.

Margaret moved on to Denver, where she fell in love with the West, a romance which she would resume in later life. Sitting by Judge Ben Lindsay of the famous Juvenile Court, she thought that at last there were men to match the mountains. Women, too, she decided when he told her that it was the feminine vote that kept him in office, for Colorado had been the second suffragist state. In Los Angeles, a women's police division welcomed her at the station, in contrast to the baleful receptions policemen gave her in the East.

From the next weeks of lectures, conferences, interviews and everlasting fatigue, Margaret recalled two incidents. Once in San Francisco, between meetings, a thoughtful lady had whisked her out to the giant redwoods, where she was left alone for fifteen minutes. The sun burst through a patch of sky, and Margaret was filled with peace.

The second memory was of the only time when she ran out on her self-imposed schedule. Being indisposed, she had given only a tentative acceptance to speak at the close of a church service, but as usual she went, slipping in, unseen at the back. A few moments later she was horrified to hear the minister describe her as a modern Joan of Arc. This was too much. With the old sick feeling at the pit of her stomach, she rose and tiptoed, still unseen, out of the church.

In the Northwest she ran into lumbermen who had helped distribute *Family Limitation,* and to her surprise, she found that they were still selling it. Since it was not copyrighted, it had been reprinted, not only to boost the cause but the income of those who handled it. This was all right with her, but as she skimmed through the reprint, she saw that it needed revision. Although it had served its purpose, it had been hastily written and did not include much of her current knowledge. Between meetings and with the help of a pioneer woman doctor, Marie Esqui, she drafted another edition.

Since there were no restrictive Oregon laws, friends planned to sell the pamphlet at the Portland meeting, but they had not reckoned with the police, who arrested the distributors. The City Council then condemned *Family Limitation,* offering a retroactive reason for the arrest. In the next week the free-wheeling ways of western justice held several surprises, some agreeable, as when the hearings were postponed to fit in with Margaret's lecture schedule in Seattle and Spokane. She had asked to testify as a special witness, but in the end appeared as a defendant. Dr. Esqui had called a protest rally the night before the hearings and at that time both she and Margaret were arrested. Some hundred supporters followed them to jail, clamoring to be arrested too. To keep the crowd out, the doors were finally bolted. Another pleasant surprise was Margaret's first jail, which was warm and clean.

Next morning, after the court had condemned the pamphlet and found the prisoners guilty, the judge gallantly waived the penalties for the ladies, fined each man $10, but advised them not to pay. When the defendants left the courthouse they were greeted by a friendly crowd, enlivened with sandwich-board men whose signs proclaimed: "Poverty and large families go hand in hand" and "Poor women are denied what the rich possess." Naturally, all this free advertising launched a flourishing new league, along with two others in Spokane and Seattle.

Measured by publicity, the tour was a triumph, but Margaret was unhappy as she rode east. Not only was she exhausted, but she was not sure that her efforts had been worthwhile. She had said that she wanted to speak to working women. She had talked to tens of thousands of them, arousing them to the importance of her cause, but what these women wanted was not more speeches, but clinics to supply their needs.

During the long trip back to New York Margaret had time to assess her position. She saw that she was at another turning point both in her personal life and in public tactics. Her boys were happy at country boarding schools, undisturbed by her melodramas. Bill Sanger, if not resigned to separation, was becoming used to it, although his last months had been bitter, mostly because of her. Among his grievances was the fact that his study abroad had been cut short. There at least she might help him financially to realize his dream of going to Spain. Meanwhile, for the first time she too must learn to live alone.

As for tactics, her travel had shown that her growing sprawling movement needed a unifying force, a communication system. Once more she resolved to start a journal, this time a birth control review. This would unite her supporters and prepare them for the climax of her work, the establishment of clinics.

New Tactics

15

Thrift was Margaret's guide in choosing her home in New York, as it had been in London, and she settled for much the same, an unheated, cold-water "studio" room in a decrepit building on West Fourteenth Street. After all, Europeans lived without central heat and a few coals on her hearth gave as much warmth as Havelock's gas grate over which she had often huddled. Her yellow curtains took the place of sunshine and on the floor above lived her younger sister.

The marriage of Ethel Byrne, which had not been happy, had curiously paralleled her own. Ethel's husband, just out of high school, had meant to study medicine, but instead, to support his bride and the two children who followed rapidly, he took a job at the Corning glass works. For lack of funds, they moved in with his family, although Mrs. Byrne, Sr., who had cherished high hopes for her only son, always resented Ethel. John soon lost his ambition, and Ethel began to see her future as a bitter recapitulation of her mother's. At last she left her husband and children with her mother-in-law, and following Margaret's example, became a trained nurse. She was a quiet, intense young woman with an astringent wit and a somewhat competitive feeling toward her older sister.

Margaret also had a new associate in Frederick Blossom, who had come to her like a gift from the gods or more truly, a gift from his wife, whose money enabled him to donate his services. Charming and experienced, he had the administrative skill that Margaret never developed. He also had a flair for raising money and attracting volunteers, sucking them in like a vacuum cleaner, she said. On his own, he opened an office on lower Fifth Avenue, equipped with files and business methods with which he now attacked Margaret's mail. During the tour, letters had come to her in such torrents—1,000 from St. Louis alone—that she had sent them east unanswered, in trunks. Her mail continued at the rate of a senator's, although she had no government-paid staff to cope with it. This response had become a nightmare until Blossom set his volunteers to work. They analyzed, classified, and answered it, as does a congressional office. Eventually her mail, one of the largest ever received by a private citizen, became the basis for her book *Motherhood in Bondage*, an historic record of the tragic results of antiquated laws.

After his conquest of the mail, Blossom turned to new projects. He assumed the first responsibilities for the journal Margaret had now resolved on. He also started the New York Birth Control League to bring pressure for a change of laws.

The New York laws were the stumbling block to Margaret's immediate goal. Since federal legislation dealt only with the mails and public carriers, the legality of clinics rested with the states. Section 1142 of the New York Penal Code said that no one could give contraceptive advice for any reason, but Section 1145 offered a loophole. It allowed physicians to prescribe for the cure or prevention of disease.

After consulting two lawyers and several physicians, Margaret confirmed her belief that the exemption had been added for only one reason, to protect men from venereal disease. After all, the English Colonel Cundom had developed his eighteenth-century sheath for precisely that function. In other words, contraception was legal if its purpose was to promote male promiscuity. No doubt the New York gentlemen who wrote and voted for the law loved their wives and daughters, but they barred them, along with all women, from protection that might save a mother's life. Their only tolerance was for phallic frolics.

It was Margaret Sanger's inspired view that an enlightened judge would use the loophole to serve the needs of married women. While her critics knocked their heads against the Comstock laws, she laid the strategy for vaulting over those legal obstructions. Again it was her knowledge of the Bradlaugh-Besant trial that made her rely on the short cut of an appealed court decision. Fortunately Blossom was systematizing the office work and freeing her to develop this winning strategy, which he, along with most birth control advocates, heartily disapproved.

Since the loophole applied only to physicians, Margaret had felt fortified when two women doctors had offered to staff a clinic whenever she decided to open one, but that was before the case of Dr. Mary Halton, of Grosvenor Hospital. At her evening clinic Dr. Halton had once prescribed a pessary for a patient who had shown tubercular symptoms. By 1916 it was a common practice for doctors to protect their private patients in this way. But Dr. Halton's patient was a poor woman at a public clinic, and when the hospital's board heard of the incident, they asked Dr. Halton to resign.

Compared with some others, Dr. Halton was lucky. Her health was not broken by a six-year term in Leavenworth, as in the earlier case of Dr. Elliott, nor by three months at hard labor, as in the historic example of Dr. Knowlton. Nevertheless, her dismissal was a warning. At a period when birth control was becoming routine for the well-to-do, there was no physician to serve the poor.

Reluctantly, Margaret abandoned the hope of finding a doctor. That was a setback for her strategy, but it did not end her resolve to open a clinic. If there were no doctors to serve, there were two trained nurses, the Higgins sisters. Her tutelage under Dr. Rutgers at The Hague had qualified her for the task, but she made a major concession to the medical profession in deciding that there would be no actual fitting. They would explain the use of pessaries with charts and estimate the right size from the number of previous births and miscarriages. This was not perfect, but it would help the majority of women and at worst, it would substitute a harmless effort to stop pregnancy for the vicious ways then in use. Furthermore, if the clinic were closed, as she expected it to be, there would be another chance to test the law.

Once she had settled her tactics, she mentioned the forthcoming clinic in a press interview, saying that she was looking for a site. Because the right location was all-important, she had tramped the streets of the Bronx, Brooklyn, and lower Manhattan. She had studied the vital statistics of the boroughs, their wage scales, and the number of social agencies in the areas. Then one day the answer came to her in a delegation from the Brownsville section of Brooklyn.

One of the women had read her interview and after sharing it with the others, they had come to urge the immediate opening of this clinic. Each of them had a heartrending tale of poverty, poor health, sickly children—in no case less than four—and constant terror of another pregnancy. As she heard their stories, Margaret suffered with each, just as she had once suffered with Sadie Sachs. When the women left, she realized that Brownsville was her site. Next morning she would go out and find the exact place.

Now everything was settled, except finances, which never deterred her. When she was a young housewife, solvency had been most important, but after she had found her cause, she was psychologically Michael Higgins's daughter. On principle, she acted first and then found the practical solution. Ethel thought that she should take an occasional nursing assignment, but Margaret declared that she had "cast herself on the universe," which would provide. Soon afterward when she received a contribution, the sharp-tongued Ethel called it her "gift from God." Now God seemed to be helping again. She received a $50 donation from a Los Angeles enthusiast, the first month's rent for the Brownsville clinic!

The next morning, in cold rain, Margaret and her Chicago recruit, Fania Mindell, made their way through Brownsville's dismal streets, which were lined with run-down houses, bursting with humanity, most of whom were Jewish or Italian. After a few rebuffs, they found their landlord, Joseph Rabinowitz. So interested was he that he reduced his usual rent to the specified $50. Margaret was well pleased, not only because she thought this Jewish community would offer the best protection from harassment, but because it seemed appropriate. Starting with Sadie Sachs, Jews had played an important role in her work. They had taken the lead in birth control committees, and Jewish mothers had brought her to Brownsville.

Her landlord exceeded her hopes by donating hours of labor to make the rooms more "hospital-like." Fania's Yiddish secured the best prices at local stores for a few indispensable chairs, a desk, a stove, and curtains. Margaret ordered five thousand handbills printed in English, Yiddish, and Italian. They read:

> *Mothers,*
> *Can you afford to have a large family?*
> *Do you want any more children?*
> *If not, why do you have them?*
> *Do not kill. Do not take life, but prevent.*
> *Safe, harmless information can be obtained of trained nurses.*
> *46 Amboy Street*
> *Near Pitkin Ave., Brooklyn*
> *Tell your neighbors and friends.   All mothers welcome*
> *A registration fee of 10¢ entitles any mother to this*
> *information.*

Passing out the handbills was a good way to introduce themselves and promote their cause. They dropped them in letter boxes, pushed them under doors of rickety, condemned buildings, still crowded with people. Unkempt children swarmed through most of the corridors and alleys; they sat on fire escapes and played in the rubbish heaps of the vacant yards. In the streets, almost every mother either carried or wheeled a baby, while older children tagged along beside them.

Margaret chatted with as many as possible, offering extra handbills for friends. The women were at first startled and then excited. But would they come? She recalled that doctors claimed that the poor bred like rabbits because they liked to. Could these women understand how birth control might change their lives? Would these poor creatures dare to use her clinic?

Taking one last precaution, Margaret visited the area druggists. Since they were already selling a wide assortment of alleged and illicit preventives, they were glad to stock her material also. In this way she avoided the additional risk of selling contraceptives. Finally she notified the district attorney that she was opening a clinic but she never received a written answer.

The Brownsville Clinic

16

In October 1916 Margaret Sanger opened the first American birth control clinic. Indeed, it was the first such clinic anywhere outside of the Netherlands. On that bright autumn morning the three participants arrived early, but by seven o'clock there was already a waiting line halfway to the corner. Did the women want the clinic? The long line gave the answer.

As Margaret described them in her *Autobiography,* they came, some shawled, some bareheaded, their red hands clasping the cold, chapped smaller hands of their children. Some came alone, some in pairs, perhaps with a neighbor or a married daughter. Some had not dared tell their husbands; others had been urged on by their men. They were still coming at seven in the evening when husbands joined the line, bringing their timid wives or leaving word that they would stay home so that the wives could come. When the staff finally closed the doors, they had seen 140 women and some were waiting who promised to return the next day.

Fania welcomed each woman in the receiving room where she asked a few questions. Along with names and addresses, she took down vital statistics, not only of the living and dead, but the numbers of miscarriages and abortions. From the outset this clinic collected the data that The Hague had so sadly ignored. Whenever there was a lull in the anteroom, Fania read aloud from *What Every Girl Should Know*. She also "minded" the children when their mothers went to the rear.

All day long in separate offices the Higgins sisters repeated their simply worded instructions to small groups of anxious mothers. They showed the diaphragm pessary and with carefully drawn charts, explained how to place it. They answered personal questions, estimating, according to the number of previous births, the size of pessary for each woman, and told her where to buy it.

Yiddish and Italian papers picked up the clinic story from the handbills; wives soon appeared clutching the scraps of paper that their husbands had seen as they rode to work. Thus, the territory served by the clinic expanded. Women came from the eastern end of Long Island, from New Jersey, even from Pennsylvania and Massachusetts. Some had never before left their own neighborhoods, but were drawn by the urgency of their needs. The appeal cut across ethnic lines, being the same for Catholics as for Protestants and Jews. Each applicant had a pent-up, pitiful tale that gushed out when she registered.

Once a gaunt skeleton of a woman addressed the startled waiting line. Someday, she declared, there should be a monument to Margaret Sanger right on that spot. She herself had been married fifteen years and lost her health with eleven births and twenty-eight self-induced abortions. Before the opening of this clinic, she announced, when poor mothers had too many babies, they were given charity. When they were worn out by pregnancies, they were given charity talks. Rather than share their secret, the rich would let them die!

Sometimes even Catholics joined in the testimonials. Babies were a mother's business, one observed. If your man had a bad heart and could earn only a few dollars a week, what should you do? The priest had told her to have many babies, said another. She had fifteen, only six of whom lived, but the priest had made money on fifteen baptismal fees, nine funerals, masses and candles for the little ones.

The word "clinic" kept some women away, in the belief that it was an abortion office, but it brought others for the same reason. These were the most tragic of the applicants. Some threatened suicide, as did the mother of eight, who had suffered two abortions and was hysterical about the future. She threatened to grind up a glass and swallow it when she went home.

Neighborhood good will relieved both the tension and the pressure of the work. When there was no time for lunch, Mrs. Rabinowitz, the landlord's wife, brought tea, and the baker across the street sent over doughnuts. The postman, delivering some hundred letters daily, usually expressed his hope that the ladies would still be around on his next call. Good-natured policemen often dropped in apparently to discuss the weather.

So the days and the first week passed. The waiting line continued, and there was no interference. On the ninth day Margaret was out, hopefully on the trail of a doctor. In the afternoon Fania noticed a large, grim-faced woman, wearing the usual shabby shawl, but under it a well-cut suit. When the woman bought a copy of *What Every Girl Should Know* and insisted on paying $2.00 instead of 10 cents to register, Fania went back to notify Ethel that there was a policewoman in the crowd. To Ethel, caution was the same as cowardice and so she gave her usual talk.

Near closing time the next day and after Ethel had left, the same large woman pushed her way into the still crowded office to confront and arrest its chief. Mrs. Whitehurst of the vice squad was, indeed, a policewoman, who now went through her routine, scarcely altered, although in a different setting. With plainclothesmen guarding the door, she took down the names and addresses of the frightened mothers, as though they were inmates of a brothel. Some of them whimpered, one shrieked, and this set off wails from every child in the place. In a moment it was pandemonium and then Margaret despite her arrest, took charge. Going from one to another, she explained that the police had come for her alone. If they would be quiet, they might all leave. After she had secured peace, it was a harder task to convince the police that these decent, hard-working mothers had every right to go home. Meanwhile, Mrs. Whitehurst was ransacking the place, confiscating the demonstration supplies and 460 intimate case records. Not until the patrol wagon rattled up to the door did the two women face each other again.

The press account, taken from the police, said that Margaret called Mrs. Whitehurst "a dirty thing" and "no woman." She herself wrote that she was "white hot with indignation" at the treatment of her patients. Certainly she refused to ride with the vice squad and instead, marched ahead of the Black Maria, right down the street to the Raymond Street jail, where she spent the night.

This jail made her Portland quarters look like the Ritz Hotel. There was a terrible stench, the mattress was stained with filth, and the blankets were stiff with grime. Only her towel was clean, and with it around her head and her coat over her, she tried to sleep. Soon she was aroused by roaches, bedbugs, and finally a rat.

The crowning indignity, a psychological one, came the next morning with a visit from a prison reform society. The ladies peered at the inmates as though they were caged animals. Was there anything they might do, one of them asked. Knowing that they liked to pray over the prostitutes and pickpockets, Margaret turned savagely on these pious do-gooders. Yes, there was something they could do, she told them. "Clean up the filthy place." As she itemized the needs, the ladies hastily retreated.

Later at a press conference, Margaret notified the Brooklyn taxpayers that their money was being wasted on a jail that would disgrace any community. When her $500 bail was arranged, she returned at once to the clinic.

With incorrigible hope, she thought that a court decision might allow her to continue. When a few women appeared, she agreed to see them and then others began to come. So did the police. This time they settled the matter, not only by arresting her again, but by forcing the reluctant landlord to sign ejection papers for sheltering "a public nuisance." At The Hague, Queen Wilhelmina had cited a clinic as a public benefaction; in New York it was a public nuisance.

Since the police, not the vice squad, had come, Margaret went quietly to the patrol wagon. As they rode off, she looked back at the mute, frustrated crowd of women who watched her taken away. In *My Fight for Birth Control,* she wrote that she believed something had gone out of the human race. Something had silenced these women and made them impotent to defend their rights.

Although Ethel had escaped the raid, she too was served with a warrant. In all, there were four separate charges: Fania had sold an indecent book, Margaret was running a public nuisance, and both sisters were violating Section 1142 of the New York Penal Code. This section, banning the spread of contraceptive information, Margaret believed unconstitutional because no state was allowed to interfere with a person's right to life and liberty. Of course she knew that no lower court would share her view, but her hope always lay in the judgment of an upper court. Because she meant this to be a test case, she decided that she must have an attorney.

A rising young Tammany lawyer, J. J. Goldstein, who would one day run for mayor and later become a distinguished judge, offered his services. In his youth he had been guided by Lillian Wald and Mary Simkhovitch, founders respectively of New York's two most famous settlement houses. Margaret was often impatient with the "feather dusting" of welfare work, but in the case of the popularly known "J. J.," she conceded that "the seed of a social vision had been planted in him," although she thought that his legal training had slowed its growth.

Often in the next months the lawyer and his client despaired of each other's tactics, but nevertheless, they joined in a fruitful four-year association, which ripened into affection. For him, the rewards were as intangible as for her, but he suggested to his Tammany colleagues that his profits were large. Otherwise, they would never have forgiven his working for birth control.

J. J. insisted that the record must be perfect, if the case was to be appealed and that the defense must take every step that the law allowed. His client was infinitely irked by what she saw as senseless rituals and court pomposities, and as it turned out, the one concession that they gained followed from her direct action.

They all pleaded not guilty on November twentieth and J. J. asked to have them tried together, but in this he failed. He was also denied a jury trial and a change from the November schedule. Judge McInerney, who had presided at Bill's trial, would again preside.

Since J. J.'s efforts had failed, Margaret wrote an open letter to the judge, ending, "To come before you implies conviction. Now in all fairness do you want a case of this character brought forcibly before you, when the defendant feels and believes that you are prejudiced against her?" His reply was an official request to be taken off the case; the trial was therefore postponed until January.

The Ordeal

17

The year 1917 began with Margaret again under indictment, but this time with allies ready to share her battles. Along with many of her last year's sponsors were new recruits, among whom Mrs. George Rublee was outstanding for practical aid and enduring friendship.

Juliet Rublee was the handsome wife of an international lawyer whom Wilson had named to the Federal Trade Commission. When she first heard Margaret speak, she decided that birth control was the most important issue in the world, and so the two women gradually became intimates. As Margaret once wrote, others brought their personal friends into the movement, but Juliet brought her husband's associates also, including the Dwight Morrows and the Thomas Lamonts.

This new support changed Margaret's tactics. In the past she had tried to rouse deprived women to liberate themselves. They wanted her help, but like the Brownsville mothers, they left her to fight their battles. She had called them biologically enslaved, and slowly realized that just because they were enslaved, they had no courage to win their own rights.

The emancipation of the poor mothers must come through the efforts of privileged women, on whom Margaret would in future depend to finance her defense and to educate the public. This was the purpose of the Committee of One Hundred, which Juliet helped to organize, but whose leadership was given to Mrs. Amos Pinchot, aristocratic in background, compassionate in views and, not to be overlooked, the family friend of New York's governor. In spite of J. J.'s protests, Ethel alone was tried on January eighth. Until then few had heard of her, but in the next weeks her name would be headlined more than any other woman's. Those in the courtroom saw a close replica of her famous sister, although a little younger and, according to one brother, the prettiest of the daughters. She had less to say than Margaret, but said it with more emotion.

Ethel acknowledged that she had taught contraceptive methods, but sharply denied that a 10-cent fee made the clinic a money-making institution. Neither she nor J. J. tried to answer the fantastic charge that the clinic, located in a Jewish neighborhood, was actually trying to do away with Jews. This was put in the record, carried in the tabloid press, and was a forerunner to the similar accusations made about birth control a half century later in the Negro ghettos.

Dr. Morris Kahn was to be the main witness for the defense, but was not allowed to testify on the grounds that his physician's experience was "irrelevant, incompetent and immaterial." J. J. was given only fifteen minutes to explain why Section 1142 of the Penal Code was unconstitutional. He argued that the law fell unfairly on different groups of citizens. After all, if the purpose of the law was to encourage more children, why not penalize bachelors and childless couples unless they could prove themselves impotent? When his time was up, the court ruled that the section was constitutional.

There was still hope of only a minor penalty, although the defendants knew that they could face either a long or short term in the workhouse. While Ethel's sentence was deferred for two weeks, the sisters reviewed all possibilities. Both of them had been impressed by the hunger strikes of the English suffragettes and thought that such tactics would be a powerful weapon in shaping public opinion for birth control. In case of a long term, they agreed that it might be worth the agony, but for a short term, submission would be wiser.

On January twenty-second Ethel was sentenced to thirty days in the workhouse on Blackwell's Island. She looked stunned. Then in a tremulous voice she announced that she would go on a hunger strike. She would touch neither food nor drink nor would she perform any work. The previous night she had made her will and arranged for the care of her two children. Then she had eaten a farewell dinner with plenty of turkey and ice cream. Now, if need be, she would die for the cause.

As Ethel was taken off to jail, J. J. reassured Margaret that in the morning he would have a chance to secure a suspension of the sentence. But in the morning he failed. Ethel looking pale and excited, whispered that she had eaten nothing at the Tombs, where she had spent the night. They had tempted her with the odor of eggs and bacon wafted into her room, but now she would give up liquids also, lest her warders dissolve food in them.

Margaret gazed fearfully at this younger sister with the red glint in her hair and the dogged family look of resolution. She reminded her that the strike was not necessary for so short a sentence and that it would be wise to say nothing more until she had carefully reconsidered the matter.

Perhaps a little heady with her fasting, Ethel turned at once to the reporters. In a frightened voice she told them that to change the archaic law she was ready to fast to death. What was one life compared to the eight thousand lost in New York each year through illegal operations? Later, in the patrol wagon on the way to Blackwell's Island, she indulged in a last defiance by lecturing to the women prisoners on birth control.

Commissioner of Corrections Burdette G. Lewis informed the press that he was used to threats of hunger strikes and they meant nothing. To show his indifference, he ordered no food at all for Mrs. Byrne. The warden's wife felt differently and lest the girl die on her hands, coaxed Ethel to eat. No one would know, she promised. "I would," said Ethel.

Giving up liquids greatly magnified Ethel's suffering. At night the woman who brought round drinking water stood outside her cell, calling "Water! Water!" From her window Ethel heard the everlasting swish of the river and from the hallway this enticement, but for her, like the Ancient Mariner, it was "Water, water, everywhere, nor any drop to drink."

For Margaret, the turn of events was cruel. After her first indictment, Bill had borne the brunt of the punishment; and now her younger sister was risking her life for a cause which she had only recently espoused. Better than most people, Margaret realized the dangers of dehydration, but she also knew that Ethel was as stubborn as herself. She decided that her immediate task was to secure all possible publicity for her sister's sacrifice. With this in mind, she made a deal with the *New York World*. She would give them every news break if they would put a special reporter on the case. Perhaps it was this man who ferreted out the daily reports of Ethel's condition.

After the first blast of news on the hunger strike, Lewis banned reporters from the workhouse and all visitors, except her lawyer, to Mrs. Byrne. Lewis himself refused any word about his prisoner on the grounds that the strike was a publicity stunt. This news embargo whetted the public interest, especially since Mrs. Sanger always seemed to have precise knowledge of her sister's pulse and temperature. Soon she warned that Mrs. Byrne's vision was affected and that for lack of liquids, her heart had begun to miss beats.

Suddenly right across the nation the hunger strike was the big domestic news. It competed with headlines that the Kaiser might accept Wilson's plan for mediation. As Mrs. Byrne started her fifth day of fasting, the United Press announced that "the pale little advocate of birth control is rapidly reaching the climax of her struggle against imprisonment." Franklin P. Adams of the *New York Tribune* predicted that "it will be hard to make the youth of 1967 believe that in 1917 a woman was imprisoned for doing what Mrs. Byrne did."

When the strike had lasted 103 hours Lewis announced something new in American penal history, the forcible feeding of a woman. A simple matter, he told the press, in which you roll the prisoner in a blanket and then administer milk, eggs, and a stimulant through a rubber tube reaching into the stomach. The whole thing was trivial, but he would charge Mrs. Byrne for the expense of hiring an expert. Far from finding the news trivial, the press gave it banner headlines and editorials. From a sampling of the week, we read:

JANUARY 25   New York *Globe*: Court May End Strike
              Boston *Transcript*: Take Birth Control to Wilson

JANUARY 26   Associated Press: New York Hunger Strike Resolute
              Fitchburg *Sentinel*: Weakens Under Hunger Strike
              Pittsburgh *Sun*: Starving Self

JANUARY 27   New York *Sun*: Woman Hunger Striker Forcibly
                  Fed
              Philadelphia *Bulletin*: Hunger Striker Forcibly Fed

JANUARY 28   New York *Times*: Mrs. Byrne Now Fed by Force
              Boston *Globe*: Hunger Striker Passive
              Chicago *Record Herald*: Hunger Striker Fed 2nd
                  Time
              Peoria *Star*: Drive on Congress to Alter Birth
                  Control Laws

JANUARY 29   New York *Globe*: Mrs. Byrne Will Win or Die
              Greenville, South Carolina: Hunger Striker Hoax

JANUARY 30   Detroit *Tribune*: Feed Her by Force

JANUARY 31   Baltimore *Sun*: A Defense of Mrs. Byrne
              Ithaca *Journal*: Whitman Promises Pardon
              New York *Evening Mail*: Mrs. Sanger Worried

"The country seemed to stand still," said one reporter, "watching the lone woman who was giving her life to fight an unjust cause." But neither Margaret nor the Committee of One Hundred was standing still. Within an hour of Ethel's conviction, the committee had hired Carnegie Hall for a protest meeting January twenty-ninth. Trying every publicity angle, they bombarded the press with letters and sent a delegation to Washington to pressure Congress. Although her husband was a Wilson appointee, Mrs. Rublee joined in a demonstration before the White House and later in another in Albany.

On January twenty-ninth the committee packed the Brooklyn courthouse where Margaret's case was to be heard, giving the drab chamber a curiously gala look. Society women filled the front rows, said the *New York Tribune,* and Mrs. Sanger, with a bouquet of American beauty roses might have been the guest of honor at a reception. "A demure, rather shy looking woman," she was attended by the imposing, red-headed Mrs. Pinchot and the white-haired Mrs. Lewis Delafield, whose husband was an outstanding lawyer.

In the eyes of the defendant, it was no gala occasion. It was the crucial day in a life filled with crises. The hearings that afternoon might determine her own fate and that of her cause. In the evening, she must make the main address at Carnegie Hall. Every moment she must keep her wits about her, although she was sick with worry over Ethel. In discounting the feeding operation, Lewis had said that Mrs. Byrne did not resist. That in itself was frightening, for if the resolute Ethel was passive, she must be very weak.

Sometime between the court proceedings, which were continued, and the rally, she told a Baltimore *Sun* reporter that the evening might turn into a memorial instead of a testimonial meeting. She had learned that her sister was spitting blood and had been unconscious for twenty-four hours.

Against this nightmare background, the rally was extraordinary. Years later a participant, John Haynes Holmes, a famous Unitarian minister, said that he had never known such a meeting. It had the spirit of Abolition days. Margaret Sanger "took the audience and lifted it up. . . . She had the dramatic air of a woman in danger. She had the power of a saint and the mind of a statesman." In brief, her message was that a nation founded on self-government still denied its women the basic right to control their own persons. The audience pledged "unwavering moral and financial support" for the embattled sisters.

The *World*'s special reporter soon warned that Ethel's strength was ebbing. Margaret had been torn between loyalty to her sister's decision and her own wish to end the martyrdom. Now, she saw that she must use the full power of the committee. That afternoon

Michael Hennessy Higgins

Anne Purcell Higgins

Ethel, Margaret, Nan, and Mary Higgins

Facing page, top With Stuart

Facing page, bottom With Grant and Stuart, 1916

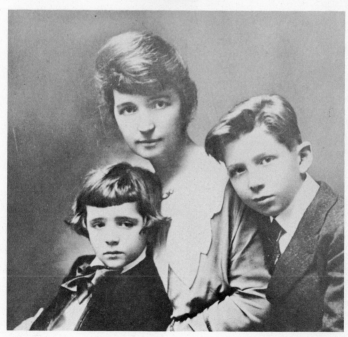

1916

Photos: Planned Parenthood—World Population

Leaving Brooklyn Court of Special Sessions after arraignment, January 1917

Photos: Planned Parenthood—World Population

Release from jail, 1917

Facing page, top Margaret in early 1920s

Facing page, bottom With Otis Skinner and H. G. Wells in England about 1920

Havelock Ellis

With Noah Slee in Germany, 1927

Facing page, top Testifying for birth-control information before Senate sub-committee, 1931

Facing page, bottom Willowlake, Fishkill, New York

With Baroness Ishimoto, 1932

Facing page, top With Gandhi, 1936

Facing page, bottom With Nehru

Fathers of "the Pill"

Dr. John Rock

Dr. Min Chueh Chang

Dr. Gregory Pincus

Mrs. Stanley McCormick   *Courtesy Chicago Historical Society*

Reprinted from Anthony
Comstock, Traps for the Young
(edited by Robert Bremner
and published by The Belknap Press
of Harvard University
Press)

"Your Honor, this woman gave birth to a naked child!"
BY ROBERT MINOR, FROM "THE MASSES," 1915.

From Birth Contro
Review, *June 1918*

Cartoons:
1915
1918
1968

Mrs. Poor Patient:—"If you're rich, the law don't count."

"PATIENCE—IN TIME THEY ACCEPTED
MY PILL."
9/8/68

All photos not otherwise
credited are from the
Margaret Sanger Papers,
Sophia Smith Collection,
Smith College Library

© *From the*
Herblock Gallery
(Simon and
Schuster, 1968)

Mrs. Pinchot, Jessie Ashley, the lawyer, and Margaret took the train to Albany.

Governor Whitman was an independent person who thought that Mrs. Byrne's imprisonment was a disgrace. Out of sympathy with both the laws and court decisions in regard to birth control, he readily accepted the delegation's proposal for a study commission to report back to the legislature.

As an emergency measure, he offered to pardon Mrs. Byrne if she would abide in the future by the present laws. To Mrs. Pinchot's dismay, Margaret would not make such an agreement without her sister's consent. However, she gladly accepted the offer of a pass so that she might see Ethel. Because she had to be in court the next morning, the visit was postponed until evening when Amos Pinchot and his wife accompanied her to the workhouse, and waited downstairs.

On a cot in a dark and dirty cell lay the wreck of Ethel Byrne. Her face was gaunt and drained, the once white skin was covered with bruises, and her eyes had the chilling look of death. When she finally recognized her sister, she whispered, "Liberty! I want liberty!"

That was enough. Margaret decided to guarantee the Governor's terms, although Ethel would probably resent the interference after her recovery. At the moment, survival was all that mattered. Hurrying downstairs, Margaret rejoined the Pinchots, who had just learned that the Governor had already acted and was en route to New York with the pardon.

When word finally came that Ethel was on her way out, Margaret and Mrs. Pinchot rushed to meet her in the corridor. Two burly men were dragging along one small figure whose head rolled helplessly from side to side. The orderlies ignored Margaret's protests because Lewis had told them that Mrs. Byrne must be seen by the press, on her feet, walking out of the building. Born to command, Mrs. Pinchot ended that nonsense with an imperious clap of the hands. She told the men to lay Mrs. Byrne on the floor and fetch a stretcher. Then slipping off her long fur coat, she wrapped it around the cold little form. For the first time Ethel seemed to know that she was safe.

It was two weeks before doctors promised that she would live. It was a year before she regained her health. Ethel Byrne was allowed just one chance to work for birth control, but in ten days she alerted millions to the movement. Her courage lifted the issue to its emotional peak. In her first book, *Woman and the New Race,* Margaret declared that "No single act of self-sacrifice in the history of the birth-control movement had done more to awaken the conscience of the public or to arouse the courage of women . . ."

On January twenty-ninth the Court of Special Sessions first took up the case of Fania Mindell. She was charged with having sold an obscene book, and since the court found *What Every Girl Should Know* indecent, she was convicted and later fined $50, which Mrs. Pinchot paid.

The court then opened its case against the principal defendant, Margaret Sanger. J. J. Goldstein pinned his hopes on the young Italian, John Freschi, who presided over a panel of three. On this first day Judge Freschi was most understanding. Picking up the cervical cap or pessary which the prosecution had put in evidence, he asked why this proved a legal violation, since the law allowed the use of contraception to prevent disease.

The district attorney had subpoenaed thirty mothers from the clinic list, and they had come with their children, equipped with lunches, pacifiers, and diapers. They nodded reassuringly to Margaret, trying to tell her that they would put in a good word. One by one they were called to the witness stand.

When asked by the prosecutor why she had gone to Mrs. Sanger's clinic, each mother answered, "To stop the babies." At this point the mother might beam at Margaret, telling how helpful she had been. Each answer seemed to the defendant like another nail in her seal of doom.

At last J. J. had a chance to turn this testimony to his client's advantage. He brought out the background of these mothers, the number of children, the poverty and bad health. The climax came with a pitiful little woman whose husband had a bad heart.

"How many children have you?" he asked.

"Eight and three that didn't live."

"What does your husband earn?"

"Ten dollars a veek—ven he verks."

Judge Freschi slammed down his gavel. "I can't stand this any longer," he muttered and adjourned the court for the week end.

J. J. was jubilant, and on this auspicious note Margaret had gone to the Carnegie Hall rally.

At the next session the district attorney produced a copy of *Family Limitation* with a picture of the same cervical cap. Reading aloud the author's instructions for use in preventing conception, he then gave irrefutable proof that Margaret Sanger had recommended the article for purposes banned by the law.

As for Section 1142, he argued that a citizen's liberty was safeguarded by the law's exemption of physicians. Since Mrs. Sanger was not a physician, she was of course not exempt and was guilty. The court agreed, but deferred sentence.

On good authority, J. J. learned that if his client would change her plea to guilty, her sentence would be suspended. The panel was relieved to have Mrs. Byrne finally off the front page and wanted neither to stir up the issue again nor to inflict punishment. J. J. was delighted, for to him, as to most lawyers, prison was the ultimate defeat. Besides, as he shrewdly pointed out, world events had changed since the first trial. Because the Kaiser had declared unrestricted submarine warfare, the United States had severed diplomatic relations with Germany. In the next weeks there would not be the same concern over birth control. Admitting all this, Margaret nevertheless refused to plead guilty.

The panel and J. J. now entered into a long legal discussion and Margaret, who was exhausted, began to drowse. When she dimly heard her lawyer promising something, she aroused herself with new apprehension. He had planted himself directly in front of her so that she could neither hear nor see much. She tried to peer around him, but each time she moved, he shifted to obstruct her view. At last she grabbed his coattail which ended the conference. Then the court asked her to rise and in brief, this is what followed:

THE COURT: Your counsel had made the statement that pending the prosecution of appeal, neither you nor those affiliated with you in this so called movement will violate the law. . . . Do you personally make that promise?

THE DEFENDANT: Pending the appeal.

THE COURT: If Mrs. Sanger will state publicly and openly that she will be a law-abiding citizen without any qualifications whatsoever, this Court is prepared to exercise the highest degree of leniency.

THE DEFENDANT: I'd like to have it understood by the gentlemen of the Court that the offer of leniency is very kind and I appreciate it very much. It is with me not a question of personal imprisonment or personal disadvantage. I am today and always have been more concerned with changing the law regardless of what I have to undergo to have it done.

THE COURT: Then I take it that you are indifferent about this matter entirely.

THE DEFENDANT: No, I am not indifferent. I am indifferent as to the personal consequences to myself, but I am not indifferent to the cause and the influence which can be attained for the cause.

THE COURT: Since you are of that mind, am I to infer that you intend to go on in this matter, violating the law, irrespective of the consequences?

THE DEFENDANT: I haven't said that. I said I am perfectly willing not to violate Section 1142—pending the appeal.

THE COURT (*to Mr. Goldstein*): What is the use of beating around the bush? You have communicated to me in my chambers the physical condition of your client, and you told me that this woman would respect the law. The law was not made by us. We are simply here to judge the case. We harbor no feeling against Mrs. Sanger. . . . We ask her openly and above board, "Will you publicly declare that you will respect the law and not violate it?" and then we get an answer with a qualification. Now what can the prisoner at the bar for sentence expect? I don't know that a prisoner under such circumstances is entitled to very much consideration after all. (*To the Defendant*) We don't want you to do impossible things, Mrs. Sanger, only the reasonable thing and that is to comply with this law as long as it remains law. . . . If you succeed in changing the law, well and good. If you fail, then you have to bow in submission to the majority rule.

THE DEFENDANT: It is just the chance, the opportunity to test it.

THE COURT: Very good. You have had your day in Court. . . . Now we are prepared to be extremely lenient with you if you will tell us that you will respect this law and not violate it.

THE DEFENDANT: I have given you my answer.

THE COURT: We don't want any qualifications. . . . We are not concerned with the appeal. . . . What is your answer, Mrs. Sanger? Is it yes or no?

Everyone's eyes were on the defendant. Juliet Rublee, sitting close by, later described that moment. Margaret looked so small and frail that it seemed impossible that she could be challenging this panel of justices. When the Court said, "Is it yes or no?" her body stiffened and the muscles in her face grew so tight that they seemed to be bursting out of her skin. She was risking a long prison term and a fine of up to $5,000 although Juliet knew that she had not a penny in the bank. There was a terrible silence while the whole room seemed to hold its breath. Then Margaret spoke in "that quiet brave little voice":

"I cannot promise to obey a law I do not respect."

The tension broke as every woman in the room began to shout and clap. A gavel sounded and the sentence was pronounced:

"The judgment of the Court is that you be confined to the Workhouse for the period of thirty days."

Someone cried, "Shame!" and then it was over.

For a few minutes life went on just as before. J. J. was busy with legal formalities while Margaret sat there, rather relieved at the sentence. For thirty days there was no need for a hunger strike, which at best would be an anticlimax after Ethel's. She had no wish to be a martyr, and with her past record she did not think that she could survive what Ethel had endured.

Her thoughts were cut short by a reminder of her new status when someone took her into the anteroom to be fingerprinted. Fingerprinted! She reacted in fury. She was being classified along with thieves and prostitutes. This should not be, for she was a political prisoner, not a criminal. When she balked, the clerk consulted the justices and, worn out by trying to keep her out of prison, they refused to become involved. So she won a technical victory before being herded with the other prisoners out of the rear of the building into a waiting van.

Now she entered a new world. Some young men were joking about their "sleeping time," the three or more years which they would serve behind bars. At the Raymond Street jail, where she spent the night, Margaret scored another victory by refusing a physical examination. Her reputation had preceded her, and when the attendants learned that she was Mrs. Sanger, they let her alone.

The workhouse apparently refused to care for a second Higgins sister, and next morning she was taken to her unknown destination, which turned out to be the Queens County penitentiary on Long Island. On meeting her, Joseph McCann, the jovial warden, asked if she had lunched and was pleased to hear that she would only fast if the food was too bad to eat.

It was reassuring that the building was laid out something like a hospital and she was used to uniforms. Furthermore her cell was a happy surprise, for unlike Ethel's, it was clean and equipped with a washstand and toilet. Mrs. Sullivan, the matron, added a table for her books and papers, and when Margaret asked why she was not given a job assignment, Mrs. Sullivan chuckled. Margaret looked better, she said, with a pen in her hand. To their mutual comfort, she and the administration cooperated. Following the young men's theory that prison was sleeping time, Margaret tried to catch up on sleep and on reading and writing.

A few excerpts from her diary describe her routine.

February 8th . . . Afternoon drags slowly and supper—bread and molasses and tea—seemed tasteless. Locked in at 6 p.m., lights out at 9 o'clock. . . .

Wednesday . . . Cells open at 7 a.m., but bell rings at 6 o'clock. Breakfast—oatmeal with salt and milk and coffee, two slices of bread (saltpeter said to make it taste so queer).

Clean cells . . . walk in air. Talked with little colored girl, Liza [who knew of Mrs. Sanger and called out], "you'se eats, don't you?" referring to Mrs. Byrne's hunger strike.

Dinner of stew and bread. Afternoon four letters. Called to warden's room to be fingerprinted. Told him I objected to being classed as a criminal and would not submit.

Supper of tea, bread and stewed peaches.

Women here seem to like Warden McCann and matron. Atmosphere here very different from Workhouse or Raymond St. Jail. Women are not treated so well as men though—not allowed papers, nor to send out for anything like food, papers or cigarettes as men are allowed to do. No visitors except two a month. All letters read going and coming—which is an outrage.

Since she was to be there for a month, she decided that it was a chance to study penology. Her fellow prisoners fascinated her, especially in their class snobbery. There was a pecking order in the prison yard as rigid as in a chicken coop. A high-class thief or "Tiffany," warned her not to associate with the pickpockets. They were the lowest order, in part because they filched from the poor, which in the eyes of the others was not cricket.

In the first quarter of this century, instead of being given any therapy, young drug addicts were locked up with criminals for as much as three years. There were also young illiterates, whom she proposed to teach, until she found a better solution.

One stately white-haired woman, "the Duchess," who held herself aloof from her fellow prisoners, told her story to Margaret. She had been a teacher for many years before she married a retired minister; when he died, years later, she not only found herself penniless, but too old to be reemployed. In her predicament, she had fled from several unpaid landlords until the law caught up with her. Margaret thought the broken-spirited woman might regain her self-respect by teaching once more. With the help of J. J., she obtained a set of primers, and the Duchess happily opened literacy classes. Hers turned into a rags-to-riches tale with Margaret as the fairy godmother. Later when the elderly Cinderella was released, Margaret found her a position as hostess in an Adirondacks summer camp, where she met her prince, a retired millionaire, and they were soon honeymooning on his yacht.

Margaret saw prison as a good social laboratory to test a favorite

thesis. Recently Dr. Alice Hamilton of Hull House had shown that
the nation's child labor was recruited from the large families of the
poor. From these same families, Margaret believed, came most
of the nation's prostitutes and petty criminals. Warden McCann,
with whom she discussed the matter, offered to relay whatever facts
she wanted, but he warned her that her theory would be disproved.
Most of the inmates, according to him, had been single children.
This seemed incredible until some of the old timers explained that
every prisoner tried to keep his family out of his affairs by claiming
that he was an "only" child. Margaret's personal poll of thirty-one
in her corridor refuted the warden's report. The average home
had seven children.

Her fellow prisoners wanted to know about "sex hygiene," and
never missing a chance to tell her story, Margaret asked Mrs. Sullivan if she might lecture to them in the corridor. The matron's
first response was that the girls "knew bad enough already!" Soon,
however, Margaret was lecturing almost daily in one corridor or another.

By chance, a sidelight from a fellow prisoner is included in the
privately printed *Our Margaret Sanger* in the Smith College Collection. Hannah Voorsinger was secretary of a church committee
which tried to help the women at the penitentiary. In talking
to "the Queen" of New York's pickpockets, she heard of "a wonderful woman" who ought never to have been locked up. Miss Voorsinger was so impressed that she asked McCann to point out this
remarkable Mrs. Sanger. She caught a glimpse of Margaret talking
with other prisoners, dressed like them in the cotton uniform, but
conspicuous for her "gorgeous red hair."

Although Margaret had gained some insight and perhaps some
rest, the month was not therapeutic. Because of the poor food, she
had lost fifteen pounds, which reactivated her tuberculosis. Furthermore, her last two hours were so brutal that they wiped out
the memory of otherwise decent treatment.

McCann had hoped that by cooperating with her, she would re-
lent about the fingerprinting, which was mandatory. He could not
guess the steel underlying her ladylike presence, and in the end he
turned her over to his strong-arm men. Even she could not ex-

plain where she found the strength to keep them from their purpose. Finally, police headquarters, prodded by J. J., ordered McCann to forget the fingerprinting.

It was a stinging cold day when the metal doors clanged behind her. In front stood her friends, nearly frozen by the delay, but now lifting their voices in the Marseillaise. Behind and above her at the upper windows were new friends, waving good-by. Nothing in her life, she said later, touched her more than this moment. The waiting escort, which included a delegation from the Brownsville mothers, strewed her way with flowers, helped her into a warm limousine and whisked her off to a breakfast fragrant with real coffee, grapefruit, eggs, and toast. It was her "coming out party."

The euphoria of her coming out of prison lingered for a while that spring. The press had never been as friendly, the governor had promised action, and her *Birth Control Review* had materialized. Since she had planned the first number long in advance, Fred Blossom, the managing editor, had brought it out on schedule while she was in prison.

There was glamor too in those first weeks when she and Blossom plunged into the motion picture business. Much as he had opposed the clinic, he had been so impressed by her publicity that he wanted an instant substitute to keep the issue in the public eye. Together they tried a scenario, to which they gave the disarmingly banal title, *The Hand that Rocks the Cradle*. Still the miracle-worker, Blossom found an angel to finance it, and the film was shot.

The scene was the lower East Side of New York, Margaret played herself, a nurse who cared for someone resembling Sadie Sachs; the trial provided the climax. Briefly she fulfilled her childhood ambition to be a leading lady, but no one saw her in the part. The Commissioner of Licenses suppressed the amateur effort before it was released. Before this verdict could be challenged, a crisis developed in the production partnership.

Six months earlier, when Blossom had arrived in New York, Margaret was absorbed in her clinic plans; after that, first the trials and then prison took her away from her usual functions. Filling the vacuum, Blossom had deftly directed most phases of the work. He had opened the New York office, answered the huge volume of mail, organized a New York Birth Control League, with himself as president and then, as editor as well as manager, had launched the *Review*.

Officially, he called Margaret the Joan of Arc of the movement, but increasingly he thought her erratic and sensational. Although he had no use for Mrs. Dennett who, as president of the National Birth Control League, was the only one who had challenged Margaret's leadership, he agreed that Margaret Sanger lacked the background for her role. His academic Ph.D. fitted him for that part.

Since it never occurred to Margaret to give up either her life work or the *Review*, an adjustment between these two, sharing undefined responsibilities, required the utmost tact and good will. By that time it was doubtful that this able and charming man possessed either trait. Certainly he was unstable. During this period, in which he had broken with his wife, relinquishing his only apparent income, he kept changing his professional ties, leaving his former colleagues puzzled, if not mistrustful. At best he was careless in finances.

This partnership with Margaret broke over the seemingly irrelevant, but overwhelming, issue of the day. After Germany began unrestricted submarine warfare, President Wilson declared to a joint session of Congress, that "the world must be made safe for democracy. . . . It is a fearful thing to lead this great peaceful people into war, into the most terrible and disastrous of all wars. . . . But the right is more precious than the peace . . ."

Margaret was appalled, as were her friends in the labor movement. While they believed that wars were imperial nonsense, ruinous to the common man, she saw them also as the fulfillment of Malthusian laws. Once more men were bringing their numbers into balance with the available subsistence by slaughtering surplus people, who as usual were the young. Why talk of democracy? The civilized answer was birth control. War was a male vice and women were forced to proliferate the cannon fodder. Margaret, trying to explain all this in an editorial for the *Review*, reverted in tone to the shrill vehemence of *The Woman Rebel*.

To Blossom the article was horrible and pro-German. A Francophile, he welcomed the long-delayed declaration of war, and felt so strongly that when Margaret insisted on the editorial, he resigned. After working for six months as a volunteer, he had a right to leave, but not in the way he chose.

One May morning when Margaret unlocked the door, she found the office stripped bare. Again, Blossom had a right to take the furniture, for which he had paid, but he had also taken the files, records, and funds. The *Review* had two thousand paid-up subscribers, each entitled to nine more issues, but without the payments and records the editor was stymied. Besides, Blossom was treasurer of the sisters' legal defense fund, which had received some large contributions of which he had never made an accounting.

Blossom always claimed that he had advanced more money than he had received. At first he was too busy even to sort out the papers, for he had plunged at once into the management of a Socialist candidate's congressional campaign. When time dragged on, Margaret's lawyer started a suit against him, but this brought the intervention of Blossom's new friends. They guaranteed to secure a full accounting if Margaret would drop the suit and give them her evidence of Blossom's questionable acts. Finally in the interest of harmony, she agreed.

Soon afterward, she was shocked to read in a morning paper that the Socialist Party had condemned Margaret Sanger's conduct in her dispute with Frederick Blossom. Later this report proved to be an error perpetrated by Blossom. After an investigation, her position was upheld and his censured, but by that time it was ancient history. Blossom had left the Socialist Party for a brief stay with the I.W.W., and the fact that both of these organizations also opposed the war, simply made his motives more mysterious. In any case, he never returned to Margaret either records or funds.

Beyond the bitterness of this experience, Margaret was left in such serious straits that for six months there was no *Review*. The printer carried her account for some weeks, after which, in order to pay him, Margaret again borrowed from her older sisters.

In June Congress passed an Espionage Act which triggered a crackdown on all subversives. After that, raids on pacifists, conscientious objectors, and labor's left wing swept the country along with the influenza. Bill Haywood went to Leavenworth with hundreds of his Wobblies; the nonviolent Eugene Debs started a ten-year sentence in Atlanta. Some months earlier Debs had written to Margaret at the Queen's County penitentiary that his blood boiled when he thought of her "locked up like a beast." Now, like a beast, he was locked up for failing to give the war his "moral" support.

The war turned the clock back on all progress. As people channeled their surplus time and funds into that effort they had no energy for other causes. New York's Governor Whitman did not name his birth control committee; three states passed new laws banning birth control. Teddy Roosevelt, exhorting mothers to have more children, thundered against race suicide; Billy Sunday fulminated to huge crowds on the sins of contraception.

With no way to capture the headlines for factual answers, Margaret brooded over tactics for preserving her hard-won gains. Finally she decided to make the *Review* her holding operation, as well as communication system. To revive the short-lived paper in wartime was in itself an uphill effort, but to consider it without personal income or financial backing was both audacious and characteristic of Margaret Sanger.

Reminiscing of this period in *My Fight for Birth Control,* the author says that she was sustained by faith that she was working in accord with the universal law of evolution. Her conviction not only gave her strength for her daily schedule, but it also opened locked doors. Certainly it unlocked the resources of some of her friends.

Juliet Rublee, who had often bailed Margaret out of crises, was the first to see that if the *Review*'s editor-manager was to survive, there must be a steadier financial base than the haphazard largesse of a few supporters. Her initiative led to the incorporation of the New York Women's Publishing Company with shares at $10, each share carrying one vote on the paper's policy. The first goals were to raise $10,000 and to cut costs by securing second-class mailing privileges. During the next decade these stockholders, with Frances Ackerman, the permanent treasurer and most responsible member, kept the journal solvent. While they never raised enough funds to cover all needs, which Margaret often paid for from her lecture fees, they assured survival during the national emergency.

After its erratic start, the *Review* became the movement's forward thrust. Not only was it the link among adherents, but also the reporter of local, national, and world developments and the special resource for speakers in all parts of the country. For sales appeal, it relied on Margaret's distinguished friends; inevitably, the lead article of the first number had been by Havelock Ellis, whose prestige was at its peak, and whom the editor honored with an annual birthday number. With a growing circulation, rising to ten thousand in the next few years, Margaret found that she need no longer rely on chance contributions. Distinguished experts were glad to write special articles. These files today offer a rich commentary on the era, with timeless and often amusing arguments for birth control.

In a random sampling, we learn from Luther Burbank that man uses the worst seed in the worst soil in only his human harvest. A fourth of the nation's parents, living in squalor, bring forth a half of America's children, "unwillingly and in passion and ignorance." The biologist, Gideon Diedrich, struck down the church argument that contraception, like abortion, kills life. Since all reproduction is based on cell division, no life is involved before any cell is divided.

A news reprint tells of a Georgia hen that laid twelve double eggs on successive days but on the thirteenth day died of the strain. Thomas Nixon Carver of Harvard compared employers who wanted large supplies of cheap labor, priests who wanted large numbers of parishioners, military leaders who wanted large numbers of soldiers for cannon fodder, with foxes who enjoyed large families of rabbits. Meanwhile, the paper reported that three judges with small families sent Kitty Marion to prison for advising the poor how to limit the number of their children.

Kitty Marion was a gift from the English suffragettes. A large Valkyrian blond, she had fled from her German home after a paternal beating, and in London did a turn in the music halls before she read about Mrs. Pankhurst. Her own suffrage services included seven jail sentences with forcible feedings, but when war broke out, lest she be interned as an enemy alien, her friends shipped her to the United States. In New York, the congenial exploits of the Higgins sisters brought her into their movement. Since she had sold *The Suffragette* on London streets, she volunteered to sell the *Review* at Times Square.

From morning until midnight, day after day for thirteen years, she was a landmark. Passers-by assumed that she was Margaret Sanger, and for the rest of her life people told the latter how she had changed since she had patrolled Forty-second Street. Actually, Margaret did take her turn, but found it torture. Only the robust Kitty Marion could long endure the jibes and insults. When reminded of God's command to "be fruitful and multiply," she answered good humoredly that this had already been done. Then she quoted Ecclesiastes 16:1: "Desire not a multitude of unprofitable children." Right on her beat, she claimed to witness the most fascinating, comic, tragic, and moving spectacle in the world.

New policemen always arrested her and although she knew that her case would be thrown out of court, she often had to wake Margaret to bail her out. Once, however, she did serve thirty days, trapped into giving illegal advice to the same stooge who had trapped Bill Sanger three years previously.

Margaret called these the "leaden years." Since her cause was overshadowed by the nation's emergency and brought no dramatic or public response, most people were indifferent, if not hostile, to her efforts. Among her few intimates, J. J. Goldstein had become a favorite. Having defended her in court, he was now her chivalrous and frequent escort, to whom she refers in her journal as "J. J. —dear, generous one." "A queer lad," she also calls him, "fascinating at times, but does not try to be or is not conscious of it. . . ." In spite of a keen mind, he was "quite undeveloped emotionally and in some things intellectually and artistically."

More than three decades later Judge Goldstein gave his views of her in a recording for the Planned Parenthood Federation. Margaret Sanger was "charming . . . charming," he began, "with a great sense of humor and no touch of the battle-ax." As for integrity, he doubted that she could think dishonestly. He never knew her to lie, and she never made promises. To her, money was nothing. He himself neither received a fee, nor asked for one. To serve her was a privilege.

Then the distinguished judge summed up his experience. It had been "the thrill of a lifetime to be her friend and to represent her." The world was a better place because of Margaret Sanger, and the more he thought about her, the happier he felt.

From J. J., Margaret received a homely and practical legacy, his cook, Daisy Mitchell, commonly known as "Old Faithful." For forty years she served the Sangers, freeing Margaret from endless chores.

During the war when public response to birth control was again almost as frosty as in the days of *The Woman Rebel,* there was a continuing link in the person of Jessie Ashley, who had followed Margaret into the movement. This radical daughter of one of the nation's first families relieved her friend of many burdens by accepting the position of managing editor of the *Review*. She poured such zeal into her work that, while convalescing from the flu, she contracted pneumonia and was another war casualty. Propped up on her pillows, her last words were a written exhortation to women in "every hamlet and every city" to spread the message and, following Kitty Marion's example, to sell the *Review.*

William E. Williams, former managing editor of the Kansas City *Star,* did most to professionalize the paper by teaching Margaret whatever technical skills she acquired. Later he edited her first book. His payment, according to his letters, was "the happiest and most inspiring" time in his life. She had awakened "depths to his nature that he did not know existed." In her journal, Margaret soberly noted that "when men, so big and generous and devoted, offer their all, their strength, labor, energy, talents and love at our feet," it does not necessarily awaken a responsive feeling. She thought perhaps love was a chemical matter and J. J. had more of that. Years later when someone asked about Billy Williams, she answered guardedly that he might have thought he loved her, but it was not her physical self, but that which "emerged from her to touch the same quality in him."

Perhaps a truer example of her gift for arousing disinterested enthusiasm was Anna Lifshiz. Her young stenographer was the only one to receive a salary, if her uncertain pittance could be called one. She worked excessive hours without complaint because she too was enlisted in the cause. So was her mother who volunteered to distribute literature and on holidays sent wine and cakes with prayers for Margaret's health and happiness. Like most of Margaret's colleagues, Anna Lifshiz remained steadfastly loyal throughout the years. Much later she said that working for the movement was "like a religious crusade. The office was bedlam, volunteers rushing in and out. . . . Through it all she [Margaret] moved, serenely confident, giving us all some added strength that would make us work thirteen hours that day when we were sure that we couldn't last ten."

Historic events were taking place abroad, and sometimes they brought personal repercussions. After the Kerensky revolution, John Reed telephoned Margaret with the offer of a house which they had seen together six years before in the village of Truro, near Provincetown. This captivating cabin of an old sea captain was what they each had wanted but since the Sangers were about to leave for France, Reed bought the place. Now, as a free-lance writer, he was taking off for Russia, where he would write his famous *Ten Days that Shook the World,* and he needed money. Margaret had just had a windfall, a thousand dollars for a series of lectures, which she gladly exchanged for the house. She hoped to make this a family homestead where she might vacation three months a year with the boys. Her sons did vacation there, but usually under the care of Grandfather Higgins, Aunt Nan, and "Old Faithful." Margaret seldom had time for more than a week's stay.

Truro, she may also have realized, could simplify her divorce. With property, she could establish a residence there and then with Bill's cooperation, which now seemed likely, since he was interested in another woman, she might win her freedom without publicity under the more lenient Massachusetts law.

One day a "bright bugle sounded." Margaret learned that the army was using the section on venereal disease from *What Every Girl Should Know.* Five years previously the Post Office had suppressed this chapter as obscene; now the army had reprinted it as educational material to protect the health of American soldiers.

This reprint, albeit with no acknowledgment to the author, should suffice to reverse Fania Mindell's conviction for selling an indecent pamphlet.

If she heard a bright bugle in 1917, she must have heard a whole fanfare at the start of the New Year. J. J. Goldstein had carried her case to the State Supreme Court where Judge Frederick E. Crane of the Appellate Division gave the decision. To most people the fanfare was muted, if they heard it at all, for Margaret's conviction was upheld. This was based on the fact that as a nurse, not a doctor, she was not covered by the law's exemption.

However, the historic part of the decision was an interpretative phrase which said that a licensed physician might give contraceptive advice "for the cure and *prevention* of disease." Crane had taken Webster's definition of "disease" as "any change in the state of the body which caused or threatened pain and sickness." In this way he stretched the meaning of the word far beyond the law's original intent.

Crane fulfilled Margaret's faith in what an enlightened judge would do. His interpretation had changed an outrageous law, meant only to protect male promiscuity, into one which would protect ailing mothers. Her strategy had won. Even J. J. conceded that "in the long run she was right, unassailably right."

On November 11, 1918, pandemonium broke out with Armistice Day. Christmas was never more jubilant. The boys were coming home and President Wilson's European reception on his way to the Peace Conference was stupendous. The New Year would ring in a brand new world order, safe for democracy, with war forever banned.

In the midst of national rejoicing Margaret was told that she might not be around to enjoy the new era—unless she changed her ways. Dr. Mary Halton warned that ever since she had come out of prison, she had been overworking. She had ignored her symptoms, trudging on foot through rain and snow to give talks while she ran a temperature and should have been in bed. Her days were too long, her home was too cold, and her diet inadequate. She needed rest and sunshine. With no funds for a winter vacation, Margaret was pondering the solution when a publisher offered advance royalties if she would deliver a manuscript on labor problems. She seized the chance, hoping to combine writing of the book not only with convalescence, but with the company of her sons.

In her *Autobiography,* she explains that she put the boys in country schools directed by capable masters where they could lead healthy, regular lives. The sacrifice was hers, a loneliness that often seemed unbearable. Now, however, it became apparent that she should not interrupt Stuart's schooling. He was sixteen, preparing for Yale and earning part of his tuition at the Peddie School for Boys in New Jersey. On the other hand, since the affectionate and adaptable Grant was only ten, a three months' change of school would not hurt him and his mother's company might be reassuring. Perhaps because she had cared for him from infancy, as she had not been able to care for Stuart, their relationship was closer. Yet even in his case, she must have known that it was not easy to be the son of Margaret Sanger. Once he had attacked a larger boy for calling his mother "a jailbird." He got a black eye, but when others joined in the taunt, he ignominiously announced that she was "another Margaret Sanger."

One February evening mother and son boarded the train for the long and to Grant exciting trip west. They settled in Coronado, California, for three months during which she basked in sunshine and her favorite subject. While statesmen debated world plans, Margaret drafted what she believed was the only viable basis on which to build an enduring peace.

The publisher had asked for a book on labor problems, but Margaret Sanger wrote her "heart book," *Woman and the New Race.* She had not rejected her assignment, for the brief manuscript dealt with labor, along with most human problems, but in perspective, reducing them to the manageable scale that all would assume once mankind corrected its main error.

As she saw it, the chief cause of misery was woman's fertility. Excess people, not acts of God, created poverty, famine, and war. Craft unions had learned to better themselves by limiting their membership, but even they ignored the larger lesson. Labor itself produced the excess workers who beat down their own standards of living.

Margaret claimed that if labor would strike against the Comstock laws, it would gain more than by striking against any employer. Whatever a man's wages, they would go further in a small family than in a large one. With fewer births, there would be fewer deaths and much less illness. Mothers would have time for their children, who, rather than competing against their parents in mills, factories and coal mines, would remain in school, preparing for a better future.

All society would gain, said the author, if birth control were allowed to shut off the spigot that floods the world with weaklings. When sick and unfit mothers were not forced to breed, there would be an end to unwanted children who grow up to fill our prisons and asylums. Organized vice would dwindle, as would venereal disease.

As for war, the author confidently thought that mothers could end it by cutting off the surplus people. Of course military states always clamor for more children, first to defend the Fatherland, and when the population soars, to conquer more territory for the added millions. Napoleon had voiced the military mind when he said: "Woman is given us to bear children. She is our property. . . . Because she produces children for us, we yield none to her. She is our possession, as the fruit tree is that of the gardener."

But why, asked Margaret Sanger of the twentieth century, did women ever accept the role of chattel in a male society? Much of the slim book is her explanation of woman's built-in submissiveness, stemming not only from physical weakness, but from the man-made laws of both church and state.

To the early Christians, Margaret recalled, sex itself was evil, and marriage a carnal indulgence. A child was conceived in sin by an unclean spirit, which only baptism could exorcise. Although a woman's life was determined by sex, in her the sex impulse was thought especially shameful. Satisfaction was a man's prerogative, for which woman's body was made. St. Paul ordered wives to "subject themselves to their husbands as to the Lord." No matter what her condition, nor how brutal, drunk, or diseased her husband, he must not be denied. For this reason the outrages committed within marriage far outweighed the illegal ones.

The Comstock laws simply made permanent and explicit customs that had generally prevailed throughout the nineteenth century. Supposedly these laws applied to all, but they had become class legislation when first the rich and then the middle class learned how to evade them. Finally, only those who most needed help—the poor, who had no family doctors—were denied it.

Of all species, the author proclaimed, man alone had been given the power to perfect his race by promoting quality, instead of quantity. By fully using his gift, he would breed superior men and women. And since any code of human rights assumes that the individual controls his own person, it was high time that women gained that basic freedom. With the fear of pregnancy removed, wives would then develop healthier sex relations. They too would experience the soaring ecstasy of the consummated act.

Just as a slave race bears slave children, so mothers in bondage transmit their fears and cowardice to their offspring. But as perfect trees bear perfect fruit, so healthy, happy mothers would bear a race superior to those of former generations in both physical and spiritual robustness.

Woman and the New Race carries Margaret Sanger's enduring message. Since the author had a single great purpose, the same theme with remarkable variations, runs through her several books, countless pamphlets and short pieces.

Havelock Ellis always urged Margaret not to hurry. His method of writing was to put aside a first draft until it "ripened," then to revise it and probably repeat the process over and over again. As a busy activist, Margaret had neither the time nor temperament for such a leisured system. Instead, in her major works, she relied on a collaborator, the most congenial of whom was Rackham Holt, whose organization of material and "inspired" advice she acknowledges in the 1938 autobiography. The result was Margaret at her best, freed from chaotic structure and stylistic failings.

Margaret's unpublished journal tells how she produced *Woman and the New Race*. She wrote rapidly and sent each chapter east for Billy Williams to edit. Later, when she returned to New York, they rewrote the first draft together. After the passage of a half century, some of the material is out of date; some of it is tiresomely didactic. Much however, remains fresh and fascinating. When it appeared in 1920, it was an arresting book that sold a quarter of a million copies.

The nineteen-twenties opened brilliantly for Margaret enjoying spring once more in England now at peace. The Drysdales arranged this by booking many lectures. In the next decade Margaret returned almost yearly either to lecture or to secure speakers for meetings back home. In England, where her cause was first welcomed, she recharged her mind, while her spirit flowered in the warmth of British admiration.

Although unrelated to her speaking, the event of this 1920 visit was her friendship with H. G. Wells. In the future the highlight of every trip would be a stay in his Essex home. Wells's squeaky voice with its trace of cockney was a legacy of his youth, but in middle life he lived like landed gentry. The ivy-covered former rectory, which was his home, was set in spacious lawns, interspersed with gardens and woods. Weekend guests enjoyed an easy hospitality based on many rooms and servants.

Wells's sons, home from Cambridge, attracted young people who did not segregate themselves, as in the United States, but joined in the activities which included a Sunday morning ball game invented by the author. But conversation, usually witty although often serious, was the main diversion. According to Margaret, everyone had his turn in the spotlight. Certainly she did.

To Wells, Margaret was heroic. She was leading the world's most important crusade, but at the same time was a feminine delight, for which he was unabashedly greedy. Early in their acquaintance he wrote, "I want to see you as much as possible . . . as much as possible without people about." Sixteen years later he confided, "Now I can tell you that I have loved you very dearly ever since I first met you and I always shall."

Wells was the foremost English spokesman for a change in society's attitude toward sex. Whether or not Victorian morals had altered, frank discussion was a twentieth-century phenomenon. Among intellectuals in England, where divorce was almost impossible, there was a widespread rejection of monogamy. Margaret's friends urged several high-minded, pseudo-scientific reasons for multiple loves. On her first visit she had been exposed not only to the philosophy of Havelock Ellis, but also of Marie Stopes, who was now referred to as the high priestess of love and marriage. The influence of these two had affected Margaret's vocabulary, her thinking and finally her way of life.

According to Wells, the female's restricted role had resulted from man's "animal jealousy," which, making a fetish of her chastity, had reduced her to his property. Wells argued that a Socialist government should end the "servitude" of women, as well as that of labor. More basic than the vote, for which the suffragettes clamored, was the endowment of motherhood. With economic independence, women would gain self-respect, and then developing freely, as did their brothers, they would enter into life-enhancing, if transitory, relationships with members of the other sex.

Wells's program, enunciated some years previous, had run afoul of the most prestigious Socialists, the Fabians, led by Sidney and Beatrice Webb and George Bernard Shaw. In a paper before that group, of which Wells was then a member, he had declared that the Socialist "no more regards the institution of marriage as a permanent thing than he regards competitive industrialism as a permanent thing." Unfortunately, the cornerstone of Fabian strategy was to stress only a few major issues and refrain from stirring up irrelevant controversies. The endowment of motherhood was not on the agenda and, more important, whatever their personal habits, no other Fabian wanted to join Wells in publicly endorsing free love.

Beatrice Webb, one of the great women of the age, had discussed Wells's views in her journal, referring to the thesis of his novel,

In the Days of the Comet. "Education through promiscuity," she noted, "was familiar to intellectuals and seemed to have some validity. Friendship between particular men and women has an enormous educational value to both [especially to the woman]. If you could have been the beloved of the dozen ablest men you had known, it would have greatly extended your knowledge of human nature and human affairs . . . but there remains the question whether, with all the perturbation caused by such intimacies, you would have any brain left to think with . . . moreover, it would mean a great increase in sexual emotion for its own sake and not for the sake of bearing children. And that way madness lies."

To Margaret Sanger the educational value of such friendships might have had a great appeal, as would the chance of winning strong allies for her cause. On first meeting Wells, she observed in her diary that he was a "sort of naughty boy man" with twinkling, laughing eyes. In the *Autobiography* her comments were disingenuous, for she was trying to deflect gossip when she said that Wells was the "Don Juan of spinsterhood . . . that there was a Mrs. Wells, for whom Mr. Wells cared deeply, did not matter in the least."

In this case, Margaret may have been equally indebted to Catherine Wells, who, through an obscure gift, diagnosed the infection that had long plagued the former nurse. Instead of applying an ice pack every night to her "tubercular glands," Mrs. Wells thought she should have her tonsils out. Embedded tonsils did prove to be the root of her twenty-three years of unnecessary suffering. After the operation, she enjoyed better health than she had known since childhood.

Meanwhile, Wells's contributions to Margaret's cause, by way of his speaking, writing and entertaining, were impressive. Once after a visit, he scrawled, "Wonderful! Unforgettable." But over the years their encounters were mostly at banquets and formal meetings where their wit and praise of each other were shared by large audiences, as when Wells announced, "Alexander the Great changed a few boundaries and killed a few men. Both he and Napoleon were forced into fame by circumstances outside of themselves and by currents of the time, but Margaret Sanger made currents and circumstances. When the history of our civilization is written, it will be a biological history and Margaret Sanger will be its heroine."

If friendship with the famous H. G. was the high point of 1920, he was only one among many admirers. Five years after she and Ellis had parted, they toured Ireland together. Ostensibly, they were trying to trace her forebears, especially the link with the poet Edward Fitzgerald of *Rubaiyat* fame, but lack of contacts, plus the Sinn Fein rebellion, raised too many roadblocks. Finally, they hired a two wheel cart, in which they sat back to back, bumping through a misty drizzle until they reached Killarney. There, Ellis, feeling a chill, took to his bed while she chatted downstairs with three young priests. They volunteered that the ablest youths, for lack of jobs in an overcrowded country, were emigrating. It is not clear how much of her standard speech Margaret Sanger made to the friendly priests.

If Margaret and Ellis had ever seriously considered marriage, they dropped the idea now that it was possible. Edith was gone and after years of pleading, Margaret was gaining her divorce. But they both must have realized that a union between an aging recluse and a crusading reformer would be disastrous. Besides, Margaret had known for two years that someone else shared Havelock's love. He had assured her that the little Frenchwoman, Françoise de Lisle, would never drive the Irish woman from his heart, but Françoise was close at hand and worshipful. Perhaps he offered a chivalrous compensation when he introduced Margaret to his young disciple, the poet, Hugh de Selincourt.

This year and in the next ones Margaret often relaxed at Hugh's Sussex home, Wantley. Enchanting she found this thatched and memory-haunted birthplace of Shelley and lyrical the evenings filled with poetry read by Hugh, music played by his wife and daughter and moonlit walks on the lonely moor.

Wantley was unique in its attempt to fulfill Shelley's dream that "to live and love are one." Disdaining the vulgar and promiscuous, Hugh once set down his own fastidious standards in a note to Margaret, commenting on the dancer, Isadora Duncan, also in the vanguard of the sexual revolution. This other famous American, who had supported Margaret during the 1916 trial by taking a box at the Carnegie rally, had seen herself as a chaste Diana when she made her European debut, but she had emerged an insatiate Bacchante. "Gallant and adorable" she was, wrote Hugh, but "It" used her; she could not use "It." She was so greedy that her loves led no-where, certainly not to the tenderness and understanding for which he aimed.

To the sensitive Hugh, love was a psychic force as powerful as electricity sending out waves of creativity. Blake, Shelley, and Have-lock Ellis had all sensed this phenomenon and knew that it was as futile to judge or condemn love as it was to judge or condemn electricity. Instead, they urged its use. As a start, Hugh believed that those who loved the same person should love each other. To-gether they should drink the cup of bliss, which meant sexual rela-tions, thus breeding new happiness in a cumulative way.

Insane and immoral as his ideas were to most people, he lived consistently and encouraged his wife Janet to do the same. She wrote Margaret that at first she had been a "grudging little pig," but over the years and in spite of their complex ménage, the affec-tion of the Selincourts proved remarkably durable. Eventually they shared a new home, Sand-Pit, with Harold Child, author of lead articles for the London *Times*. Having lost both his wife and wealth in her long illness, Child was partly consoled by drinking the cup of bliss with Janet. But that was only the start of their en-tanglements. Janet's sympathy went out to a neighbor doctor whose wife was institutionalized. Gallantly Janet's husband and lover picked the daily bouquet which she presented for the doctor's of-fice.

First Hugh and then Harold Child became enthralled with Margaret, although, true to their principles, they were not jeal-ous. On the contrary, Hugh rejoiced at the workings of "cumula-tive" love. A note from Child suggests his feelings: "My Margaret —mine because you gave it to me and you can spare it without tak-ing away from the Margarets of all the other people who love you."

Like Ellis and Wells, they were captivated by her mixture of the heroic and the feminine. Hugh put it variously as "the delicious blend of the great queen and little girl," and the fact that she, while moving the world, was "delicate and fragrant." For him, she was the "creative, unifying woman, helping all that's lovely to thrive." Shamelessly he bragged of kissing her feet. Harold Child, less whimsical, asked, "Great and lovely lady, are you real or are you a most wonderful dream?" She was to them a crusading goddess, half Athena, half Aphrodite.

And how did Margaret take this adulation? She found it delightful, the more so after years of Spartan, even ascetic existence. She had worked relentlessly, living alone in a comfortless room and, lest she hurt her cause, she had been very discreet. Yet she was no Puritan, in fact, she was part hedonist with a gift for laughter, "the laughter of the Gods," Harold Child called hers. She too was a product of the sexual revolution which was sweeping the Western world.

For ten years she had been associated with New York's radical left, innovators of changing mores. As Bill Sanger's letters from Paris show, he had become convinced that the "so-called Labor Revolutionary Movement was nothing but a Saturnalia of Sexualism." He suspected that its free lovers were after his wife, "her body"; yet she would never break with them.

On her first visit to England, Margaret had readily accepted Ellis's views, which among other points, stressed a single sexual standard, with the right of women to the same freedoms that men had always enjoyed. Her own speciality, birth control, merged with Ellis's studies on the art of love. She also recognized that a major cause of marital unhappiness was the disregard of the wife's erotic needs. Enlightened love-making would not only enhance life, but release a many-sided creativity.

In her *Intimate Memories*, Mabel Dodge gives a revealing sidelight from a private conversation after Margaret's first stay in England. Never before had Mrs. Dodge heard anyone speak of the "mysteries and mightiness of physical love as a sacred and scientific reality." At a time when a sense of sin was always mixed with the sense of pleasure, Margaret openly acclaimed "the joys of the flesh." She was trying to rehabilitate sex, to teach people to accept "the life in the cells, developing it, expanding it and enjoying it with a conscious attainment of its possibilities that would make previous relations between men and women, with their associations of smirking shame and secretive lubricities, seem ignoble in their limitations and stupid beyond words in their awkward ignorance." Margaret Sanger stressed the "conscious, careful selection of a lover, that is the mate, if only for an hour, for a lifetime maybe."

Mabel Dodge was not always reliable, but she publicly thanked Margaret for liberating her future, which was one of the more flamboyant examples of changing mores. Her emancipation began with the much publicized affair with John Reed. Once he fled from her "smothering" love, but she finally turned her passion to others, including two more husbands. The last of these, Toni Luhan the Indian, saw her always "goin' by, goin' by, just like water." Unstable as water! She caught his point. With no inner purpose, she tried to fill the vacuum with physical love. She made a cult of it, but "It" used her; she never used "It."

Margaret left no intimate memories, and since her autobiographies recorded her leadership in birth control, she excluded that which would create irrelevant hostility. Nevertheless, Mrs. Dodge's report was consistent with Margaret's frankest writing on sex, which appeared in 1926 under the unimpeachable title, *Married Happiness*.

According to her thesis, happiness in marriage, as elsewhere, is an achievement won by conscious effort. The first requisite, a single standard of purity, is not enough, for ignorance is the great destroyer. Rightly understood, sex fulfillment is an art, requiring complete mastery over the instrument through which it is expressed.

Using an Ellis simile, Margaret likened the average man's approach to the orangutan trying to play a violin. As in a symphony, each part of the sex act should unfold its own delight, while leading without break into the next part. It is the husband's function to attune the mind as well as the body of his mate for the harmonic consummation. She must fall into the rhythm of the love flight, "a dance in which two humans are no longer separate and distinct persons, but in which their beings are commingled in a new and higher unity, a mutual rhythm and ecstasy."

The author saw sex as a sacred gift, as well as the most valuable human inheritance. Misuse or precocious use of it, which surprisingly, she said was before the age of twenty-three, wastes the forces needed for the individual's development. Eventually, sex should supply the radiant strength for all types of endeavor. "To deny its expression cuts one off from the zest and beauty of life."

In England on the eve of her divorce, Margaret saw no reason to cut herself off from the zest and beauty of life. In the postwar world, repression was the villain, but it was absent from Wantley. For a brief period Margaret welcomed many loves. Her admirers were outstanding men, all sympathetic to her cause. Transmuting their interest into enduring friendships, she never ended any with a bang or a whimper.

With Hugh de Selincourt the attachment produced such a prodigious correspondence that one wonders why Margaret, in the midst of important events, bothered. She once wrote that he was the man of her "adolescent dreams" and since they met rarely, for the most part he remained just that, a disembodied love. The tonic of his letters she declared was better than a health cure topped by a case of champagne. For one facing constant public attack, his large doses of undiluted adoration were important ego-lifters.

Over the years while her one-time lovers continued to aid her, she brightened their lives with her affection until one by one they died. Hers was the gift, which Ellis preached, of spiritualizing erotic relationships, but her success was unique. Even the happiness of Ellis, "the king" of the Wantley, then the Sand-Pit group, was a casualty to the multiple concept.

The bitter shadow over Ellis's last years is fully chronicled in *Friendship's Odyssey,* a book written after his death, but at his request by Françoise de Lisle. Françoise had come to him in 1918, distraught over an unhappy marriage and the burden of supporting two children. Always at his best with ladies in distress, Ellis had restored her confidence, as he had done for Margaret four years earlier. Suddenly the impulsive Françoise declared her love and, as she faithfully recorded, within a week they were "naked in each other's arms."

This swift-paced attachment was the culmination of his loves and, according to Françoise, the only consummated one. By sheer faith in his virility, she overcame his self-doubts and induced a miracle in this man of sixty. Love for them became a beautiful game that inspired his essay, *The Play Function in Sex*. He scarcely knew whether he was on research or pleasure bent. But if Olive Schreiner, his earliest love, had detected the satyr in him, Françoise, a third of a century later, felt that word conveyed too much age. Archly answering to the name of Naiad, she called him "the Faun."

Yet the blessings of Françoise eventually brought equal torments. When Ellis introduced her to Hugh, the two young people began to collaborate on a book about their "king." The theme was Woman's Debt to Havelock Ellis. Together they talked Ellis by the hour, sharing a mystic sense that they were extensions of their beloved sage. In this curious cult, they merged until one day Françoise awoke to find she had two lovers. Although a faithful type, she had been led astray by the Shelley-Ellis-Selincourt dreams of passionate friendships.

When her elderly lover learned the facts, she found his "volcanic" reaction out of place. After all, she had been drawn to Hugh only because he was Ellis's disciple. Besides, she never quarreled over the Faun's passionate friendships, and the number of lovely ladies seeking his counsel had increased with his fame. Perhaps it was his own record that made the blow so harsh. Naturally, he rejected the charge of jealousy, which he had always condemned, but he declared that Hugh had distorted his beliefs. People who preached plural attachments, such as Shelley and Selincourt, made a mess of their own lives as well as those with whom they consorted.

What he had always feared had taken place. The young woman, whom he cherished, had succumbed to a man twenty years his junior, "a sexual athlete," who in a few months had given Françoise more rapture than he had given her over several years. Ellis proposed to withdraw quietly, but that was the last thing that the lovers wished. For weeks, months, and even years all three analyzed and dissected their predicament. Furthermore, all members of this articulate triangle poured out their separate views to Margaret Sanger across the ocean.

To Françoise it became clear that Hugh had lit the flame of a gigantic fire that threatened to consume them all. To the king, it also seemed like *Götterdämmerung,* the twilight of the gods. Deep in his conscience smoldered the fact that, like the legendary king, his own philanderings had laid the basis for this almost incestuous love between the young couple who claimed to be his "children." His hard-won kingdom, built on amorous play and irrelevant philosophy, was crashing about him.

Françoise, although still madly in love with Hugh, finally renounced him. She hoped to salvage a Platonic friendship among the three, but in this she failed. When Hugh lost his king, he bitterly repudiated Françoise. Out of their years of agony, she thought that she had learned two profound truths: You cannot love by proxy, and sexual love is not cumulative when shared by several. Still ardent, in the prime of life, Françoise then settled down with her Faun, who had suddenly grown very old.

For Ellis, the ordeal had been excruciating. In the last test, spiritual love had transcended sex, but curiously, that drew him closer to the memory of his long dead wife. Again he heard her beautiful voice, vainly calling him from the nursing home, "Havelock! Havelock!" Now basking in the care of Françoise, he decided that Edith had been his one great love. In *My Life,* he hardly mentions Françoise, and referring to his wife's jealousy of "M," wrote, "Beautiful as my new friend was to me and continues to be to this day, I have sometimes been tempted to wish that I had not met her."

Yet Margaret transmuted even that passionate friendship into an enduring relationship. She was probably the best friend that Ellis ever had and continued to enhance his days with extraordinary gifts. She not only lavished upon him such conventional delicacies as wines, fruits, flowers, and a phonograph with fine records, which he could not afford, but she looked after his interests in the United States. She interviewed publishers for him, stimulated articles by and about him, and wrote some of the latter herself. For his eightieth birthday she rounded up cabled greetings

from celebrities, along with a princely gift of money. She helped
finance a house for his old age and most remarkable, for two years
paid Françoise a salary equal to her teacher's pay, so that she could
care for the king.

Of all the Sand-Pit circle, Margaret alone emerged serene, admired by all and untouched by the backlash of cumulative love.
In part, this was because she came infrequently, never living in
the emotional maze. More important, erotic love never controlled
her destiny. During his last years Hugh wrote brokenheartedly of
the havoc caused by his entanglement with Françoise. Not only had
he lost his king, but all that Havelock had taught him about love
and the Woman Spirit came "leering back" at him until he thought
he might go mad.

Margaret tried to lead him back to equanimity: "I am so happy
in a cause, Hugh. . . . All the world of human beings is a passing
show. They come and go . . . but the idea of human freedom
grows ever closer around one's heart and comforts and consoles and
delights."

The Ellis group was only one of the manifestations of the sexual
revolution that affected Margaret. Writing years later, Mrs. Dodge
had said that it was as though Margaret Sanger had been "arbitrarily chosen by the powers that be to voice a new gospel of not only
sex knowledge in regard to conception but about copulation and
its intrinsic importance." However, the phrase "new gospel," had
been taken from Dr. Marie Stopes and so had the stress on sex as a
"prophylactic part of right living," which Mrs. Dodge attributed
to Margaret.

For a period Margaret Sanger and Marie Stopes were potent
influences upon each other. Margaret had introduced the English-
woman to the subject of birth control and clinics, which started a
new phase in the latter's career. In turn, Dr. Stopes's sexual the-
ories obviously, if briefly, colored Margaret's ideas. More important,
her open letter to President Wilson, signed by famous British writers, was, as Margaret gratefully acknowledged, a major factor in
changing public opinion during the 1916 trial.

When they met at Margaret's Fabian lecture, Dr. Stopes had

just secured an annulment as "virgo intacto," to a short marriage. She had turned her ordeal, as well as weeks of study about sex, into a manuscript called *Married Love*. No English publisher would take it, but in New York Margaret found one who brought out an expurgated version. The cuts, however, determined the author to bring out a privately printed British edition.

Thanks to a new friend, Colonel Humphrey Verdon Roe, of the Royal Air Force, Dr. Stopes could now finance the book. She had persuaded him not only to put up the funds, but to break with his fiancée, so that he might marry his new author. For some time both decisions seemed supremely right. In their pristine and almost primeval delight, she called him "Tiger" and signed herself "Wood-nymph."

The book was always a fine investment, in fact, a runaway success, selling more than a million copies. Today this is hard to account for, except that it was the first popularly written book explaining the physiology of sex. According to Dr. Stopes, her unique contribution was material which today is dismissed as chimerical. Science was investigating the newly discovered sex glands and hormones when she announced that the sexual act enriched and vitalized the partners by the mutual exchange of "substances materially presented as chemical and ultrachemical molecules."

She talked of chemicals, instead of electricity, but like Selincourt, created her own hypothesis that exalted sex as a panacea for spiritual and physical well being. Scientifically, she was as irresponsible as a medieval schoolman and although she used her academic title to give her words authority, she was not a medical doctor.

In the twenties, Aylmer Maude, who had written a biography of Tolstoi, the ablest man he had known, decided to do the same for the ablest woman, his dear friend Dr. Stopes. He claimed that her achievements, which were substantial, derived from the fact that she was "attuned to the universe." This cosmic association inspired her *New Gospel to All Peoples,* directed in 1920 to the Anglican Bishops of Lambeth. The amazing message starts: "My Lords, I speak to you in the name of God. You are his priests. I am his prophet . . . I speak to you of the mysteries of the union of man and woman." At this point she explained about the interchange of molecules. "Without the balance of these subtle, internal secretions, neither child, nor unmated man or woman can be a whole individual."

A posthumous biographer, Keith Bryant, who had access to the tons of papers Dr. Stopes left to the British Museum, says that she suffered increasingly from megalomania, which Colonel Roe confirmed. Because of a war-time injury, he became deficient as a husband and apparently when the tiger in him left, her love went also. Nostalgically, he settled alone near the fiancée, whom he had once jilted.

Before Margaret's second visit to England, a rift had already divided the two somewhat parallel women leaders. A third and lesser one, Mary Ware Dennett, then president of the Voluntary Parenthood League had arranged the break. She had not only started an American cult of Dr. Stopes, bringing her to New York for a mass meeting, but had never ceased to circulate reports that Margaret was a sensational, ineffectual leader without background. Dr. Stopes now adopted these views and the former friendship turned into the one bitter rivalry of Margaret's life. However, at this period, probably no one in the same field could have maintained a friendship with Dr. Stopes.

Marie Stopes, who had risen swiftly from obscure poverty and loneliness to wealth, fame and a coterie of admirers, decided in her late fifties to start a third career. She had spent twenty years in science, twenty years in sex education and now would pursue poetry and drama. She meant to continue her world contributions for another sixty years, but to do so she must maintain her creative forces through the subtle secretions which she had described. As caretaker of genius, she needed those vitalizing molecules.

The author of *Married Love* and *Enduring Passion* kept neither love nor passion, for she separated from her second husband for the same reason as from her first. She who wrote *Radiant Motherhood* and *Wise Parentage* broke forever with her only child when he dared to marry. Somewhat indignantly, with only half her life schedule fulfilled, Dr. Stopes died in 1958 at the age of seventy-seven.

Marie Stopes was perhaps the most gifted and certainly the most repellent spokeswoman for the many-faceted sexual revolution. Her extravagant claims for physical love made a gargantuan joke out of her ill-balanced life. The omnipotent molecules which were supposed to spiritualize passion destroyed both her affection and common sense. By comparison, Margaret Sanger appears singularly level-headed and self-disciplined.

But what have these erotic excesses to do with birth control? Opponents claimed that they were the inevitable corollary. Margaret always answered that the use of contraceptives was not related to morality. Women inclined toward promiscuity would surrender to it whether or not they had protection against pregnancy. Modern permissiveness in rearing unchaperoned girls, along with the opportunities provided by parked cars, had created new temptations. Contraceptives merely prevented the tragedy of illegitimate and unwanted children.

Neither Margaret nor her friends were promiscuous since they chose their lovers carefully, believing, in the words of Havelock Ellis, that sometimes "the communion of bodies becomes the communion of souls." Margaret was so discreet that most of her associates did not know that she had other than conventional habits. Since she succeeded during her life in hiding her loves, the question therefore arises, why they should be exhumed in death. The first answer is that they have already been exposed. She talked freely to her intimates about her loves and in the early fifties she did so to her biographer, Lawrence Lader. He wrote about the Sand-Pit group in detail and, according to Françoise de Lisle, with many inaccuracies. Beyond that, Margaret left her uncensored correspondence to the libraries.

As the custodian of a great cause, Margaret tried to protect it during its critical years, but she never repudiated her own views. Her loves were bright strands in her life, wholly consistent with the ethos to which she subscribed. With a sense of her historic role, Margaret Sanger was content to let posterity make the final judgments.

Among the upper classes and opinion-makers of England, birth control was fast being accepted, but the Drysdales had invited Margaret to reach the workers, who remained curiously alienated. Unlike Dr. Stopes, who was an impressive orator but spoke only to large gatherings, Margaret addressed dozens of small cooperative guilds, to reach which she cheerfully rode the underground. Later she made a three-week speaking tour of Scotland.

Glasgow was her first booking, the Socialist city whose poverty had overwhelmed her seven years earlier. On the green, one Sunday noon, she celebrated Fourth of July with her own declaration of independence from excess children. Nearly two thousand shipyard workers in caps and baggy corduroys crowded around as she explained that labor itself produced the surplus workers who dragged down their living standards.

That evening she appeared at a Socialist-sponsored forum where women for the first time outnumbered men. The latter came to re-fight the historic battle between Marx and Malthus. Socialist dogma held that any reform dulling the edge of poverty retarded the main goal, the fall of capitalism. This doctrinaire view had kept the party from endorsing family limitation. To demolish the argument, Margaret asked, "Why do you fight for higher wages? If misery is your weapon, why ask for an eight-hour day instead of a twelve- or fourteen-hour one?"

She reminded her audience that the Socialist Party had always endorsed women's rights, but these rights were meaningless to those who still lacked freedom to protect themselves from unwanted pregnancies. When she was done, the men were strangely silent, but women who had never before spoken in public poured out their personal testimonials.

In the next weeks Margaret, the veteran trouper, made one-night stands in towns which boasted neither inns nor taxis. Once she shared the only bed in the house with her hostess and was remarkably comforted to learn that Sylvia Pankhurst had recently enjoyed the same accommodations.

Near Andrew Carnegie's birthplace in Dunfermline, she found child labor reminiscent of the early years of the Industrial Revolution. Most of the population had been brought in to do munitions work and had remained after the war, although conditions became worse than elsewhere. Children were apprenticed to the mills at eight or nine, and because schooling was thought unnecessary for girls, they worked ten to twelve hours a day right through adolescence, through their own marriages, and up to birth of the first child. These young mothers had a built-in tiredness which, according to the local doctor, they transmitted to their children. In the first grade the pupils, who were pitiful examples of reckless breeding, kept falling asleep at their desks.

Although Margaret's talks made friends for the Malthusians, she grew increasingly aware that for the very poor and ignorant, there should be cheaper, easier methods of contraception than were then available. Ellis had told her of a chemical product that he had read about in a German medical journal just before the outbreak of the war. Apparently it had met all standards, but after the war he could find nothing more about it. Margaret decided to go to Germany and track it down. It might be the technical breakthrough which would democratize birth control.

Eventually Margaret located the chemist family that was again quietly manufacturing its contraceptive jelly, this time in Friedrichshaven. She was disappointed to find the materials too costly for her purposes, but she brought home samples of the jelly and a suggestion for a new approach, a commercial, chemical one.

In her search, she had interviewed many doctors, at first courteous, but who turned on her as though she were the enemy when she mentioned birth control. All of them insisted that the Fatherland needed as many children as possible to make up for war losses. If a woman could not survive another pregnancy, she might be aborted. Since abortion was illegal, Margaret did not follow the logic until a gynecologist blurted out that Germany would never turn the future of the race over to its mothers; in the case of an abortion, doctors made the decision. As Napoleon had put it, children belonged to the state, as the fruit to the gardener.

In France, she found the counterpart to this view in one of the least publicized war casualties. Although the nation had been the first to stabilize its population, the government now demanded large families. The loss of its youth, plus fear of Germany, had reversed its policy. In the future not only were contraceptives banned, but bonuses were offered to the parents of many children.

At the end of her trip Margaret met the Drysdales in Holland for a tour of the clinics that she had studied five years earlier. Her English friends were now convinced that instruction in the poorer areas was the great hope for birth control. Since there were no legal barriers in Britain, they began to plan for a clinic staffed by doctors to be opened in London within the year. Before they fulfilled their plan, however, Dr. Stopes opened the first clinic, although hers was staffed by midwives.

Home once more, Margaret began to see the medical profession as an obstacle to progress, as it had become in Germany. Just before America's entrance into the war, the New York Medical Society had voted three to one against birth control and apparently it had not changed its views. The Crane decision of 1918 had explicitly stretched the right of physicians to prescribe contraceptives for health reasons, but no doctor had done so for the poor.

On Margaret's suggestion, Dr. Mary Halton had made a citywide test of twenty-nine hospitals. Two women, one with tuberculosis and the other with a kidney ailment, were refused help everywhere, although in each case another pregnancy might be fatal. As in Germany, the doctors hinted that if a woman were already pregnant, she might be aborted, but they could not compromise their standing by giving contraceptives to charity patients.

Well aware of the profession's hostility toward outsiders' meddling in health matters, Margaret nevertheless did not waver in her plan to start a doctor-staffed clinic. With this in mind, she addressed letters to many child specialists, outlining her project and asking for support. Never would she forget the lighthearted cynicism of the replies, most of them reminding her that since babies were their business, they did not want to limit the supply.

In sharp contrast, Dr. Emmett Holt, author of *The Care and Feeding of Children,* the Bible for young mothers, wrote that a reliable contraceptive would be a godsend. With his aid, a small medical committee was formed, headed by a woman doctor pledged to set up the clinic. Since Margaret wanted nothing more than to have doctors take the initiative, she now gratefully turned her attention elsewhere.

At this time the future was bright with promises and new support. One of these involved a trip to the Orient, another, equally exotic, a tycoon. The latter's incredulous response, on being introduced, was, "You can't be *the* Margaret Sanger!"

She was confronting a tall, white-haired man with the ruddy glow of an English country squire. Brusque he was often called, but when he smiled, she saw a "radiant personality." J. Noah Slee was the founder of the Three-in-One Oil Company and an arch-conservative. Margaret and he were at once vividly aware of each other, although when he asked to drive her home, she did not want him to see her shabby flat. However, there was no putting him off and with disarming frankness, he pronounced her neighborhood unsafe. He also reproved her for impairing the health of a national leader by living in deprivation.

In the next months he courted her in all conventional ways, but most persuasively by applying his expertise to her office. Along with bouquets, he gave her a date stamper, a mechanical letter opener, and a new filing system. She was entranced by these attentions and impressed by his competence and reliability, traits in which the men of her family had been in short supply. However, she continued to doubt that his big-business outlook could be compatible with hers. Besides, he was eighteen years her senior. Still, Margaret had always liked older men, and he was two years younger than Havelock Ellis. He was, as she once wrote, "in the full plenitude of his powers with the vigor of youth."

Born in South Africa, Noah Slee had made his fortune, as well as an unhappy marriage, in the United States. After a divorce, he had lived bleakly, confining his great energies to the promotion of his business, a few charities and his Episcopal church, the fashionable St. George's, where he served as Sunday school superintendent. He looked askance at social innovations, but after falling in love with the leader of the most controversial one, his sympathies expanded. Since he claimed that Margaret was the great adventure of his life, her cause became his cause and he supported all of her projects, often substantially, but always quietly.

In 1921, Margaret's chief project was the first National Birth Control Conference. Public opinion seemed ready at last to support a three-day educational program which she scheduled at the Plaza Hotel, shrewdly choosing the dates of the American Public Health Conference, so that delegates might attend some of her sessions.

On the eve of her meeting, she launched a new sponsoring group, the American Birth Control League, to take the place of the now defunct National League. Being a lone worker, she did this reluctantly and almost as casually as seven years before when she started the original league. This time it began under the aegis of the Rublee home and with able trustees to guide it through the first year while she would be in the Orient.

As she had planned, the conference opened in a dignified, rather than news-making, way. It looked as though the memorable feature would be the doctors' session at which a thousand crowded into a room designed for half the number. Margaret, who had once tried to learn from the profession, was now instructing physicians in the techniques and current methods of contraception. In view of their past indifference, it was ironic that some were disgruntled because she could neither guarantee adequate testing nor 100 per cent safety for any method. The session was an historic milestone, not only because it was unprecedented, but because it opened the eyes of so many to their new responsibilities.

The conference was to end with an evening rally at Town Hall, the most ambitious meeting that Margaret had ever planned and for which she had inveigled Harold Cox to come from England. This former member of Parliament and editor of the *Edinburgh*

Review, had startled the British Establishment by pointing out that neither the Anglican clergy nor most physicians practiced what they preached. Although denouncing contraception, they showed the lowest birth rates of all professional groups. To make the most of her prestigious speaker, Margaret invited leaders of all denominations, including Catholic Archbishop Patrick J. Hayes. Borrowing the theme of her opponents, she had billed the subject as "Birth Control: Is It Moral?"

Shortly before eight, Margaret, Cox and their dinner hostess, Juliet Rublee, drove to West Forty-third Street, rejoicing at the overflow crowd. Pushing their way up to the entrance, they were astonished when a policeman told them that the meeting was canceled.

Back rolled the years as Margaret saw again the locked door at Corning, the locked theater in St. Louis, and all of the locked doors that she had faced. But this was New York, and the speaker was a distinguished Englishman! It was incredible and humiliating. The officer had no further information except that no one, not even those who had rented the place, might enter. Margaret called police headquarters. Curiously, the officer in charge knew nothing of the meeting and had issued no orders.

As she considered what to do, Margaret noticed a few people emerging from the hall. Swiftly she wedged her way back to the door and when it opened with another trickle from those inside she ducked under the policeman's arm, into the partly filled hall and down the long aisle. Another officer stopped her at the stairs of the platform. Again frustrated, she was looking up at the seemingly unattainable stage, when she was lifted bodily and tossed up where she wanted to be. The tosser, a large man who had spoken earlier on her program, sprang up beside her. Thrusting into her arms a bouquet of American beauties that a messenger had been trying to deliver, he roared to the departing audience, "Here's Mrs. Sanger!" The crowd burst into tumultuous applause; those in the lobby stampeded back into the hall.

During the ensuing turmoil, Anne Kennedy, Margaret's aide, explained what had happened. As the hall was filling, several police arrived with Monsignor Dineen, secretary to the archbishop.

Finding Mrs. Kennedy in charge, he told her that the meeting was canceled on the archbishop's orders. The hall must be cleared at once and the doors barred. The police confirmed his authority and in her predicament, Mrs. Kennedy asked Monsignor Dineen to put his message in writing so that she might read it to the audience. He did so, she read it, but the crowd just sat there incredulous.

This outrage convinced Margaret that she must settle the matter with a court ruling, even at the cost of another arrest. Both the hall and stage were jammed as she moved forward to start the meeting. The uproar subsided, but she had not said a dozen words when two policemen grabbed her. Why shouldn't she speak, she asked. Had they a warrant? What were the charges? They did not try to answer, but in the next hour were as busy as fire fighters stamping out sporadic flames, as they squelched each person who tried to speak.

Down below was bedlam as the police tried to herd the stubborn crowd out of the hall. When they failed to clear the platform, Captain Donohue, the officer in charge, arrested Margaret and her most voluble supporter. They marched the two women off to the nearby station house, with some hundreds following as a noisy protective guard. The night court put the cases off until morning, letting the defendants return to their homes.

Outside, reporters were clamoring for the facts. They had meant to dismiss the matter as police bungling, until the *Times* man, checking on Mrs. Kennedy's story, called the "Power House." At St. Patrick's Cathedral, he reached Monsignor Dineen himself, who calmly accepted responsibility. Next morning the *Times* headline ran, "Suppression of Town Hall Meeting Under Direct Orders of Archbishop Hayes."

Never had there been such unanimity about a birth control incident. Perhaps because Mrs. Ogden Reid had been a shocked spectator, her family paper, the *Tribune,* carried an editorial on "Police Prussianism." Said the *Evening Post*: "Every liberty loving citizen of New York is hot with indignation." The *World* summed it up: "The issue Sunday night was bigger than the right to advocate birth control. It is part of the eternal fight for free speech, free assembly and democratic government. It is a principle which must always find defenders if democracy is to survive."

Captain Donohue did not bother to appear in court the next morning and so with no charges against them, the cases were dismissed. Margaret at once rescheduled the meeting for the next week and since Town Hall was booked long in advance, she took the Park Theater with twice the seating. Even so, there was an overflow of two thousand. The program proceeded as originally planned, but on the platform sat one impressive new sponsor, Karl Reiland, pastor of St. George's Episcopal Church, of which Noah Slee was an influential member.

The triumphant mass meeting by no means closed the matter. Archbishop Hayes issued extensive statements, ending with his Christmas Pastoral: "Children troop down from Heaven because God wills it. . . . Even though some little angels in the flesh through moral, mental or physical deformity of parents may appear to human eyes hideous, misshapen, a blot on civilized society, we must not lose sight of this Christian thought that under and within such visible malformation there lives an immortal soul to be saved and glorified for all eternity among the blessed in Heaven. . . . To take life after its inception is a horrible crime; but to prevent human life that the Creator is about to bring into being, is satanic."

Among the floods of protests were so many demands for an investigation that the Police Department finally volunteered to review the action. But their closed hearings investigated the sponsors of the meeting rather than the ban. Their guilt-by-association technique was a forerunner of the later McCarthy hearings. However, for their own good, the questioner should not have called two witnesses. J. Noah Slee was not only a pillar of orthodoxy, but a most effective champion for Mrs. Sanger. Juliet Rublee proved a worse mistake.

Mrs. Rublee's published answer to the archbishop's first statement had already brought an anonymous threat on her life; now she was given a prolonged questioning. Suddenly she was arrested for an alleged violation of the criminal code. In court, her case was at once dismissed, but the malice of the hearings backfired. Since she was the wife of an important lawyer, the elite of the bar closed ranks to defend her in an open letter to Mayor Hylan. What they demanded was in effect an investigation of the investigation. The signers included Henry Morgenthau, Sr., Charles C. Burlingham, and Herbert L. Satterlee, son-in-law of J. Pierpont Morgan.

The new hearings dragged on for months with no effectual action. Again the *World* summed up the melodrama: "The effort to muzzle the birth control propagandists is as stupid an attempt at obstruction as ever helped a minority movement. It is a puzzle to see how anyone can imagine that police abuses, star chamber sessions, inquisitorial investigations, false arrests, farcical persecutions, dummy complaints . . . will suppress the advocates. . . . The score today is all in favor of the birth control advocates, not because of the excellence of their case, but because of the sheer stupidity of the opposition."

The Gentlemen's Paradise

22

Alien backgrounds had not hampered an instant meeting of minds in the fall of 1920 when Margaret met the Baroness Shidzue Ishimoto. Although the baroness was the hothouse flower of Japanese culture, trained in calligraphy, correct posture, elaborate rituals, and obedience to her husband, she was in New York trying to convert her stylized perfection into utility. Beyond that, her aim was the same as Margaret's—to help the forgotten women of her country.

Her transformation started at the suggestion of her husband, a leader of the Kaizo or Young Reconstruction League, who thought that Japan's progress depended on rejection of medieval customs, including the role of high-caste ladies. Trained as an engineer, he had taken his bride to live in a squalid coal mining camp where he worked for nearly three years. After she had produced her second son, he told her to leave the children with his mother and follow him to New York, where he was then studying Western ways.

In New York, he enrolled her in a Y.W.C.A. business school and left her for a tour of Europe. He counseled her to "swim abreast the world's new tide," but she had never learned to swim; in fact she had not even learned to speak English. Nevertheless, with great dexterity she managed to survive. With her unpracticed English, but a bright mind and hard work, she mastered all of her studies with the highest marks. This success was so exhilarating that she developed a confidence and initiative usually suppressed in Japanese ladies.

In her autobiography, *Facing Two Ways,* Baroness Ishimoto says that her "God of Fortune" brought her in contact with Margaret Sanger, "one of the greatest women of the world." At once she wanted to emulate the American, although she feared that she lacked the courage. She underestimated herself, for she became a somewhat parallel figure for her country.

Margaret gave a tea for the Baroness, who, used to rigid protocol, was surprised when the hostess opened the door herself. She also marveled that so important a person was not built in "manly proportions." Instead, she saw "a delicate little figure with charm of a thoroughly feminine type—with bright shining eyes, thick shining hair which gave a touch of eternal youth to her appearance."

Margaret too, admired her guest, "tall for her race, equally beautiful by our standards, very smart in her American dress." The Baroness was compassionate about the women in the mining camps and she grasped the possibility of birth control, not only to relieve personal tragedy, but to raise the status of Japanese women. She wanted to establish a birth control league and asked Margaret about visiting her country. This possibility seemed remote, but the Baroness left with a supply of literature, much of which was translated and used in the Kaizo journal.

In the summer of 1921 Margaret received an extraordinary invitation. The Kaizo had scheduled lectures by three leaders of Western thought, Albert Einstein, Bertrand Russell, and H. G. Wells. Would Margaret Sanger be the fourth, the only American and the only woman? Aside from the honor, she would have a chance to introduce birth control to the country which in Western eyes represented the Yellow Peril with its exploding population and warrior tradition. At that time Margaret herself was predicting that Asia's teeming millions were the chief threat to world peace. So she gladly signed the contract, which required a late February departure.

Meanwhile, the first weeks of 1922 were fully booked with Midwestern lectures, a schedule which became frantic when the Town Hall hearings were prolonged. In the rush, Margaret postponed several decisions, but at last resolved to take Grant with her. This meant a new passport and with the time so short, she asked that it be sent to San Francisco, where she would also secure her visa. All went smoothly until she appeared at the Japanese consulate. There, with many apologies, she was told that she could not have a visa. Was this a personal ban, she asked, or a ban on her subject? "Both," was the reply.

Because she had no visa, the Japanese liner promptly canceled her reservation, and the story exploded in the press. Some journalists claimed that the exclusion of Margaret Sanger was an official retaliation for the United States Exclusion Act. In the midst of this hullabaloo, a Japanese, returning with his country's delegation from the Washington Naval Disarmament Conference, suggested that Margaret take out a Chinese visa. The ship's last stop was Shanghai, but he thought that her presence on the passage over would create enough support for her to gain clearance for Japan. Taking this chance, she and Grant sailed as originally planned.

Noah Slee sailed also. According to most evidence, his future was one of the decisions that Margaret had postponed. For the last two years, bouquet in hand, he had usually seen her off on trips and often had materialized en route. What his exact status was at this time is not certain. Even the family is in disagreement. Grant Sanger, who was on the spot, believes that they had been married in Paris the previous year. Noah's obituary said that they had been married in 1920. Most of the evidence contradicts this. On the Japanese trip they carried separate passports, which are today in the Library of Congress, and although his was for Mr. and Mrs. Noah Slee, the picture of his wife was not of Margaret.

During the trip there was no public mention of Noah's presence. It seems likely that Margaret took Grant with her to act as a disarming chaperon, in case her elderly admirer might come along. To the latter, a slow boat to China must have seemed the ideal spot to press his suit. He had even made preparations. Learning that Margaret loved to dance, the devout churchman, who had never even waltzed, signed up for ten lessons at Arthur Murray's Studio.

More than 150 Japanese were returning from the Washington conference, among them the two official delegates, Admiral Kato, later prime minister, and Masanoa Hanihara, vice minister of foreign affairs and future ambassador to the United States. Shortly after sailing, they made Margaret's acquaintance and during the next weeks often questioned her about birth control.

The scheduled stop in Honolulu allowed Margaret to speak to a large meeting, where she inspired the organization of a birth control league, as well as boosting her stock throughout the Orient. Two Japanese journalists scooped all others with their reports; immediately the conference delegation asked her to address them in the ship's dining room. Then on their own initiative, the official delegates cabled Tokyo in her behalf.

As in the United States, the attempt to suppress Margaret's message had increased public interest, and protests were deluging the Japanese government. Editors regretted her exclusion, while the foreign press condemned it. For a fortnight the official position fluctuated. First it suggested that Margaret Sanger might land but make no talks. The protests mounted. All right! She might talk, but not in public. No one was satisfied. The final rumor was that she might talk, but not on birth control. Meanwhile, radio invitations poured in for her to address medical, cultural, business, and labor groups.

On shipboard Margaret was besieged with interviews and questions. Noah did not resent this, for he wanted her success, but he must have rejoiced at his precautions. In the evenings when the orchestra struck up dance music for the Occidentals, he monopolized her. Together they fox-trotted, holding the Orient at bay.

On reaching Japan, Margaret was lengthily questioned by officials who finally said that she might land on two conditions: (1) She must not lecture publicly on birth control. (2) The American consul must make a formal request for her. Although she had already asked the consul's help, she sent him a second message, which, like the first, was ignored. After many hours of delay, she was at last grudgingly admitted.

Next morning the *Japan Times* reported:

Mrs. Sanger was allowed to land in this country after a series of negotiations that made the diplomacy of the Washington Conference look like child's play. . . . An army of star writers from Tokyo—the authorities said that they had issued seventy passes to these men alone—a dozen regular waterfront reporters and a few foreign correspondents swarmed up the gangway of the ship. . . . The eager newsmen scurried about in search of a notable story. Was it Admiral Baron Kato they sought? It was not. . . . A dozen disgruntled shorthand men dropped out of the herd to take notes on the Envoy's address in the dining room, but the others flocked onward until they found the modest quarters wherein abode a modest little American woman and her handsome young son. Mrs. Sanger and the cause of birth control were what the press of Japan was interested in. . . . The Peace Conference was an old story.

Shidzue Ishimoto was waiting to welcome and drive the Sangers to her home in Tokyo; Noah lingered discreetly in Yokohama for business talks. The Kaizo group had been both angry and humiliated at the treatment of their guest, but they had come to realize that if the government had deliberately tried to focus interest on birth control, it could not have done so more effectively. The dramatic entry had made Margaret Sanger big news.

To clarify the situation and if possible remove the last restrictions, Margaret called on the chief of police, who had made the original decision. He met her with a courtesy, a cup of tea, and a flash of humor. In their language, he explained, her name sounded like "Sangai San" or "destructive to production." At this time there was before the Japanese Diet a bill called Dangerous Thought, which would exclude from the country all ideas not conforming with tradition. Since birth control came under this category, he could not let her lecture publicly. Later she learned that it was also rumored that she was a secret agent commissioned to deplete the Japanese population before an American invasion.

Margaret had to scrap her prepared lectures and improvise new ones on war and population, using European examples. The contract called for eight to ten lectures of five hours each, although she had reassured herself that the latter was an error. It was not. She found that standing five long hours was in itself an endurance test. Translation took half of the time, and the freewheeling questions might have gone on forever had it not been for the five-hour clause, which she now considered a protection. Otherwise, the lectures were a pleasure, for Margaret had never known more intelligent and appreciative audiences. She talked to the exclusive Peers' Club, the Tokyo Medical Association, the Chamber of Commerce, the large Y.M.C.A., and, in all, made thirteen major addresses.

What puzzled her at first was that she spoke chiefly to men. In some places, where the Baroness, who always accompanied her, was the only other woman, she felt cut off from her own sex. And yet people always asked her about the American woman. Was it true that she was all things to her husband: companion, mother to his children, mistress, business manager, and friend? This, Margaret tried to explain, was the ideal, however imperfectly fulfilled. Slowly she realized that it was not the ideal in Japan.

Living in a Japanese home, Margaret gained insights on the family structure and the role of women. Trying to "face two ways," her hostess was putting her new skills to work. With a triple purpose, she had opened the Minerva Yarn Shop, which helped to finance a leper colony, taught women to make useful articles, and gave a precedent for ladies to work outside the home. Mostly her friends looked askance at a peeress in this revolutionary role. Tactfully, Shidzue conformed in matters which did not interfere with her major purposes.

Japanese girls were brought up to believe that a husband always came first, a wife second because man was superior. A husband represented Heaven and one who disobeyed Heaven incurred a righteous punishment. Girls were taught to smile, listen, and say little. When they spoke, it should be in a soft, fluttering voice. Sacrifice and endurance were their lot and it was a matter of honor that even in childbirth they should suppress all sounds. The feudal code required that a wife should rise early, retire late, and never pamper herself with naps or excess tea or sake. At dawn, after her own bridal night, Shidzue had risen at five to serve her mother-in-law.

Although marriage was predetermined for girls, all laws and customs favored the husband. A wife had no property rights since even her dowry was turned over to her in-laws. Concubines were common, and a man might rid himself of his wife by stating that she did not "meet the needs of his family." Like a broken mirror, a divorced woman had no value.

Margaret came to believe that in Japan the upper-caste lady was an exquisite work of art created by the imagination of generations of gentlemen. The confection had no personal will and in her pitiful need of security, merely reflected the stereotype men had prescribed. Shidzue, with her own mind awakened abroad, was more blunt. Her countrywomen, she wrote, were either "toys, petted by men or slaves driven by their masters."

Grant's presence constantly highlighted the fact that Japan was a man's country. Wherever they went, hotels, restaurants, or private homes, the servants hovered about him, trying to anticipate his wishes, while his famous mother trailed unnoticed behind.

But the chief evidence of its being a man's country was the number of girls dedicated, without choice, to male pleasure. In extolling the perfection of the geisha girls, Count Keyserling, in his popular *Travel Diary of a Philosopher,* described an atmosphere of harmless cheer, like that of children around a Christmas tree. Shidzue saw it differently. These children, whose training started very young, were often whipped into their seemingly artless charms. The top ones earned more than any Japanese professional woman, but their managers and clothes took most of their pay. Nor was it reasonable to suppose that young girls, virtually imprisoned in the pleasure enclaves, and often serving fat old men several times an evening, felt the spontaneous joy of children around a Christmas tree. Some geishas only sang, danced, and flirted; others were licensed prostitutes.

In her *Autobiography* Margaret says that some missionaries escorted her through the Yoshiwara red light district, starting with the unlicensed quarter where the muddy, unpaved alleys were lined with huts. Dark eyes peered through slits in the screen walls, while outside, as at a restaurant, prices were listed for each girl per hour and per night. When a man entered a house, the light below went off and another went on upstairs. Thousands of lights behind paper windows flickered on and off like fireflies while crowds of workmen seemed like swarming insects, driven by sex needs.

The licensed quarter was the most modern and attractive part of the city. Trees, festooned with gay lanterns, lined boulevards where luxury hotels presented lobbies gay as Broadway theaters, with photographs of pretty girls. In some empty frames was the notice, "Just arrived. No time for pictures." These were the new ones, fresh from the country, very young and most desired. They might have eight or nine visitors an evening.

Everyone, from the police chief to high-caste ladies, had told Margaret that the trouble with birth control was the effect on public morals. In the Yoshiwara she wondered what they meant. Physical pleasure in Japan was relieved of all responsibility just as the men wanted.

"Since the time of Commodore Perry," wrote Shidzue Ishimoto, "no American has created a greater sensation in the land of the Mikado than Margaret Sanger." The author was quite serious. When Perry aroused Japan from its timeless isolation, he catapulted a feudal, slow-paced society, devoted to cherry blossoms and tea ceremonies, into the twentieth century. Huge smokestacks were soon belching soot into clear skies, factory whistles shattered the peace and even the benign gifts of the West, such as modern sanitation and a more humane outlook, had increased the nation's foremost problem.

In 1853 when Perry first called, the empire counted some 26 million people, but in the next seventy years the once stable population had more than doubled. True to the laws of Malthus, the figures increased in terrifying geometric ratio. By the early twenties a country smaller than California had half as many people as the whole United States. Furthermore, since only a sixth of the area could be cultivated, the lowlands reached a density of 2,000 persons a square mile, four times higher than that of the other industrial island, Great Britain.

Every inch of soil was used, with hillsides laboriously terraced for rice paddies. There was no space for lawns, parks, or playgrounds and, to the terror of motorists, youngsters played all day in the streets. Children were everywhere. Fathers carried babies in their arms, mothers and the older boys and girls had them strapped to their backs. Sometimes small children carried smaller ones. It was a land of one-story houses, Margaret observed, but two-story children. Even in baseball, boys played with infants on their backs.

Small farmers could scarcely feed their own families, and the once self-sufficient nation was importing vast amounts of food. This had to be paid for by manufactured exports, produced in large part by cheap female labor. At least parents might profit from their daughters by contracting them out for several years at a time. Margaret visited some of the cotton mills, including the largest which compared favorably in most ways with Western ones. However, during the First World War, protective legislation had been suspended and these mills still required twelve hour shifts. In a silk factory she saw seven hundred girls from ten years up twirling the threads from cocoons and catching them on spindles. Stunted little creatures, they worked from dawn to dusk in a building without any ventilation so that the air would remain suitably hot and moist for the silk. It was no idle threat when parents talked of selling their daughters to the mills.

Conditions in the mines, Shidzue said, were worse. Babies were born without love and brought up without care. Half-naked men, women, and children worked together underground, competing with the forced labor prisoners. Throughout the country man was waging a bitter race to keep his productive forces equal to his reproductive ones.

Thoughtful Japanese knew that there were only three alternatives. They could let living standards drop still further, although for millions this would be disastrous. They could ship the excess people elsewhere, although this would be hard without colonies and with the United States and Australia barring them by exclusion acts. Nevertheless, for the military, territorial expansion was the only honorable solution. Finally, they could adopt a program to curtail the birth rate.

If Perry's coming had triggered the events causing the population explosion, Shidzue believed that Margaret Sanger might launch the peaceful solution. When Shidzue wrote her book a dozen years later, the visit still seemed like the passage of a brilliant comet, leaving a luminous trail of incalculable value. No woman, foreign or native, had ever been so well received. Margaret's modest manner had disarmed her listeners as she presented facts never before discussed in Japan.

Besides her thirteen lectures, Margaret gave an almost incredible number of interviews (estimated as five hundred), most of them attended by more than one reporter. In addition to her enormous daily press coverage, 81 of the 101 monthly magazines carried featured articles on birth control.

The Kaizo set up a permanent birth control committee, with its first project the publication of a Japanese edition of *Family Limitation*. Margaret also stimulated a committee among the graduates of the Imperial University Medical College. This group sent a member to Europe to investigate contraceptive practices. In the next years the general movement, under the steady guidance of Shidzue, continued to grow.

The Japanese interlude was delightful for Grant, now a tall young male, always the center of attention. Before he landed, he was expert with chopsticks and soon outdid his hosts in courtesies; in fact, he always bowed three times before answering his mother. The latter also found her reception wonderful, but so exhausting that she briefly succumbed to pneumonia. Finally, the two Sangers, accompanied by Noah Slee, sailed off together in April through the beautiful Sea of Japan. Margaret had to be in London by July, but in the intervening weeks she would often tell her story, and all three were to visit other parts of the Orient, starting with Korea.

Margaret wrote extensively about this trip in her *Autobiography,* a vivid record of what she saw and felt. The origin of the American Indian was still disputed, but the travelers were struck by the familiar look of the coolies. Their reddish skin, ragged black hair, the long pipes that they smoked, and the way they carried burdens on their backs should have fortified the theory of the Bering Straits crossing to Alaska.

At Seoul, Margaret spoke to an audience of missionaries, doctors, bankers, and businessmen to whom her cause came as a "sparkling new theory," unmarred by any prejudice. Korea reinforced her chief impression of Asia—the cheapness of life. In a silk factory, little girls, "almost like babies," crouched over large pots to lift the cocoons out of boiling water. The Japanese superintendent explained that an adult's fingers were not sufficiently sensitive, but he denied that the children's tender fingers could be hurt.

In China, all of their senses were assailed by the dust, the mingling odors of garlic, opium, incense, and sewage, the constant beat of drums and chanting from Buddhist temples, and the groans and pleas of beggars. Not until they saw China's beggars did they know how filthy human beings could be. But their hearts went out to the rickshaw boys. In Japan, they had disliked man-powered transportation, although the runners had been sturdy. Here they were half-starved, half-naked youngsters with varicose veins and other ailments. When one of their regular boys returned after a few days absence, Margaret recognized his unhealed smallpox scabs and sent him home. Against this background, however, she could not concentrate on the beauties of the Temple of Heaven and the Ming tombs. The oldest civilization was indifferent to its children.

Margaret contrasted Marco Polo's description of fifteenth-century Cathay, "a pleasant haven of silks, spices and fine manners." Yet China had always been unique among the great nations in putting a permanent mark of subjection on its privileged ladies. As she watched three women holding each other up as they tottered along together, she surmised that a bound foot kept a wife from running away. The binding, she learned, began when the child was three, and the torture continued for two years. Sometimes the bones were broken and the mother slept with a switch beside her to beat the little girl when her cries disturbed the family. In the big cities, happily, the custom was dying out.

In Shanghai, once more escorted by a missionary and no doubt with Noah, whom she never mentions on the tour, Margaret visited another red-light district. In open doorways stood the vividly dressed entertainers, like colorful posters against a drab background. Margaret talked to some of the singsong girls, of whom Shanghai boasted a hundred thousand. Sold as infants and brought up in the trade, many belonged completely to their buyers. Some were only ten years old. If they tried to run away, they might have a leg broken. Occasionally they were rented out for a month or so to foreigners. Margaret's gloom deepened as she watched American sailors bargaining for the bodies of these children.

On the whole, she did not like the American image in China. She saw her countrymen living in the pampered international settlements with more luxuries than they ever had at home and yet boasting of how little they paid their servants. In the United States they might have been humane citizens; here they were oblivious to native hardships. The infinite misery of China eroded one's conscience.

The missionaries of course were exceptions, but some of their efforts seemed misguided. Because of the slim margin of subsistence, even success in cutting infanticide raised new problems. When parents spared an infant girl, they often sold another to a brothel; and, indeed, the recent increase in singsong girls exactly paralleled the decrease in infanticide.

Americans gave generously to Chinese flood and famine relief, but these calamities were nature's way of bringing the population into balance with the food supply. Only a widespread birth control program would correct the basic problem. Indeed, China was the terrible example of the struggle that Malthus had described. Surrounded by bestial conditions, this ancient cradle of wisdom and the arts was spawning its worst elements. In her *Autobiography,* Margaret describes a scene of ultimate degradation.

"Once while a missionary was guiding me though the Chinese City [Shanghai], we noted a crowd, children included, gathered in curiosity about a leper woman. She was on the ground, sighing and breathing heavily. Nobody offered to help her. 'Maybe she's dying,' said my companion. Just then the woman gave a fearful groan and took a baby from under her rags. She knew what to do, manipulated her thighs and abdomen, got the afterbirth, bit the cord with her teeth, put the baby aside, turned over and rested. No trace of emotion showed on the faces of the watchers."

If this had been all she saw, it would have been unbearable, but Margaret also experienced the best of China. Dr. Hu Shih, still young, but home from Cornell and Harvard and already recognized as an intellectual leader, as well as a delightful human being, arranged her happiest hours. These included a banquet given in her honor by the chancellor of Peking University and a lecture to two thousand students. This talk created such excitement that within twenty-four hours *Family Limitation* had been translated into Chinese: five thousand printed copies were distributed. A year later she was still hearing aftereffects of the meeting.

From Hong Kong the travelers started their long journey through the South China Sea, the Indian Ocean, and up the Red Sea. By the time they reached Shepheard's Hotel in Cairo, Grant had come down with a bad case of dysentery and fever. For three nights a Western-trained doctor stayed with him, but could not reduce the temperature.

Meanwhile, a fortune teller announced an imminent death at Shepheard's. This inspired a group of natives to keep vigil on their prayer rugs outside of Grant's door. His mother, always susceptible to portents and in this case feeling guilty for having brought Grant with her over the protests of his headmaster, was terribly shaken. Watching her son grow weaker, as she had once watched Peggy, she thought that she was losing another child.

On the fourth morning, when the doctor left for his office, the thermometer was still at 104. Then Margaret took over. She called for a dishpan of ice and bathed her son in frosty water. At once the temperature dropped. In two hours the fever was gone and Grant was sleeping peacefully.

Grant's improvement was steady, but the time came for his mother to be in London, which was not a good place to convalesce. Noah then performed his finest service, taking the boy to Switzerland and a rapid recovery.

Grant, however, was through with sightseeing. He had been a cheerful, interested young traveler, but he had seen more than he could assimilate. As he later said, he felt as though he had been dragged around the world at the tail of a typhoon. Now all he wanted was to be home with his contemporaries. Understanding, his mother shipped him back to friends at a boys' camp in the Poconos. Nevertheless, neither regretted the trip. Grant managed to keep abreast of his class, with a mind enriched by world travel.

Era of Achievement

24

Before Margaret went to her first international congress, the venerable sponsoring group, in tribute to her, added three words to an already ponderous name. It was the Fifth International Neo-Malthusian *and Birth Control* Conference that met in London during July 1922.

Back from the Orient, Margaret Sanger was billed as "the greatest pioneer of the modern movement," at a rally presided over by H. G. Wells. Exotic proof of her influence was the presence of the "Japanese Margaret Sanger," Shiduze Ishimoto, who had journeyed all the way from Tokyo to participate. There were delegates from most European nations, including former enemy ones, but for the first time the largest foreign group came from the United States.

John Maynard Keynes, the newly famous author, struck the keynote when he declared that population was not only an economist's problem, but would soon be recognized as the "greatest of all political questions." This was censored news in countries which were demanding large families. Mussolini had sharpened the issue by claiming that Italy had three alternatives: It could "addict itself to voluntary sterility," but his people were too intelligent for that; it could try to find outlets for its surplus millions; or it could forcibly seize such outlets.

As the first requisite to international peace, the conference urged the League of Nations to advise its members to limit their populations according to their resources, since excess numbers did not justify aggression. Although the league did not act on the Malthusian advice, Margaret was so impressed by the informative world-wide news coverage that she longed to repeat it back home. Since the American delegation, including Juliet Rublee, was enthusiastic, she invited the other delegations to the United States for a sixth international meeting in 1925.

During this exhilarating week, Margaret's thoughts must often have strayed to a personal problem. She had once told Juliet that she was not inclined toward matrimony. "Where is the man," she asked, "to give me what the movement does—joy, interest, freedom?" But, as she also repeatedly wrote, she was often desolate in her cold little flat. Occasionally she thought she would go mad, not only stripped of comforts and pleasures that she knew so well how to enjoy, but existing only for her cause.

Presumably she remarried a few weeks after the conference, although she did not publicize the fact until the press discovered it in February 1924. She then announced that she had been Mrs. Noah Slee for eighteen months or since September 1922. September eighteenth was, indeed, the anniversary that the couple celebrated and the 1930 edition of *Who's Who*—the only one with any of her dates—gives 1922 as the year. True, this edition puts her first marriage in 1900, although Bill Sanger's letter in the Library of Congress establishes 1902 as the correct year. That Margaret was quite unreliable about dates is corroborated by Dorothy Brush, her frequent traveling companion. Once when a customs official pointed out that her answer to a routine question about age did not agree with her passport, she airily dismissed the matter. She thought that everyone made up such dates!

In 1922, according to her lighthearted story to relatives, she had to marry Noah because he had followed her around the world. Had she married earlier, as some believed, she could have ended any ambiguity by saying so. She had received her quiet Massachusetts divorce in 1920, and yet her two autobiographical accounts, both devoid of dates, do not mention Noah until after the tour. *The Margaret Sanger Story,* based on "hundreds of hours of interviews with Mrs. Sanger," implies that the wedding service, "before an English Justice of the Peace," took place in the fall of 1922. The author further embellishes the account by adding that the bridegroom had agreed in advance to her continued independence in both personal and professional life.

There was no apparent reason for secrecy, and Margaret denied to the press that there had been any. The Slees had informed their friends about the step and did not believe that their personal lives were of public interest. Nevertheless, in *My Fight for Birth Control,* Margaret notes that she was "amused" to have achieved an unpublicized divorce and remarriage. The truth seems to be that since her field of work made her vulnerable to attack, she went to great lengths to suppress controversial items in her private life. Besides, her *Autobiography* admits to "apprehension" about this union, and letters in the Library of Congress show that during 1922 she consulted both Hugh de Selincourt and Havelock Ellis. The latter replied dubiously that "however nice, kind and generous" Slee was, if he was a "committed reactionary," disapproving and disliking everything Margaret really was, the marriage would not work. On the other hand, if Slee was "a sort of repentant millionaire," who deep inside felt that she was doing what he wanted, the union might turn out very well.

Unlike most of her friends, Noah Slee was neither liberal nor intellectual. In *My Fight,* Margaret says that when her heart "was awakening to love again," she was troubled and perplexed. In the end she came to believe that he was "a spiritual radical and revolutionist in common sense." The last trait had been so lacking in the first two men in her life, Michael Higgins and Bill Sanger, that she doubly appreciated Noah's practical competence. In part, as she recognized, they were drawn together because they both cherished a somewhat naive regard for success, which both had attained through uncommon stamina and courage.

The good executive, Noah Slee, was softened by much kindliness, some humor, and "the heart of a child." In spite of incompatibility with his own grown sons, his care of Grant during convalescence suggested a good relationship with her sons, whose education he proposed to finance. Margaret would not discuss money and curtly declined his suggestion of an English-style premarital settlement. As she said in *My Fight,* she had grown proud of her own earning capacity from royalties and from lectures at $150 each, and had no intention of managing any but her own income. Nevertheless, ever mindful of her cause, she did not underestimate what money could do for birth control. Explicitly, she wrote, "I knew that the cooperation of a man whose experience had been gained in building up for thirty years a well known business, with such backing and interest as he could give, would help enormously in extending the work and expanding it along the lines I had mapped out on an international scale."

From the first, she had warned that her work would interfere with a conventional marriage. Noah would tire of kissing her good-by at depots and waving farewell as gangplanks lifted. He shrugged this off, reminding her that he too had commitments. They would go their own ways, but always reinforce each other.

Because the marriage was not announced, the Slees continued to have separate apartments, although she moved at once to Noah's modern building at 39 Fifth Avenue. The individual apartments helped to maintain her independence and followed the Havelock Ellis pattern of semi-detached living that she had approved. Nevertheless, once the marriage was publicized, they established their real home in the country.

On their return to New York, Margaret faced a major disappointment. The promised doctors' clinic had not materialized. Frightened by the furor of the Town Hall raid and with no help from her medical colleagues, the physician in charge had simply given up. If anything was to be done, Margaret again must resume full responsibility.

Since working for the clinic might ruin a doctor's future, no gynecologist was found available. However, Dr. Dorothy Bocker, then employed by the Georgia Public Health Service, had the necessary New York license. She was enthusiastic, willing to learn, and with a two-year contract, ready to accept a salary of only $5,000.

At first even this sum threatened to stymie the plan. Former donors refused to give anything for a project that might put Margaret back in jail. Never, she wrote, had she so desperately wanted money, although it seems strange that Noah did not provide it. He would soon give far larger sums for projects about which she cared less. Perhaps she wanted to prove that she could do it on her own.

Three years earlier Clinton Chance, a wealthy Malthusian, had told Margaret that if she ever started a clinic, he might help. It was to him that she now turned. His cabled answer assured Dr. Bocker's two-year salary and therefore the English financing of the first enduring birth control clinic in the United States.

Both thrift and caution suggested a quiet start. In the first years Margaret simply referred the many women who still called at her office to Dr. Bocker, installed in two rooms in the same building. Except for word of mouth, there was no promotion for the work behind the door obscurely labeled Clinical Research Bureau. Technically, it was not yet a clinic, but from the first there was research based on the growing case records.

In its second year the bureau's existence was anounced at a public lunch, where the response seemed to justify expansion. Margaret knew that a medical advisory committee would be her best aid, but she soon found that in professional eyes, Dr. Bocker's lack of experience was a great handicap. She also learned that Dr. Hannah Stone of Lying-In Hospital might donate her services. Margaret did not hesitate. It was one of her swift, ruthless, and farseeing decisions, and it accounted for one of Margaret's few abrasive breaks with a staff member.

If the whole of the profession had been available, there would have been no better choice than Dr. Stone. She not only impressed physicians, but had rapport with her patients. When Lying-In Hospital made her choose between her associations, she stayed with the nonpaying, controversial clinic. "It needs some of us who care," she explained. She made the clinic her life's work and the most powerful argument for the eventual reversal of the professional attitude toward birth control.

This professional outlook remained as lethargic, if not as hostile, as before the Crane decision. The less a doctor knew, the more violently he reacted against contraception. Margaret used to say that she longed to send a missionary out to preach to the benighted medical societies. In the mid-twenties, that is precisely what she did. Dr. James F. Cooper, as a gynecologist and former medical missionary in China, had swiftly been converted to birth control. His wealth of experience as well as his platform presence inspired Margaret to engage him, at $10,000 a year, to preach to his profession throughout the nation.

And where did she find the money? As usual, she first approached the board of the American Birth Control League—"charming women," she described them, "whose instinctive reaction to new ideas was always negative." They were appalled at her irresponsibility. Certainly no cautious trustee would approve such a sum for a project with no direct returns. Luckily, as she related in *My Fight for Birth Control,* "a noble friend," who had sufficient faith in her, pledged the money. Who was this noble friend of great faith? Her husband, we discover in the later written *Autobiography.* In a note preserved in the Library of Congress, she frankly wheedled him. The tide was turning in her favor, and if Dr. Cooper succeeded in putting over her program, she would "please J. Noah H. Slee and retire with him to the Garden of Paradise."

She was premature about the tide, but she never regretted Dr. Cooper. In two years, visiting all of the states, he made more than seven hundred speeches, mostly to physicians. Always in demand and with access to groups which would have barred most speakers, he brought the first accurate understanding of birth control to thousands of doctors who had been abysmally misinformed. With charts and exhibits, he taught the techniques of contraception.

A by-product of his lectures proved a real breakthrough; some twenty thousand physicians agreed to instruct patients referred to them. Margaret was still receiving a gargantuan volume of mail, more than a million inquiries in five years and at last she could refer the writers to doctors in most areas.

Now began a race to secure safe and adequate supplies to meet the growing demand. Jointly Dr. Cooper and Dr. Stone created a chemical contraceptive with a lactic acid and glycerine base, far cheaper than the German one that Margaret had brought home. Used with a diaphragm pessary, it was highly effective. But since pessaries were not made in the United States and were barred from the mails and common carriers, they were hard to come by.

Margaret never told how she secured the supply used at the clinic or by Dr. Cooper. Titillating rumors of socialites returning from abroad with a few dozen contrabands in their pockets or strapped around their waists explained an occasional windfall, but not the steady provisioning of 500 to 1,000 a week.

In the days of Al Capone, there was no more picaresque and certainly not as altruistic a case of bootlegging as that carried on by a staunch pillar of St. George's Episcopal Church. I found the key to the mystery in an uncatalogued memorandum in container 110, among the 272 containers in the Margaret Sanger Collection of the Manuscript Division of the Library of Congress. On November 25, 1925, Noah Slee dictated a statement saying that his Canadian factory had received a large shipment of German diaphragms, which were repacked in three-in-one cartons and sent to his factory at Rahway, New Jersey. This subterfuge made possible the effective growth of the clinic, as well as Dr. Cooper's crusade.

Smuggling was only the exotic part of Noah's aid. With his business acumen, he found the proper way to package the lactic acid paste and then turned his attention to the domestic production of pessaries. No American rubber company would touch the project, but two of Margaret's supporters, an engineer and a public relations man, formed the Holland-Rantos Company to reproduce the Mensigna cap for sale on prescription of physicians. Noah loaned $15,000, but would take no stock in the company.

Both Slees were sure that Holland-Rantos would make money, as it did, but lest their motives in promoting birth control be misunderstood, they did not enter any profit-making concern. Margaret reluctantly declined several radio offers which would have made a fortune, but the policy proved wise when John Sumner, Comstock's successor as head of the Society for the Suppression of Vice, once asked her how much she made on her birth control "racket" she silenced him with her files of letters refusing to sponsor any kind of article.

After the Holland-Rantos Company proved the market potential, a German company brought over a group of skilled workmen who became the world's largest producers of contraceptives. During the depression, the manufacture of such articles was not only big business, but one of the fastest growing ones.

With a physician in charge of the clinic and another out lecturing, Margaret began to concentrate on the project in which she had involved the League while she was in London. To a group of wealthy supporters she broke the exciting news of the upcoming Sixth International Conference. Her audience stared back incredulously. The *Review,* they reminded her, was again in the red and she wanted $25,000 for an international congress! Together this group of ladies might painlessly have underwritten the whole amount, but it was impossible to convey to them the value of such an event to the American movement.

Margaret decided to raise the money herself from the subscribers of the *Review.* This was the hard way, with few large gifts, but with small donations from all over the country. As the date of the Congress approached, she converted the trickle of funds into one-way passages from Europe to fetch speakers and needed delegates. She only hoped that later she would be able to send her distinguished visitors home.

It was another history-making meeting. Some eight hundred delegates came from eighteen nations as well as twenty-four colleges and universities. From the press angle, it was superlative. With no sensational incident, it yielded eight hundred articles, of which two hundred were editorials, all informative and mostly favorable. This coverage accelerated donations until the debts were paid and was banked with a surplus.

The endearing session was the Pioneers' Dinner, presided over by columnist Heywood Broun and with double stars, C. V. Drysdale, representing two generations of his family, and Dr. Aletta Jacobs of Amsterdam. Ten years earlier she had refused to meet Margaret in Holland, but now the old lady crossed the ocean to explain her mistake, receive the plaudits of the congress, and confess that the New York Clinical Research Bureau was the only place where her standards had been fully realized.

The most important session was for physicians, so unexpectedly crowded that an overflow group had to be accommodated in a second nearby hotel. The subject was unprecedented. For decades the Malthusians had been debating social doctrines, oblivious of the fact that contraceptives had never been evaluated. They were naively unaware that many of their prescribed methods were not reliable and that none could be used in every case. Dr. Cooper updated their information.

Dr. Stone's report of the clinic's first eleven hundred cases was the sensation. She knew who came to the clinic and why. All groups in the community used it, 38 per cent being Protestant, 32 per cent Jewish, and 26 per cent Catholic, which closely paralleled their numbers in the area. They came for both health and economic reasons. Most had suffered at least one abortion and some were already wrecked by self-inflicted operations.

The audience wanted statistics about methods and Dr. Stone had these also. She had inspected and made laboratory tests of most commercial devices, a large part of which were worthless. Of all types, the diaphragm pessary, used with the new lactic acid paste, gave the surest protection. It was 98 per cent effective, while the paste alone rated 92 per cent. This evidence was of prime interest. Dr. Robert L. Dickinson, dean of gynecologists, who in retirement now headed a committee on maternal health, later wrote, "For the first time in the hundred years controversy there was an analysis of a large series of followed-up histories." So valuable was the innovation that Dr. Dickinson finally arranged for the publication of the clinic's report in *The Medical Journal and Record* (M.D. Publications, Inc.). Never before had a leading professional magazine treated the subject. Eventually, Dr. Dickinson also threw the weight of his prestige behind the bureau by taking a place on its advisory committee.

By 1925 the bureau had outgrown its two rooms and had moved into more adequate quarters. Dr. Stone had secured the services of some of her colleagues, so that two physicians were always on hand, as well as nurses and a secretary to take the records. There was also a social worker for follow-up. Appointments had to be made two weeks in advance, and by the end of the twenties, nearly ten thousand patients came yearly. The shabby graystone building on West Fifteenth Street was a magnet not only to the poor women of the city, but to doctors and other visitors from all parts of the country and from abroad.

The success of this first enduring clinic was infectious, and a second soon followed in Chicago. Illinois had no restrictive legislation, but Health Commissioner Bundeson arbitrarily refused a license until its promoters, led by Dr. Rachel Yarros of Hull House, and Mrs. Benjamin Carpenter, took the matter to court. There Judge Harry Fisher gave a favorable decision. With this encouragement, the friends of birth control opened two more centers in the wide-sprawling city. Back east, Dr. Stone began to supervise a second clinic in nearby New Jersey. Then Baltimore started one, as did Cleveland and Buffalo. Out in fast-growing California, a dozen popped up like toadstools.

Noah had promised Margaret that together they would accomplish more than she could alone, and in the twenties, his partnership greatly accelerated progress. Giving his time and skills, as well as his money, he became treasurer of both the American Birth Control League and the Clinical Research Bureau. He paid off the *Review* deficits, gave generously to the league, bought Dr. Stone an examination table and other equipment, in addition to paying Dr. Cooper's salary, financing the Holland-Rantos Company, and becoming a big-time bootlegger of contraceptives.

In return, what did Noah Slee receive? The most enthralling years of his life! He had the comradeship of the woman he had courted for two years and even pursued around the world. He took vast pleasure in helping to achieve her goals.

For Margaret these years may also have been her best. After a decade of grueling effort, she was fulfilling the resolve that she had made when Sadie Sachs died. The Fifteenth Street Center was saving the lives of New York women and encouraging other centers to do the same. And, although slower than she had hoped, the tide was coming her way.

But that was not all. Her personal life expanded with new pleasures. Her marriage had not only brought a devoted husband, but security, status, and a piece of private paradise in the Dutchess County hills. Noah had owned a mansion on the Hudson, but since she thought it gloomy and overwhelming, he had made a curious exchange, suggested by his neighbor, Henry Morgenthau. The latter knew of a beautiful wooded estate on which a convent had recently burned. In their emergency, the nuns thought Noah's house with its thirty bedrooms providential, and for it gladly traded their hundred acres near Fishkill. For once the wishes of a Catholic institution and Margaret Sanger were resolved to their mutual advantage. On a spacious clearing, alongside a small lake, the Slees built their home of native fieldstones.

Margaret had feared that marriage might lessen her time with her sons, but instead, it produced the perfect vacation resort with built-in swimming, boating, riding, and tennis. While Stuart was at Yale and Grant at boarding school and then at Princeton, they came regularly for weekends, often with a troop of young people.

The place was equally attractive to Noah's children, two grown sons and a daughter, with none of whom he felt on easy terms. In summers, Margaret engaged a nurse to look after his grandchildren, and the house was full of youngsters and laughter. Noah's daughter left what must be one of the most affectionate appraisals of a stepmother. This famous wife of her father did not look like a reformer, she noted, "but just a small woman with chestnut hair, an oval face . . . and pretty sloping shoulders, like one of Godey's prints." Always a sympathetic listener, Margaret had a genius for encouraging others without flattery. The children thought her a fairy godmother who followed their fancies, helping to fulfill their dreams.

Margaret herself relished the pleasures of her new affluence. Ascetic out of necessity in the past, she now developed a taste for many luxuries. When Noah discovered her favorite beverage, he whimsically set up a trust fund to assure her a monthly allowance of $160 for champagne.

Although a thrifty man, he took a childlike joy in indulging Margaret's every wish. He should have learned long back how little material things really meant to his wife. On their honeymoon, strolling down the Rue de la Paix in Paris, he noted whatever caught her eye in the shop windows. Next day those items, including an ermine wrap and a strand of emeralds, were delivered to her. She protested that they were not appropriate for her and most be returned. Finally, they compromised, keeping only the emeralds which were lovely with her coloring. Some years later when he asked her to wear them, she confessed that they were pawned to help a project that he had not wanted to finance. As usual, she had her way, the project and the emeralds, which he redeemed.

The luxuries that she preferred at Willow Lake were not just material, but helped to lift her spirit. Instead of rising to the jangle of a telephone, she and Noah began their mornings with a canter through the quiet woods. In summer, the lake and the rock garden were her delights, and on dismal evenings nothing could surpass conversation with good friends around a roaring fire.

At such times Noah was at his country-squire, jovial best. A friend described him as being all bark, no bite and full of puns and riddles. At bedtime he might ask a guest why night was like the letter *p*. Because it puts Slee to sleep! Or if the discussion had seemed overly solemn, he told about the farmer's wife who would not take the blame for being childless because, while she might be a goose, her husband was not "a propaganda."

In this new and pampered togetherness one might expect the once single-minded crusader to grow relaxed and complacent, but there is no evidence that she ever wavered in her plans, although she readjusted her schedule. She was in her New York office less, but always commuted at least once a week.

Through the eyes of a new staff member, Elizabeth Grew Bacon, we see her coming into the office at 105 Fifth Avenue, "small, quiet, elegant in a stone beige coat trimmed with Persian lamb." Her titian hair was straight and swathed around her head. Wide-set in a small, heart-shaped face, her incredibly deep blue [they were green] eyes met the gaze of the inquirer with the steadiest, most penetrating look one has ever seen. This look reflected "a steadfast light, a steadfast faith, a steadfast dedication to her cause that had never changed nor faltered, nor weakened down the years."

Her voice, wrote Mrs. Bacon, was calm and answered questions without fuss or unnecessary elaboration. With a smile of greeting to those who caught her eye, she went to her personal office and the desk, where there was a large photograph of her husband, "who had eased the life of his beloved Margie," and who wooed her by strategy, and with such gifts as the Addressograph and an updated filing system.

Her personal secretary, Anna Lifshiz, would bring her a sheaf of mail, phone messages, a hundred and one requests for lecture dates, magazine articles, and interviews. But this was only her city office. At Willow Lake she built an aerie, Treetops, at the edge of a cliff overlooking the Hudson, where she insulated herself from the talk, laughter, and noisy bustle of those whom she had invited to her home. With or without her secretary, she worked over her enormous mail and appropriately, she wrote *Married Happiness*. Her one-time friend, Marie Stopes, suspected that she had stolen both title and theme from her own best seller, *Married Love*, but if so, it had taken eight years and Noah Slee to bring it to maturity.

In her mid-forties, although no one knew her age, Margaret had a special attractiveness. No doubt her clothes helped, for it was the first time that she could buy what she liked, and never before had the word "elegant" been applied to her. She had never wanted to be conspicuous, following the adage that the more radical one's views, the more conservative should be one's appearance, but she liked a tailored look and had found that simplicity comes high. For lack of a platform wardrobe, she had sometimes lectured in the borrowed dress of a friend.

With married happiness, improved health, and a growing sense of achievement, Margaret shed a new radiance, on which newspapers commented. Said a Denver reporter: "To keep young and beautiful, one should acquire a great faith. This recipe sprang to mind when, after seven years' absence, Margaret Sanger came into view, younger and lovelier than on her first visit before she had suffered imprisonment."

The Bitter with the Sweet

25

The last half of the nineteen-twenties was filled with paradoxes for Margaret. There was growing acclaim, but there were rebuffs from her own colleagues. There was public farce, and there were personal sorrows.

The year 1926 began with the death of Mary Higgins, the first to go since their mother, and equally a sacrifice to unplanned children. Margaret cited her as an example of "cruel immolation at the shrine of family duty" and was aware that she herself was a beneficiary. Together with Nan, Mary had helped make Margaret's career possible, first by arranging for the excellent training at Claverack and then by acting as a private social security system to which her younger sister turned in emergencies.

In August 1926 Michael Higgins died. He was eighty-four, speechless and paralyzed from a cerebral stroke, but since he was the great oak in whose shadow Margaret had grown, his fall reverberated in her thoughts. Stuart and his Uncle Bob had arrived in time to say good-by, after which most of the family escorted the body on its long hot journey from Truro, Massachusetts, to Corning. Although Michael had barred a religious service, he wanted to be buried near his wife.

Of all the children, only Joe remained in Corning, and hoping to honor his father, he had arranged a secular wake for old-timers to pay their respects. Of course most of Michael's contemporaries had died, but nobody, not one of his former acquaintances, appeared during that endless, bitter evening. He was still the town atheist, slighted even in death. Nor did the reputation of his famous daughter help to assuage the feelings of his fellow Irishmen.

It was a sad homecoming, as had been all of Margaret's last, infrequent visits with her father. Her childhood hero had shrunk into a contentious, pitiful old man. For all of his grandiose dreams, his civic projects, and controversial stands, his final influence seemed nil.

Passing the clock tower near the bank, one of her brothers remarked on how small it was, although he had considered it a second Eiffel Tower. Children's memories, thought Margaret, inflated everything. Then into her mind flashed the picture of a tall redheaded man confronting a jeering, snarling mob. "The speaking will take place within the hour," announced his resolute voice. That erect head and that will to do what he thought right were attributes of courage. Without that childhood memory, she might never have dared confront her own crises. In the next years she replaced her recent recollections of the querulous old man with her earlier ones. When she wrote about her background, she told about her father's wide-ranging social concerns, his independence and his bravery. By then she saw her own career as the extension of his influence.

Two public appearances added wry humor to this period. One year the Harvard Liberal Club invited Margaret to a dinner where, for lack of space, hundreds were turned away. The success of the dinner outraged Boston's Mayor Curley, who is recalled today in the mellowed version of *The Last Hurrah,* but whose career included a term in prison as well as one in Congress. Curley threatened to revoke the license of any hall within his jurisdiction where "the Sanger woman" spoke. In turn, this threat inspired the Ford Hall Forum to ask her to attend their annual banquet as a silent guest. Her picture, with mouth conspicuously taped, was publicized across the nation. The speaker, Arthur Schlesinger, Sr., hailed her as the "outstanding social warrior of the century." "To inflict silence on a woman," he said, "is thought to be a terrible punishment, but this silence inflicts thought upon us."

There were many attempts to silence Margaret. In Syracuse, the

Catholic dominated City Council passed an ordinance against her conference, but after protests from the university leaders, the mayor vetoed the act and the program went on as scheduled. It was the mayor of Albany who forced a hotel to break its commitment; the meeting moved to a large private home. In Cincinnati, the Knights of Columbus threatened a permanent hotel boycott, but this aroused the Masons, who won the fight by championing free speech. In Milwaukee, the Women's Marquette League demanded that Mayor Hoane stop the meeting, but he defended Margaret's constitutional rights. In Hagerstown, Maryland, the Sanger sponsors found that the only hall available was a rundown dance hall, outfitted with chairs from the undertaker.

One appearance was so secretive that Margaret never knew the names of those who invited her, nor the exact location of the place. Her invitation came from the Woman's Branch of the Ku Klux Klan of Silver Lake, New Jersey. Whether from curiosity or zeal to reach all groups, she accepted and having followed the written directions, found a parked car with a driver who might have been a deaf-mute for all her greeting. After a tortuous ride, they stopped at a large barnlike building where she was told to wait. Inside, the Klanswomen performed their rites, while outside, for three long hours their guest speaker sat alone in the cold and dark. When she finally confronted the rows of Neanderthal faces, she reduced her message to the simplest terms. In any case, she pleased them more than they pleased her, for they asked her to a dozen more meetings, which she declined.

Margaret was always busy with her vast mail, supervising the clinic and editing the *Review,* but her thoughts began to turn toward world needs. Scholars were already pointing out that it had taken unknown millenniums to produce the first billion men on earth, by about 1830, but now, after less than a century, there was a second billion, and in perhaps thirty more years there would be a third billion, and in half that time, a fourth billion, etc. etc., at implacable, geometric speed. That was bad enough, but the Fascists and all militarists were trying to accelerate the growth. The new nationalism was stimulating population as well as armament races. Her friend, the Very Reverend Dean Inge of England, who saw the issue more clearly than most clergymen, summed it up ironically: "It is a pleasant prospect if every nation with a high birth rate has a 'right' to exterminate its neighbors. The supposed duty of multiplication and the alleged right to expand, are among the chief causes of modern war."

Margaret still hoped that the League of Nations might support population controls. To jolt them into recognition of the explosive facts, she proposed to bring to Geneva the world's authorities on related matters. This could not be a Neo-Malthusian or birth control meeting, since Catholic countries would boycott such auspices; it needed a broader approach. To try out her idea she invited an international committee, which had been set up at her New York conference, for a weekend at Willow Lake. C. C. Little, President of the University of Michigan, came from Ann Arbor, Clinton Chance from London, and once more they were delighted to cooperate on a forward-looking project, for which she would do the work. Normally it took at least two years to mount an international conference, but in her urgency, she promised it within the year.

If these men grasped the importance of her plan, the women on the board of her Birth Control League did not. They viewed it as another aberration which would add to their financial burdens. To reassure them, as well as to provide for interim leadership, Margaret took a leave of absence, thus raising the conscientious Mrs. Robertson-Jones to the position of acting president.

Noah, accepting the financial responsibilities, decided to rent a villa on the French Riviera, where intermittently they could relax and entertain. Before the end of 1926, Margaret was in Geneva, settling time and place. She signed up the Salle Centrale for three days, starting at the close of August 1927. Then she went to London to develop the content of the meeting.

Since her paramount need was an advisory committee of stature, she spent a weekend with Ellis in Cornwall, where they conferred in "long walks and leisurely, heavenly talks." Next she went to Edinburgh to lasso the biologist, F. A. E. Crew, famous for making roosters lay eggs and hens crow. But of all her advisers, the most helpful was young Julian Huxley, who rounded up many of the European as well as English participants. For him, birth control was not only "something for the alleviation of distress in the present, but the means by which in the long run man can become trustee of the cosmic evolution." Finally, she picked as chairman of the conference, Sir Bernard Mallett, former president of the Royal Statistical Society, with the obvious asset of being a friend of Sir Eric Drummond, currently Secretary-General of the League of Nations.

Margaret's daily reports to Noah for once show her side of a correspondence. Her busy schedule was spiced with items such as lunch with John Maynard Keynes and his bride, Lydia Lopokouva, the ballerina, and tea with Maude Royden, the woman minister. They also reflect the relations of the couple and their problems. He was irked by her absence, while she was torn between his needs and those of the conference. With both love and tact she tried to bridge the separation:

> "Stafford Hotel, London
> "Sunday [December 5, 1926]
>
> "Dearest Noah—Darling
> "It is really always lonely to be away from you even one day. . . ."

Again on December 8, "It's a fact that I think of you a hundred times a day and laugh to myself over something we have laughed over together. You are ever in my heart and deep in my heart as you know. These little separations are not catastrophes. . . . So here's a hug and a kiss. . . . Ever your Margy." By now she accepted his money graciously and pleased him by acknowledging it. "London is expensive," she noted. "I'm happy my dearest can give me such comforts and happiness."

On Noah's insistence, she had delayed leaving him, and on December 9 explained her way of making decisions using the Quaker words, "inner voice" and "God." The latter may have been characteristic of his vocabulary, but had never been of hers. "You see, Noah dear, all my life I have acted on an inner voice and when that speaks to me, it speaks wisely and never fails me. When I disobey it for one reason or the other, for any consideration whatever I always suffer. If only I could help you to believe this and help you to understand it you would I know add to it your splendid powers and make everything I do a glorious success. But when we put our own man made minds against God's will and God's advice then disruption and disaster results everywhere."

Later she wrote in the same mood:

I have been deeply depressed today and yesterday over the affairs here. I know that were I free to work and keep on the job, I could put over a conference that would astound the world—*But*—here I am, interests divided and diverted and I cannot know what to do. The movement **now** needs one dominating force to drive it to success—The interest is alive—the time is ripe, but I shall need to give time to it if it is to succeed. No one else can do it, so it seems. It will crown my past efforts and repay my sacrifices to see this Conference a success. Will you help me? Not by money, darling one, but by seeing this thing eye to eye with me and giving me the time I need to work it up properly. . . .

You have done so much to help me make it the success it has become, that I believe you will help me again—forever. I can never believe that you have come into my life to hold me back, you who are so vigorous and glorious in your love and splendid in your ideals and generosity! You have helped others to attain their life's work, you have given support and inspiration to others you love less—and I believe with all my heart, with all my faith that you will help me to victory and success.

After spending about six weeks with her husband at Cap d'Ail, in February she was back, flitting between London and Paris. An appointment at a beauty parlor suddenly and permanently changed her appearance. Accidentally, her long bronze hair was singed off on one side and she lost her chief beauty. In the age of the bobbed hair flapper, she unwillingly followed the style. For a few hours she was inconsolable, lest Noah be distressed, but like many devoted husbands, he spent the evening with her and noticed no change until morning. By that time she never again wanted the weight of long hair. Unlike the Biblical Samson, she came to believe that hers had sapped her strength. But gone forever was the "Madonna" look that Mrs. Dodge had described when she wore her straight hair wrapped around her head or simply coiled at the back. From now on her short, slightly curled coiffeur presented a more sophisticated, if less distinguished appearance. However, change was inevitable, for although no one guessed it, she was forty-eight years old.

In April Margaret opened headquarters in Geneva, where her

staff of seventeen began to cope with the problems of an international meeting. The conference would be conducted in both French and English, but she engaged some other language interpreters with a scientific terminology. She also arranged the usual social schedule with lunches, receptions, boat rides on the lake, and a dinner at Mrs. Stanley McCormick's fifteenth-century Château de Prangins at Nyon. This was a first gesture from the lady who would become her main support.

On the Friday before the Tuesday opening, Margaret was reading final proof on the program when Sir Bernard came into her office and put his pencil through the names of all of the women workers, starting with herself and Edith How-Martyn, her able assistant. "We'll just leave these off," he announced, adding that they had no place on a scientific program.

Margaret was speechless. She had faithfully kept herself in the background, but for the chairman, whom she herself had picked, to refuse to acknowledge the services of those who had organized and largely financed the conference, was petty and unjust. Her good friend and aide, Mrs. How-Martyn, who had organized her Fabian Hall lecture and had once been jailed for suffragette activities, resigned at once from this male-dominated congress.

Antifeminism was easy to confirm in Switzerland, which to this day has not given its women suffrage. In this case, however, it was Sir Eric Drummond who had warned Sir Bernard that Europeans would ignore a conference if they thought a woman had organized it. In her erratically kept diary, Margaret privately fulminated: "An instance of the attitude of the Swiss male is this—What? A woman organized this conference? A woman brought together eminent scientists from forty countries of the world? My dear friend, don't speak of it unless you want to be the laughingstock of Europe. It is impossible to let it be known. Hide it, deny it, anything you wish, but don't openly acknowledge that!"

She had guessed that her name was the crux of the matter, but she also suspected that antifeminism was not the major enemy. In this she was also correct. Sir Bernard's Italian friends, along with others from Catholic countries, had insisted that since the words "Sanger" and "birth control" were synonymous, her name should not appear on the program.

On Saturday morning the whole secretariat followed Mrs. How-Martyn's lead and struck. Even the girl who was to return the proof to the printer refused. Whether or not there could be a Tuesday opening once more rested with Margaret. No doubt it would have been pleasant to have left Sir Bernard fumbling in the chaos of arrangements, but during the previous night she had soberly considered alternatives. She had invested a year in the meeting and at the very start had herself decided to keep birth control in the background. The chance for public education on the world's most pressing problem still remained. So she spent the day persuading the staff to resume its anonymous work.

Years later Margaret suggested that the conference was a failure. Certainly it did not change world trends, halt the rise of Hitler, or prevent World War II, which were her objectives. However, out of it sprang the Population Union which for some years was the only international group producing research studies, bulletins, and conferences on related subjects.

Of the meeting itself, C. V. Drysdale wrote: "Nothing could demonstrate more fully the immense progress in the appreciation of the importance of the population question which has recently been shown all over the world, than the brilliant conference which has just been held at Geneva. . . . In weight of authority it has far surpassed all previous gatherings [his Neo-Malthusian ones], and has been second to none in brilliance." The discerning *Manchester Guardian* called it "an intellectual treat, such as it is rarely given the ordinary mortal to enjoy."

Not until the farewell dinner was Margaret Sanger's name publicly mentioned. Then, at the prodding of Huxley and his younger colleagues, Sir Bernard thanked her for her "absolute loyalty" in furthering the interests of the meeting and praised her "real ability" and "self-effacement." At this point Drysdale reported that the whole company rose and "thundered in her honor." They also applauded Noah Slee for his many contributions, including the bilingual journal which had reached the delegates each morning on their breakfast trays.

After the farewell dinner, the distinguished participants departed, leaving Margaret with the bills, the clearing-up, and the prodigious task of editing the proceedings. Exhausted, she finally packed Noah off for sightseeing in England and retired with her work to a sanatorium.

The Slees resumed their daily correspondence, hers starting September 21:

Darling . . . I have been under great tension and high pressure. What a woman needs is to be alone, absolutely alone with God for a few days or weeks until she has filled up the reservoir of her soul again with faith, hope and courage. I have been impatient I know and really horrid at times. You have been tired and disappointed . . . so I should have been kinder and dearer to you than ever, but I was too unhappy to be anything but miserable. Now I shall get the papers to the printers and then go to the mountain top alone and meditate. . . . I need solitude as much as food and I thank you for making it possible at this time. . . . Ever your "Margy".

September 27, 1927:

. . . Are you thinking about us and our future? I am. It is not all clear sailing yet I'm afraid, because we are so much alike and yet so different. It is our interests that are so wide apart. There are none that you have that I can take up, so as to bring us into closer harmony, and you do not like me to expand my own, yet there is all the attraction between us that the world counts essential and necessary. It's really complicated.

My heart is troubled to have you lonely and apart from life's activities but I should wither up and die to be shut off from the intellectual currents of my contemporaries. All I want is a little more freedom. That is not much to ask, but I must be able to feel that I can *waste* [emphasis in original] a whole night or day or week if I feel it good for me to do so without explaining or asking. I'm too grown up and too developed to not be free. My actions so far have been tempered with intelligence and I can't go back to chattel slavery. For that is what it really is, dear, when a woman is not made to feel that she can act without asking her husband's consent. Outside of financial affairs (which is and should be a joint affair between them) there should be utter liberty for both parties to enjoy tastes and friendships utterly free from the other. You will never see this I am certain, but until you can see it there will be no real happiness for the modern woman. If you could only be made to see what riches a woman can bring into your life, not only in outside forces, but in the joyousness of her own being, when she is fully conscious that freedom and love, faith and respect are the foundations of her marriage.

I know darling Noah that one must not expect you to plunge into the depths of these thoughts but think them over now and then and talk about them to me and we will make our future. . . . I want to make your every day one of golden sunsets. Those are my desires. I worry because I am failing [in them] so I am analyzing the causes which underlie the problem. Now you can write me just as you think and what you feel about the difficulties. It will help me to see the other side.

Devotedly and lovingly ever and ever . . . no matter what we say . . .

MARGARET.

Before she had finished the editorial chore, Margaret was invited to Germany for a series of speeches under the auspices of a women's medical association. Noah went with her, and they found a different country from that she had seen seven years earlier. Now people had money to spend in hotels and restaurants, but the country was polarized between the rich and the poor. There was a new nationalism and a scarcely suppressed zeal to reassert German power. When a zeppelin appeared overhead, men took off their hats and hailed it as though it were a god. After her talk at the Town Hall of Berlin-Charlottenburg, a savage debate broke out between the extreme nationalists and the leftists. A woman, Dr. Marthe Ruben-Wolf, had all the facts and ably defended birth control. But logic would not help her, Margaret was told; Dr. Ruben-Wolf was a Communist.

Nevertheless, twenty women physicians were ready to give their services in the poorer section of Neukoln, where a friendly health commissioner, Dr. Kurt Bendix, was eager to cooperate. His was the first government agency in any land to sponsor birth control, or *Geburtenregelung,* as it was known. Margaret was so touched that she pledged $50 a month for three years toward supplies. These supplies, produced in Germany, the source of most of America's bootlegged materials, were still unknown to many German doctors, who continued to oppose contraception. This experiment in government-supported birth control flourished in a dozen centers until the Nazis took over. Dr. Ruben-Wolf escaped to Russia; Dr. Bendix committed suicide.

The Slees had planned to go to India, where Margaret was in demand for lectures, but after the German trip she relapsed with great fatigue. Wisely, they changed their schedule to spend two months at St. Moritz. It was her first extended vacation, and in the exhilarating climate she tried skating again and even took up skiing. Long before they were ready to go home, Margaret was receiving distress signals from Juliet Rublee and her faithful aide, Anne Kennedy.

The American Birth Control League had been left in the hands of those who were devoted to the cause and wanted to advance it. If none of them had Margaret's experience, some of them, especially Mrs. Robertson-Jones, the acting president, had more knowledge of organizational procedures. In the past she had been shocked by Margaret's "impulsive" decisions. She also knew that other directors, who were busy ladies, dividing their time among philanthropies, their families, and social demands, felt harassed by Margaret's unexpected plans, titanic drives, and enthusiasm for new ideas. It was easy to convince them that the league should have a fixed program and budget so that members might once and for all make their pledges for their full annual responsibilities.

With birth control becoming respectable—except among the Catholic hierarchy—a new type of leadership was indicated. The movement had outgrown its fanatic youth and it was thought that a college graduate, a woman with broad cultural and social background, would be appealing as a leader. If birth control had the right tone, Mrs. Robertson-Jones believed that it could win universal acceptance. The previous year, and mostly through her personal efforts, the New York League of Women Voters had endorsed repeal of the state Comstock laws. For the current year she had high hopes that the Junior League might accept birth control as one of its fields for service. But tone was essential for the Junior League.

Tone was the reason for the ultimate discharge of Kitty Marion, the indomitable old war-horse who still sold the *Review* at Times

Square. As a gracious gesture to soften the brusque ending of years of service, Mrs. Robertson-Jones proposed to give Kitty a farewell lunch, along with a gift of money. Kitty Marion declined to lunch with those who had fired her, took the money, and went back to England.

During her first administration, Mrs. Robertson-Jones put through a series of reforms, starting with graded memberships and the understanding that there would be no other appeals for funds. New by-laws also assured the "accountability" of the president to an executive-type board. This policy was one reason for dispensing with Anne Kennedy. Anne had practically grown up with the league, and having served for the last eight years on the executive committee, had a disconcerting way of knowing more than anyone else about the organization. Of course oldtimers, like Juliet Rublee, were indignant that Mrs. Kennedy, originally a personal aide to Mrs. Sanger, had not been allowed to present her own side to the board, but as Mrs. Robertson-Jones put it, she was "not amenable to the direction of the Board," and would be out of place in the new setup.

In spite of the unpleasantness over dropping Mrs. Kennedy, the overall success of Mrs. Robertson-Jones's efforts could be measured by the league's financial position. At the start of 1928, for the first time, there was plenty of money in the bank.

On her homecoming, Margaret, in turn, was shocked. That money in the bank had been given to advance birth control, not to lie idle. And how about the *Review* subscriptions? Unfortunately, through an oversight in not sending out reminders, these had dropped in her year's absence from 13,000 to 2,500. Margaret ordered that the renewal slips be sent at once, but she was then reminded that the new by-laws required special board authorization for any expenditure of more than five dollars.

On her first day in the office Margaret faced a more urgent crisis. Months earlier the league had agreed to take part in a Parents' Exhibition at the Grand Central Palace. The league had a contract and had paid for its booth, but on the eve of opening was asked to withdraw. William O'Shea, superintendent of schools, had threatened to remove the school exhibit unless the Birth Control League was ousted. The acting president then proposed to delete any offensive material, but O'Shea would have none of it.

Margaret at once called a lawyer to secure an injunction against the exclusion. When she hung up, she learned that only the board might take such action. Before she could gather a quorum, the league check was returned, the exhibition opened and a major chance was lost to educate the public on both civil rights and birth control.

She was no "paper president," Margaret conceded. Experience had given her judgment which should have some freedom of action, instead of being trussed up in the red tape of those who did not understand the problems. This new group thought the league a charity to be run in a routine way for the performance of a quiet, continuing service. She saw it as an urgent, current crusade, "an instrument of accomplishment," which should avail itself of every psychological factor to push on to victory and then disband. She had come home full of plans for new enterprises, while these ladies wanted to relax in their *status quo*.

In June 1928 Margaret Sanger resigned from the presidency of the league that she had founded. There was no angry severance, and since most of the directors were devoted to her, she agreed to remain on the board and continue editing the *Review*. Meanwhile, she would launch her own new plans.

Margaret's continuing influence irked the small group of dissidents, and the cleavage grew. Mrs. Robertson-Jones frankly disparaged the *Review*, which she said any staff member could handle better than its editor. Finally she reorganized the paper under an editorial board of four, leaving only nominal control in Margaret's hands.

For some months Margaret had been considering her future. Since the *Review* had been a large part of her life for a decade, she hesitated to abandon it. On the other hand, the association was becoming disruptive. She might still be able to control the board, but as she wrote Mrs. Robert Huse, who had taken Mrs. Kennedy's place, she could "fight to the last ditch against the outside enemy, but to fight old friends, women that I have loved, respected and worked with, that I cannot do."

Persuasive no doubt was the fact that her restless spirit had moved on to new fields. As she put it in *My Fight for Birth Control,* she would give "complete freedom to others to carry on as they saw best, in order to attain a new freedom for herself." In June 1929 she withdrew from the league itself, surrendering the *Review* to it as its property. Her letter of resignation was self-controlled, although she reiterated her belief in the "danger of curtailing the initiative which is essential to successful leadership." She said that she would let the current management assume entire responsibility for its policies which she might "protest but could not prevent."

Five directors resigned simultaneously, among whom was Frances Ackermann, the financial guardian of the *Review,* who had long been troubled by the new leadership. Mrs. Walter Timme, wife of a prominent physician, said that she was filled with apprehension because of the discourtesy to Margaret Sanger and the "lack of appreciation of her judgment and mission." Juliet Rublee wrote forthrightly that she could be of no use on a board whose policy she disapproved and under a president in whose wisdom and judgment she had lost faith. The stress was now on "small, technical details and overemphasis on business efficiency." There had been a deliberate effort, she said, to undermine Margaret Sanger's influence, minimize her accomplishments and to prejudice people.

There was one more resignation—an angry one—from the league treasurer, Noah Slee. If no price tag could be put on Margaret's services, he put a high one on his own. Over the last four years he had given $64,000 "for the benefit of the ideal Margaret Sanger has slaved for." He enclosed a promised check of $300, his "last contribution."

It was good therapy for Margaret that her thoughts were already on the future. By the time she wrote her *Autobiography,* she was philosophical, and the league was again begging for her help. There were many ways, she discovered, by which the same goal might be reached, and diverse ones must be tried to find the best alternative. Once she had thought of the *Review* and the league as her children and at first she had to guide their faltering steps. But unless you let children run and fall, they will never develop their own strength. "There is a biology," she wrote, "of ideas as there is a biology of cells and each goes through a process of evolution. The parent cell splits and the new entities in their turn divide and divide again. Instead of indicating breakdown, it is a sign of health. . . . Cohesion is maintained until in the end the whole is a vast mosaic cleaving in union and strength."

Research and the Tides
of Public Opinion

26

When Margaret Sanger gave up the league and the *Review,* she ceded only the façade of her movement, but she never meant to give up the Clinical Research Bureau, which was its heart. This, indeed, was the fulfillment of her work. Since the board had discouraged its creation, she had organized it as a separate entity under her personal guidance.

For more than five years the clinic quietly performed its function, but on an April morning in 1929, it was raided. The blow fell during one of the crucial moments of Margaret's life. Not only was she in the midst of her struggle with the league board and about to take off on a lecture tour, but Stuart had just come down with an excruciating case of mastoiditis. He was staying at her New York apartment, where she had come to nurse him. Having been up most of the night, she was asleep when Anna Lifshiz called to say that the police were ransacking the clinic.

Time seemed to swing backward to the decade of violence that she had hoped to have outgrown. Leaving Stuart with Daisy Mitchell, her long-time maid, Margaret grabbed a taxi and in a few moments was at her headquarters, now menaced by the parked Black Maria. The blinds of the clinic were drawn, the door was locked, but a plainclothesman from the vice squad finally admitted the owner of the building. She faced a familiar scene. Huddled in a small room were the patients, tearfully submitting their names and addresses.

After a word with Anna, Margaret resumed her Brownsville role of reassurance to the frightened mothers and children.

In the corridor outside, a burly uniformed woman shouted orders to men who were seizing books, charts, and medical supplies. The commander, Margaret was told, was Mary Sullivan, head of the Policewomen's Bureau. A second policewoman began to rummage through the files of case histories. This was too much, but when Margaret rushed over to stop that outrage, Mrs. Sullivan intervened, flashing her search warrant signed by Chief Magistrate McAdoo. For future "evidence," the cards were poured into a waste basket. Margaret protested that the files were the property of doctors; anyone who touched them would face trouble.

"Trouble!" jeered Mrs. Sullivan. "That's what you're in. This is my party."

Luckily, Anna, in a side room, was consulting Dr. Robert L. Dickinson of the Academy of Medicine. His response was to call Morris L. Ernst, a brilliant young lawyer, who in the future would carry on the work that J. J. Goldstein had begun of securing the decisive legal opinions of Margaret's career.

While Margaret was a veteran in such encounters, some of the staff were close to hysterics. Only Dr. Stone, nursing a weak heart, remained aloof and a little amused. Just that morning, she recalled, a visiting doctor had asked if they ever had police trouble; she had assured him that those days were past.

On the way to the police station, Margaret learned the background of the raid, which was almost a repeat performance of the earlier Brownsville raid. Mrs. McNamara, the second policewoman, had come as a decoy with a pitiful tale of three children and a heavy-drinking husband. Since she actually was afflicted with several pathological conditions, the doctors, after consultation, had fitted her with a pessary. This was the crime which had triggered the action. At the police station Mrs. Sullivan demanded fingerprints, to which Margaret again protested. At this point young Ernst arrived, managed to have the fingerprinting by-passed and arranged for bail, at $300 each, for the two doctors and three nurses.

Margaret hurried home to her sick boy, whom she took to a hospital. With his doctor's approval, she then rushed up to Boston for an important appearance and after this on to Chicago. En route, she heard from the hospital that Stuart was recovering from a mastoid operation. Leaving him, as she wrote Hugh de Selincourt, was "the hardest thing, next to one [when she left all three for exile] that she had ever done in her life."

In New York, both Noah and Morris Ernst were busy. It happened that Noah's minister, Karl Reiland, was a friend of Magistrate McAdoo, who was immediately consulted. McAdoo was chagrined to learn that he had signed one warrant without reading it. He ordered that the clinic files be deposited in his safe. Next morning the *New York Times* quoted his statement that the police had "gone beyond the authority of their search warrant."

Ernst assembled a Defense Committee of Five Hundred, whose quality was as impressive as its numbers. Among the well-known ministers were Reiland and Harry Emerson Fosdick; among the medical profession, the outstanding Dr. Walter Timme, and a former health commissioner; among the lawyers, the distinguised Paul Cravath. The list was studded with such names as Vanderbilt, Reid, Morgenthau, Phipps, and Lamont.

This time the press found no excuse for the police. The *Herald Tribune* said that if they could seize doctors' general files without a specific warrant, "the privileged relations of doctor and client cease to exist. The possibilities of abuse, including blackmail, are virtually unlimited." In his column, Heywood Broun suggested that if the medical profession did not resent the raid, they should all consult chiropractors to learn what ailed their spines.

In fact, the medical profession's reaction proved a turning point in their policy. Challenged on their right to privacy, dozens of doctors offered to testify. The New York Medical Society, which had once voted three to one against birth control, passed a resolution of censure on the seizure of the records. On Dr. Dickinson's proposal, the Academy of Medicine attested to its "grave concern" over the action. After this formal rebuke, Commissioner of Police Grover E. Whalen, who had called the action "routine," apologized.

This raid, like the Brownsville one, was based on Section 1142 of the penal code, barring contraceptive information. But the result of the appealed decision on the earlier raid had been the Crane interpretation, now embodied in Section 1145. Physicians giving information for the "cure and prevention of disease" were thereby exempted. Ernst's function was to show that this was exactly what the two clinic doctors were doing. To prove this, he depended on professional testimony, and here the case made history. When Goldstein had presented a physician as his star witness twelve years earlier, the testimony had been ruled out as "irrelevant, incompetent and immaterial." At this second trial, Dr. Louis T. Harris, former health commissioner, was the chief witness.

"The birth control clinic is a public health work," he asserted. "In preventing conception it may be said to cure because pregnancy can often be the cause of furthering the progress of disease." He had personally investigated the clinic and found it "quite in keeping with the spirit and purpose of the law and with the spirit of medicine, public health medicine."

To develop this point, Ernst asked about the spacing of children and frequent pregnancies. Harris explained that "so far as the mother is concerned, it [frequent pregnancy] aggravates and may, in fact, precipitate invalidism. As far as the child is concerned, it increases the hazard to the next born child very decidedly."

Equally helpful was the testimony of Policewoman McNamara. She was forced to admit both her lies and her plan to deceive the doctors. As Margaret wrote in *My Fight for Birth Control*: "Every step in the legal procedure following the raid, was an amazing revelation of progress—the fruit of long, steady plodding, the response of an awakened conscious interest which up to then had been strangely silent."

In the end Justice Abraham Rosenbluth, who at the start had seemed hostile, strengthened the Crane opinion. "But why," asked a *New York Herald* editorial, "had the raid taken place? The clinic had been in public operation for five years; it had cooperated with the City Department of Health and with the medical societies, it had never concealed its existence or its methods." Yet it was raided without warning, and the police showed animus against its staff. Why?

Since an official answer was unlikely, Margaret hired the Burns Detective Service. Social workers had always brought in a large

share of patients, but she was surprised to hear that the Catholic social workers had recently conferred with church officials for guidance about the clinic. The clergy, all the way up to Cardinal Hayes,
had been astounded to learn that a birth control clinic existed. The
very men who had maneuvered the Town Hall raid against talk on
this subject now resolved to smash the institution. Mrs. Sullivan was
chosen to lead the attack. Later she refused to answer reporters'
questions about the reason for the raid or whether the Church was
behind it. She was not put on the stand, and after a first silent appearance, was not seen again at the trial.

Once more the enemies of birth control had given it a major boost
through their arrogant interference. The hierarchy must have recognized the mistake, for this was its last strong-arm attack in New
York. Furthermore, the decision strengthened the legal position of
clinics everywhere. The law was plain, said Justice Rosenbluth: "If
a doctor, in good faith believes that the patient is a married woman
and that her health requires prevention of conception, it is no crime
to so advise and instruct her."

"At times," wrote Helena Huntington Smith in *The New Yorker*
of July 5, 1930:

the birth control question has looked like a personal encounter between
Margaret Sanger and the Catholic Church. One might ask, however,
whether the Roman hierarchy has not after all been her best friend. Several times its blundering opposition has focused public attention on the
birth control movement which was not ingenious enough to do so for
itself. . . .

Mrs. Sanger has never been adept at juggling the diableries of publicity.
Her strength is an overwhelming sincerity and great personal courage.
Although she doesn't know how to trump up an issue, she will fight
to the last ditch on a real one.

Unexpected publicity had certainly stimulated so many calls
that future appointments at the clinic had to be made weeks in advance. To ease the pressure, as well as to remove the clinic from the
whim of its Catholic landlord, Margaret hunted for larger quarters. Noah, who was no longer supporting either the league or the
Review, made another major contribution. He bought a pre-Civil

War mansion at 17 West Sixteenth Street, the final and perfect head-quarters. With an expanded staff and evening sessions, the clinic served upward of eighteen hundred patients a month.

At Sixteenth Street there also was room for research. Already the files were rich with information for students of social, economic, health, and sex data. It was news to find that in 1930 70 percent of the patients had family incomes of less than $50 a week and that for every two children born, there had been an abortion. One mother had undergone forty.

Margaret, however, was increasingly concerned with another type of research. As modern medicine and sanitation prolonged life, population problems grew. Doctors were stressing preventive medicine, but few did anything to prevent conception. In the United States the Comstock laws, which strengthened religious taboos, stymied progress. The bureau itself had taken a forward step by developing the lactic acid jelly, but only recommended it as a supplement to the pessary. In a technological age, the diaphragm that Mensigna had created sixty years previously, although cumbersome and costly, was still the best there was. This meant that contraception for the majority remained impossible.

Yet there were exciting rumors. The Soviet Union, it was said, had a spermatoxin immunizing women for several months against pregnancy. At the University of Pennsylvania, Stuart and Emily Mudd had made tests that seemed to confirm this possibility. Dr. Guyer, at the University of Wisconsin, was inoculating female rabbits with a semen taken from fowls. There was hope of a breakthrough in several fields. In California, scientists had isolated vitamin E, which some people thought was the key to fertility. Others relied for answers on the X-ray tests on animals being conducted at Johns Hopkins. Meanwhile, Margaret knew that in Scotland, F. A. E. Crew was making glandular tests on monkeys. She decided that a cross-fertilization of scientific minds would speed progress. Certainly the interchange of experience of those running birth control centers around the world would be helpful.

This was the background for another congress, the last international one that Margaret would plan for nearly two decades. For a site she returned to Switzerland, choosing Zurich, central for European delegates but removed from Geneva's intrigues and scenically refreshing. Here for five days at the end of summer in 1930, 130 scientists and clinic directors exchanged views. This Seventh International Birth Control Conference was an innovation, a meeting of professionals concerned with practical performance.

The opening session on current mechanical methods was led by Dr. Stone, director of the world's largest and leading clinic, whose six years' experience was uniquely reinforced by statistical records. Although the fifteen physicians currently attached to the bureau all relied chiefly on the Mensigna pessary, they knew it was not the final answer, since two-thirds of their patients had to be subsidized.

In Europe, the single most impressive clinic was Holland's new memorial to Dr. Aletta Jacobs. Posthumously, the nation was trying to achieve her medical standards. Elsewhere most birth control instruction was given by midwives with a wide diversity of methods in Austria, Belgium, Denmark, England, Germany, and Sweden. Some relied on intrauterine devices, others on suppositories or foam tablets.

From Japan came Dr. Majimi to tell how "Margaret Sanger's clear voice had penetrated stone walls," converting leaders to birth control, which was now taught in the health stations of the poorest quarters. There was also word from China that two Shanghai hospitals were training physicians and nurses in family limitation and that in Peking the modern Union Medical College was dispensing contraceptives. The Kuomintang government planned to use birth control as a weapon in fighting poverty.

Of all the programs, the most ideal seemed to be that of the U.S.S.R., as reported by Dr. Ruben-Wolf of Berlin. The German centers, to which she was still attached, suffered constant harassments, but the Soviet's, which Dr. Ruben-Wolf had visited four times, had developed the perfect plan. Those in need could have a skilled, cheap, rapid curettage at one of the large abortoriums run with the precision of an assembly line. More basic, all dispensaries and gynecological clinics throughout the nation gave regular birth control instruction, publicized by posters, exhibits, films, and pamphlets. In Moscow, there was mass production of rubber pessaries, chemical compounds, and intrauterine devices. The spermatoxin, which immunized women against pregnancy, was in the experimental stage.

The latter subject was the main concern of the scientists. In the many-faceted discussion that followed, Dr. Taylor, of the department of animal genetics at the University of Edinburgh, gave an impressive paper. His laboratory tests on mice had shown the influence of sex hormones on both the sex cycle and fertility. This strengthened the belief that hormones were the key to effective contraception.

As a result of the congress, several German and Swiss universities added contraceptive techniques to their medical curriculums. Clinical staff workers raised their standards by an interchange of experience and more training at the superior institutions. But the great achievement, as Margaret had hoped, was the stimulus of scientific research, especially in the United States.

Toward the close of *My Fight for Birth Control,* the author writes that she had reached a place from which she could survey the international landscape and discern the harvest from seeds she had sown. From her Alpine height, she counted fifty birth control centers in the United States, all rooted in what she had planted in New York a few years earlier. Collectively, Europe boasted the same number, more than a third of which had sprouted from the seeds that she had scattered in Germany. Meanwhile, the Far East, where she had prepared the soil, seemed on the verge of the largest crop.

"One left the Conference," she wrote, "convinced that there was the beginning of a new era in human progress, a technique of racial help inaugurated without fanfare or trumpets, without consideration of remote political ideals, but aiming to place the weapons in the hands of the individual himself, whatever his environment, whatever the condition of his previous servitude."

There was another beginning at Zurich which would lead to Margaret's last great legal case. Dr. Majimi had shown a new type of pessary, samples of which Margaret ordered for the purpose of testing. Later the New York Customs notified her that they had barred and destroyed a package from Japan. This was in accordance with Section 305 of the Revenue Act, another Comstock legacy. Margaret promptly put in a second order, this time through the Baroness Ishimoto, to be sent to Dr. Stone. At the worst, Margaret foresaw a new judicial decision. If, as the famous Mr. Dooley said, the Supreme Court followed elections, perhaps a lower court would follow public opinion.

Public opinion was moving fast, spurred by the positive action of organized women. In 1930 the National Council of Jewish Women officially endorsed birth control, followed at once by the vast General Federation of Women's Clubs. In the same year came the first church support, from the Unitarians, whose individual leaders had long been helpful. But the act that rocked Christendom was the endorsement in 1930 of the Anglican bishops at the Lambeth Conference. As the Very Reverend Dean Inge pithily put it, the bishops had notified the world that "Birth control is here to stay." The irreverent George Bernard Shaw said that the church was "belatedly trying to catch up with the twentieth century."

With accelerating speed, others were also trying to catch up. Right after the Zurich conference, New York's Academy of Medicine declared that "the public is entitled to expect counsel and information on the important and intimate matter of contraceptive advice." After mature study, started by Dr. Dickinson, the academy endorsed birth control, sex education, and changes in legislation. Because of its prestigious position, the academy's stand was impressive, although other large medical associations, moving at a glacial rate, lagged behind most churches.

In 1931 a tidal wave began with the Presbyterians, followed by the Central Conference of American Rabbis, then the Universalists, the Methodists, and on the first day of spring, the Federal Council of the Churches of Christ, the central body of more than 20 million Protestants. "There is general agreement," said a remarkable report, "that the sex union between husbands and wives as an expression of mutual affection without relation to procreation, is right." There should be a new morality, the report continued, based upon knowledge and freedom, instead of ignorance.

"It's just what I would have written myself," Margaret Sanger told the press. Most of the press agreed with the *World-Telegram* which called it "a day of triumph for Mrs. Sanger."

The changing tide of public opinion was reason enough for new tactics. Although great progress had been made over the years, the old statutes remained on the books, an affront to modern views and a constant threat to the future. The time seemed right for repeal.

Formerly, because Mrs. Dennett's Voluntary Parenthood League had focused on federal legislation, Margaret had left that field to her, although she had made some efforts to change state laws. After all, it was the New York laws that had interfered with the Brownsville clinic. As early as 1921 she had visited Albany where she had found a few legislators privately sympathetic to her purposes, but all of them certain that her bill was political dynamite. Finally, in 1924, young Samuel Rosenman, later to become a distinguished judge and then adviser to President Roosevelt, introduced it, but it never had a chance.

Connecticut also had offered a special challenge because there the very use of contraceptives was a crime. To enforce that law would have taken "a policeman under every bed." Furthermore, in this state Margaret had two outstanding aides, Mrs. George H. Day and Mrs. Thomas Hepburn.

Of all her friends, her shared memories ran deepest with Mrs. Hepburn. Daughter of the owner of Corning's glassworks, Kathy Houghton's background had discouraged early intimacy, but as a young matron, she had become an active suffragist. In 1916 she had reentered Margaret's life to pay her tribute at the Brevoort dinner. Kate Hepburn, now the wife of a well-known physician, mother of the future star—and equally attractive—added the popular word "glamour" to the birth control movement. She and Mrs. Day became perennial lobbyists at Hartford, but in spite of their efforts, reinforced by Margaret's occasional appearances, the archaic law remained intact. No logic affected the politico-theological agreements of the state establishment.

On the national level, Mrs. Dennett, resting her case on the freedoms of the First Amendment, had always asked for a straight repeal of the Comstock laws. This seemed reasonable, but Margaret believed that until contraceptive techniques had been simplified, medical supervision was essential. A simple repeal would flood the mails with quack remedies which would be harmful both to mothers and the movement. Furthermore, an amendment based on the Crane decision exempting the medical profession would probably have a better chance of passage.

Certainly Mrs. Dennett's "open" bill had frightened legislators. During her first sessions every one of the fifteen men whom she had asked to introduce it, had pleaded that he was either "too busy, too ignorant or too old!" In her fifth year, when the bill had been finally introduced and killed in committee, she may have agreed with Congressman Volstead, who had told her that the Comstock laws could only be expunged through a complete revision of the penal code. In any case, she ceased her Washington activities, although not her opposition to Margaret Sanger, and the "open" bill was never again introduced.

In 1926 Margaret asked Mrs. Day and Anne Kennedy to explore a new congressional approach. After many interviews, they were convinced that the "doctors' bill" might have a chance. By that time, however, Margaret was abroad preparing for the World Population Conference and afterward recovering from it. When at last she came home, her thoughts were on the upcoming legislative campaign. The fact that the league's board viewed this plan with alarm helped reconcile her to a parting of the ways. The five board members who resigned with her, including Mrs. Day and Mrs. Hepburn, joined in the new enterprise, which they hoped would bring final victory.

Since congressmen listen to local, not to Washington appeals, Margaret appointed regional, state, and district officers, utilizing many experienced suffrage organizers, such as Kate Hepburn as legislative chairman and Mrs. Timme as vice president. Frances Ackermann cooperated on finances with Noah.

There had to be a replacement, however, of Margaret's staunchest aide. When Dwight Morrow was named Ambassador to Mexico, George Rublee went along as adviser. With a new outlook, his wife conceived the idea of a film, *The Flame of Mexico,* to promote international good will. During the production of this, she shuttled between Mexico City and Hollywood. Eventually, her amateur movie was no more successful than Margaret's a decade earlier, and it was far more costly. In fact, she lost her personal fortune and although her intimacy with Margaret always continued, her role in the birth control movement receded. Into her place as confidante and traveling companion gradually moved a younger woman, who, in partnership with her husband, had helped build an excellent clinic in Cleveland. When widowed, Dorothy Brush moved to New York, where she became secretary of the National Committee on Federal Legislation.

Even before the committee had opened Washington headquarters at the close of the twenties, they had done much of their spade work. For years Margaret or one of her aides had regularly attended the national conventions of most of the large women's organizations. At her own expense Margaret had often traveled hundreds of miles to speak for five minutes at a meeting. It was not by chance, therefore, that the General Federation of Women's clubs, which endorsed the principle of birth control in 1930, shortly afterward supported the "doctors' bill" by a vote of 393–17.

The much respected George Norris, who had supported Mrs. Dennett's bill, encouraged the committee with his belief that the new bill would fare better than the former one. Nevertheless, absorbed as he was in Muscle Shoals and the Lame Duck Amendment, he wanted someone else to take the initiative. Senator Gillett of Massachusetts, the former Speaker of the House, finally consented. Since this urbane gentleman was about to retire from public life, he had nothing to lose and introduced the legislation at the close of the 1930 session. When Congress reconvened, the bill was sent to the Judiciary Committee, whose chairman, Norris, named a sub-committee with the famous Borah of Idaho, serving with Gillett and with Bratton of New Mexico.

For the first hearing, Margaret assembled an able and balanced group of witnesses, leading off with the obstetrician-in-chief of Johns Hopkins University. He was followed by a well-known sociologist, a minister, a rabbi and, for press appeal, the president of the Junior League.

Next day Representative Mary T. Norton, for many years the only woman in the House, played the stellar role. A motherly type, al-though she had never had a child, she spoke with euphoria on the blessings of large families even when penalized by poverty, which she called the spur to achievement. John Sumner, Comstock's suc-cessor as head of the Society for the Suppression of Vice, came next, and was followed by spokesmen for the Purity League, the Clean Books League, the Patriotic Society, the Southern Baptists, the Knights of Columbus and a barely extant professor emeritus of gynecology. One after another they reiterated that birth control was a Bolshevist invention, that it was against nature, God, and female decency. Indeed, it was a diabolical idea.

In *My Fight for Birth Control,* the author sums up the opposi-tion: "It was as though we were in some antediluvian age, some kingdom out of *Gulliver's Travels.* Under these words, these exposures of medieval mental processes, one could only sit in amaze-ment, enduring as best one could, the flood of personal abuse, mis-representation, deliberate prevarication, and false statement. At the beginning I had waited expectantly, anxious to learn what hon-est objections could be presented. . . . At last I closed my ears to this monotonous, repetitious chant of medieval dogmas . . . I sat back to collect my own thoughts . . . I was aroused by the voice of my friend, Kate Hepburn. . . . It was time for the rebuttal."

Margaret stepped forward, a youthful figure in her blue knit suit and matching hat, but with new tired lines on her face. She had only ten minutes, but began by answering some lies. Birth control was an American innovation of 1914, before there was a Bolshevist government. Neither the American Federation of Labor nor the American Medical Association had taken any stand on the bill. In reply to Mrs. Norton's paean to large families, she launched the verbal sensation of the day. "Jesus Christ," she observed, "was said to be an only child." At this point the opposition crossed themselves and muttered, "Blasphemy!"

Since most of the antagonists were Catholic, Margaret pointed out that only one sixth of the 120 million Americans were of that faith. No one tried to impose birth control on them and they might continue to practice self-control. But non-Catholics also had their rights and wanted to have "children conceived in love, born of parents' conscious desire . . . and with healthy and sound bodies and minds."

In the end, Gillett supported his bill, Bratton opposed it, and Borah, who had not come to the hearings, cast the decisive, negative vote. The bill was killed for 1931. Before returning to New York, the indomitable leader drafted a letter to her cohorts, asking them to start their next year's campaign.

By this time there were few persons brash enough to debate with Margaret Sanger, but one did. Chief Justice Richard Russell of Georgia's Supreme Court had fathered eighteen children, fifteen of whom had survived birth. For this reason he felt himself an authority on procreation, as well as law. Articulate about a man's right to paternity, he seems never to have thought of a woman's right to decide her maternity.

When Margaret reached Atlanta's Erlanger Theater, she found it filled with two thousand people, the first rows being Russell's progeny and their in-laws. The Chief Justice himself, an erect, white-haired patriarch, looked as though he had stepped out of the Old Testament. His main argument was, "I have followed God's command to increase and multiply."

"That command," Margaret informed him, "was given to Noah after the flood. The earth had just been depopulated."

"We don't need birth control in Georgia," Russell shifted his attack. "We need more voters because we have just lost two congressional seats. Besides, our people can't afford those contraptions."

"If they can't afford birth control," answered Margaret, "they are too poor to raise large families."

In spite of the Russell claque down front, the New York *Herald Tribune*, which covered the meeting, reported that Margaret received the most applause. Perhaps her final rebuttal was the next generation. Russell's famous namesake and thirteenth child, soon started his long senatorial career, but remaining a bachelor, he did not follow the paternal practice of multiplying.

Margaret was pleased at one congressional session when Representative Gassaway, father of fourteen, introduced her bill. He did so, believing that birth control might have spared the lives of his first wife and seven children. He used an earthy argument. "If we were as reckless to the interests of our cows, sows, and mares, it wouldn't be long before they became a scrub bunch of stock."

Since Senator Gillett had retired in 1932, Margaret had to find a new sponsor. For two years the bill was killed in committee. In 1934 the highlight was the testimony of the famous Nazi-enthusiast, radio priest, Father Coughlin. As a representative of the church, he refused to stand before a body of the state, and seated, ruddy-faced, cocksure of himself, he began facetiously. "You gentlemen are married and know more about this than I ever will." He arched his eyebrows and leered significantly. Then becoming serious, he shouted, "But I know how these materials are bootlegged in the corner drugstores near high schools. To teach children to fornicate and not get caught! All this bill means is how to commit adultery and not get caught!"

At one point a congressman interrupted to speculate as to whether any member of the House had ever used such horrible devices. Statistics suggested that they had. Out of 225 families, only a dozen had six or more children, 80 had two children and 46 a single child.

During the depression it seemed that economics would be the ultimate persuader. As Margaret kept repeating, the nation spent eight billions to support the mentally and physically degenerate. Furthermore, there were fifteen million jobless, whose birth rate was the highest in the country. Even employers who had always wanted a reservoir of cheap labor, shuddered at the thought of taxes to prevent starvation. Better perhaps to turn off the spigot of this profligate fertility than to keep on with government doles!

The main opposition was suddenly fortified. In 1931, the year after the Anglican Bishops had acted and the very year that the Federal Council of Churches endorsed birth control, Pope Pius XI issued an Encyclical. The message condemned as a "sin against nature" and a "deed shameful and intrinsically vicious" any deliberate frustration of the purpose of the conjugal act. The message was inspired by the words of St. Augustine, another bachelor, dead for fifteen centuries.

As Margaret often recalled, the celibate always glorifies undisciplined fertility. Even Luther, the onetime monk and father of Protestantism, had said, "What if a woman dies in childbirth?" After all, she was created to bear children! Priests, who talked in mystical abstractions, never consulted the mothers of the race. Neither did governments consider their needs. In the year of the Encyclical and in Rome, as though in collaboration with the pope, Mussolini launched a Five Year Baby Marathon among his poorest people—those with incomes under $1,000. He posted prizes for those producing three or more children in three years. The idea traveled around the world, finally climaxed by Toronto's "Stork Derby." There, a half million dollars was offered to the mother bearing the most babies in ten years. Margaret called it a race reducing mothers to the role of animals. When the New York Assembly voted a $75 bonus for every birth, she called for a two year moratorium on all babies. Instead, let the nation, in depression days concentrate on care of its millions of neglected children.

At the peak of the legislative campaigns a thousand organizations, representing more than twelve million women, endorsed the bill and the committee blanketed the country with hundreds of speeches. Even some Catholics were sympathetic enough to bring Margaret into a conference with Dr. Joseph J. Mundell, Professor of Obstetrics at Georgetown University. He offered to drop some objections, if she would delete a few points. The proponents believed that they had agreed upon a bill, and at the hearings they felt betrayed. Instead of supporting the revised measure, Dr. Mundell announced that there was no longer any need of legislation. Recent discoveries had shown the right solution.

The new insights were based on studies of the reproductive cycle, popularized in a book, *The Rhythm of Fertility and Sterility in Women* by L. J. Latz, issued with "ecclesiastical approval." This knowledge made it possible to assess a period safe from pregnancy with "almost mathematical precision." Since the recent Papal encyclical had condemned sexual intercourse except for the purpose of progeny, this guide to frustrate that purpose through "calendar contraception," in itself sounded paradoxical.

In rebuttal, Dr. Prentiss Williams testified that the rhythm theory had no medical standing. Dr. C. C. Little held that there had been no dependable tests on human beings or animals. Margaret summed up the pros and cons as the one favoring a scientific method under the guidance of doctors, while the other upheld "an untested method, which could be tried by any literate boy and girl."

In 1934 the Senate committee voted the bill out and it was put on the unanimous consent calendar. In the rush of the session's last day, it was passed by a voice vote. For a few minutes the supporters thought it was as good as law. Then Pat McCarran of Reno, the Catholic divorce lawyer, asked unanimous consent to recall the "doctors' bill." With senatorial courtesy, the sponsor granted the request and the bill went back to committee. Never again did it advance that far. In the next two years neither House nor Senate acted on it.

In the midst of these rebuffs, came the unexpected victory. After long delay the case of the United States *v.* One Package reached Judge Grover Moscowitz, presiding over the Federal District Court of Southern New York. This was the suit challenging the seizure of materials sent two years earlier to Dr. Stone. The government's case was based on Section 305 of the Revenue Act, which barred the importation of articles for the purpose of "preventing conception." Morris Ernst, again relying on the Crane decision, reinforced by his case before Justice Rosenbluth, argued for a broader interpretation of the law. Once more he presented former Health Commissioner Harris and other doctors who testified that contraceptives could save the lives of mothers and children. Judge Moscowitz, accepting this view, said, "We cannot assume that Congress intended to interfere with doctors prescribing for the health of the people."

The government at once appealed the case, which finally reached the Circuit Court of Appeals. Speaking for the court, Judge Augustus N. Hand not only upheld the opinion, but added that Section 305 and similar statutes had a common origin in the Comstock Law. "Its design, in our opinion, was not to prevent the importation, sale or carriage by mail of things which might intelligently be employed by conscientious and competent physicians for the purpose of saving life or promoting the well-being of their patients. . . ."

Since the unanimous opinion of this court, which included Learned Hand and Thomas Swan, was seldom reversed by the Supreme Court, birth control supporters were jubilant. Only Margaret Sanger, who had been disappointed too often, grimly went on preparing for the next legislative fight. The government still had time to appeal when at the close of January 1937, Attorney General Homer Cummings announced that it would accept the court's decision. This was the greatest single victory of the movement, and was known as the One-Package Victory.

What did the victory achieve? Once and for all, wrote Dr. Stone for the *Nation*, "it established contraception as a recognized part of medical practice and removes the last legal barriers to the dissemination of contraceptive knowledge." It opened up the mails, domestic as well as from abroad, for the carriage of materials and literature from doctors and other qualified persons. This meant that the Comstock walls were irretrievably breached.

From his own experience, Morris Ernst wrote: "In the United States we almost never repeal outmoded legislation in the field of morals. We either allow it to fall into disuse by ignoring it . . . or we bring persuasive cases to the courts and get the obsolete laws modified by judicial interpretation." Twenty years of effort to change the laws had failed, but most of the restrictions were now modified by judicial interpretation.

Margaret said that the decision closed one epoch, bringing in a new one. The sixty-three year tyranny of the Comstock Law was ended with the rights of physicians clarified. At last even the medical profession recognized this. Margaret was at Willow Lake one June morning when she read that the American Medical Association had endorsed birth control. The *Autobiography* says that she was so excited that she fell downstairs. "Here was the culmination of unremitting labor ever since my return from Europe in 1915, the gratification of seeing a dream come true." It was also the culmination of a decade of effort on the part of Dr. Dickinson and of organizational work by Dr. Prentiss Wilson.

The court decision had immediate as well as long-time effects on Margaret. It may have saved her life. For two years doctors had been urging a gall bladder operation, but she would never take time off for her own care, when her cause needed her. Now she had the operation, but was still convalescing when her conscience stirred again. From the Harkness Pavilion, she wrote a memorandum to all her field workers and supporters: "Make known to hospitals, relief agencies, philanthropic, and public health officials that the decision . . . frees their hands. Call on public health officials and ask that birth control instruction be included in their services. Establish clinics. There are today approximately 320 birth control centers in America. I look forward to seeing not twice that number, but ten times that number at the close of 1937."

The year's victories did not mean that any more women were being helped, but merely that it would be easier to help them. Now was the time for wholesale action by the states. Margaret meant to use her own army of workers and her four hundred country and congressional committees to spur the program.

There were two areas of special opportunity. In the South, where Catholic opposition was minimal, the birth rates among poor whites, as well as Negroes, were very high. Since a doctor on North Carolina's Board of Health had been converted to birth control and since Doris Duke, the tobacco heiress, would finance a pilot project, Margaret cooperated on a program of state services, which finally spread to other southern states.

The second neediest area was the "Okie" camps of the West. Uprooted and dispossessed, these migrants continued to breed. Here the Federal Security Agency offered to set up clinics, actually establishing twenty-five in the Arizona and California camps, advertising the services along with square dances and typhoid vaccinations.

On her visits to these centers, as in the South, Margaret was dissatisfied. The women were so pitifully ignorant, even of their own anatomy, that they needed other techniques. Where was the pill or hypodermic that would one day supplant them? How could she speed their development?

Before Margaret could chart the next phase of her work, she had to settle some unfinished business. The government's decision had cut short the legislative campaign that for six years had taken most of her time and taxed her strength more than any former effort. She never regretted the work, since it had been an important educational program, but it had been expensive, costing more than $150,000 in depression days. She could always raise money for special projects, but left with a deficit, she found that no one wanted to contribute for past efforts.

For twenty years Margaret had scanned obituary columns, vainly hoping that someone had left a million dollars for her cause, but she could never have foreseen the first bequest for birth control. Once, after a Los Angeles meeting, a thin, shabbily dressed woman had introduced herself as Viola Kauffman. She knew the name because there had always been a small donation since her earliest campaigns from this hard working school teacher. A year later Miss Kauffman wrote that she was leaving whatever she possessed for Margaret's work. As a courtesy, the latter asked her former secretary, Anna Lifshiz, now living in Los Angeles, to give a personal thanks to Miss Kauffman. After she had done so, Anna wrote that she doubted that the poor woman had money to keep body and soul together.

Two years later the Salvation Army notified Margaret of Miss Kauffman's death. She seemed to have only some change tied up in a handkerchief, but since Mrs. Sanger was her designated beneficiary, she must order the specified cremation, after which she would receive the remains. Margaret held a little ceremony with her staff before scattering the ashes on Willow Lake. Eventually, she learned that Viola Kauffman had invested $30,000 in real estate. It was the lifetime savings of a teacher who had lived in poverty that liquidated the congressional venture.

Meanwhile, the American Birth Control League was harassed with problems. Their affiliates, the state and local leagues, had developed a sense of territorial imperative, which instinctively repelled invasions of their areas by Margaret's zealous field workers, eager to open clinics. Furthermore, fund raisers had learned that they got nowhere without the Sanger name. Finally, a professional insisted that the two groups reunite. Under new leadership, negotiations were possible and the merger took place in 1939. Margaret, living at that time in the West, accepted the title of Honorary President. A few years later when the same fund raiser persuaded the board to change the organization's name to Planned Parenthood, she regretfully wondered if her child was again repudiating her.

By this time, however, Margaret Sanger's efforts were irretrievably committed to the world movement. Moreover, her spirits were buoyed by widespread recognition. The first great honor had come back in 1931 with the Medal of Achievement from the American Women's Association under Ann Morgan's chairmanship. Its citation said that she had "fought a battle single-handed . . . a pioneer of pioneers." Pioneer she remained above all and having crossed the last frontier in her own land, she turned to new horizons.

Sixteen years after the raid on her Town Hall meeting, Town Hall gave her their annual medal "for contributing to the enlargement and enrichment of life." Pearl Buck, the recent Nobel Prize winner, had written that Margaret Sanger's name would go down in history "as one of the company of pioneers"—again that word— "who have not been afraid to do what was to be done. . . . Such men and women live in the life of humanity to come."

In sheer amount of travel, Margaret Sanger must have made some kind of record, although she usually went abroad for the sole purpose of extending her crusade. The exceptions were her trips for information: her first to France, her wartime crossing of the English Channel to see the Dutch clinics, and her later search for contraceptives in Germany. In 1934 she had the same reason for going to Russia. At Zurich, Dr. Ruben-Wolf had given a panegyric on the Soviet Union's birth control program which Margaret wanted to inspect, especially the spermatoxin tested by a Dr. Tushnov of the Institute of Experimental Medicine.

There was much besides that she was eager to see in the vast new social laboratory, but Noah, who was seventy-four and who always fussed about accommodations, had no stomach for roughing it in a Communist country. He would go to England and after her trip, they would vacation in *gemütlich* Marienbad. Since Grant, who had finished his second year at Cornell Medical School, wanted to examine Soviet hospitals, he would accompany his mother, together with Florence Rose, her efficient new aide.

During this trip Margaret's reactions fluctuated from a chronic frustration, often close to anger, to highest admiration. She was deeply impressed to find that every child in the Soviet Union was a wanted child. Callous as the system was to both the old regime and even to old people, children always held priority. During a milk shortage, they received what there was. Legally, they were protected from exploitation and corporal punishment. In contrast to the past, most of them had superior care and schooling, and if the pupil was considered promising, he would be paid while going to college.

Because the state assumed guardianship of its youth, it relieved parents of many financial responsibilities and in some ways had upgraded its human resources. For the first time Russia's young people were literate. The best side of the system, as Margaret saw it, was the Institute for the Protection of Motherhood and Childhood, a great establishment with model clinics, nurseries, milk centers, and educational laboratories. In her *Autobiography* Margaret says that it represented an impressive effort to teach "the rudiments of hygiene to an enormous population that had previously known nothing about it." Public nurseries near every factory helped free mothers from constant child care and cooking.

At the start of her trip, in Leningrad, Margaret managed to see Dr. Tushnov, who had become the Soviets' forgotten man. He volunteered that some years back he had indeed given long-term immunization by spermatoxin against pregnancy to twenty-two out of thirty women tested. However, in the midst of his tests, the state had changed its policy and shifted his assistants to more utilitarian tasks. Furthermore, under penalty of arrest, he was forbidden to publish anything on the subject. This bitter news persuaded Margaret to promote American tests.

In Moscow she found Dr. Ruben-Wolf, who had escaped from Germany with her family when the Nazis took over. The German doctor was now in charge of one of the large abortoriums that she had described at Zurich. Although the operation was discouraged, for health reasons a skilled surgeon would perform it for the equivalent of $2.50, and it could be done in two to six minutes. Afterward, the patient was allowed an adequate convalescence with no deduction in her pay.

With Dr. Ruben-Wolf as interpreter, Margaret talked to many of the patients, who were well cared for and grateful for the operation. However, in her journal, she noted that the doctors did not use anesthesia, and she suspected that there must be needless infections because they did not wear gloves. When she asked some of the women who had returned for repeated operations, why they did not use birth control, they all said that they did not know how.

Physicians everywhere claimed that birth control was available and when the superintendent of one hospital claimed that there was a department right in his building, she insisted on seeing it. She was shown some posters and a dusty exhibit of condoms and diaphragms, but the door to the consultation room was locked. On inquiry, a young assistant explained that it had been closed for two years, while they awaited supplies.

At a reception given by Dr. Kaminsky, the Commissariat of Health, Margaret learned the current policy. It had been a pleasant social occasion at which the host had explained that the old regime's worst legacy was medical backwardness. With a new concern for their patients' welfare instead of profits, Russian doctors now stressed preventive medicine. Since preventive medicine sounded like her cue, in the question period Margaret asked about birth control. Aghast, the interpreter exploded with a tirade against Malthusianism. When he subsided, she explained her point.

Because the Soviet Union had long-range plans for farm and factory output, she thought they might have one for people. Under communism, there had been a population growth of 50 million. She had seen an abortorium and had been told that there were 400,000 such operations a year. Obviously women did not want so many pregnancies, but abortion was a cruel way to achieve family limitation. Was there no preventive plan?

When Dr. Kaminsky understood her question, he answered coldly that there had been a labor shortage for six years and so the government did not wish to restrict the population. Evidently her question seemed to him in as poor taste as it would have to the Catholic hierarchy. The People's Government was not concerned with the people's needs; instead, it insisted that they follow dictates from above. This fact would be repeatedly demonstrated. Two years after her visit, the state outlawed abortion under criminal penalties. Twenty years later, with a change of leadership, abortion was again legalized.

One day a voice from the past startled Margaret in her Moscow hotel. She did not recognize the ill-dressed, beaten-looking fellow until he identified himself as the young labor leader who had helped set up her Seattle meetings eighteen years earlier. Then she asked him to lunch, where she heard the story of this man who remained nameless in both of her accounts.

During the months when Bill Haywood was in Leavenworth and the Wobblies were being arrested, he had hired out as a ship's stoker, making his way to Russia, where he hoped to usher in the glorious new society. His dream was so far from being fulfilled that he rated her lunch the best meal he had eaten since leaving home. In her private journal she quoted his observations on the "workers' republic." Shock troops were used to speed up production, and factory machines were cleaned before and after use, on a man's own time. Why not return to the United States, she asked? He assured her that he would grab the chance, but could not get in.

Bill Haywood had succumbed to diabetes in Russia, but some said that he also had been disillusioned. He had renounced conventional loyalties to help the workers of the world, but in the end he too was a displaced person, lonely and ignored. There were rumors also of John Reed's disaffection, although he had been buried as a hero in the Kremlin. His erratic widow, Louise Bryant, was one of those who claimed that he had been spiritually as well as physically sick.

Lunch at the American embassy turned Margaret's thoughts back to those friends of her *Woman Rebel* days. Before her untimely death, Louise Bryant had married William C. Bullitt, currently the first United States ambassador to the Soviet Union. Now presiding at his table was their ten-year-old daughter. In her *Autobiography,* Margaret noted that the Russians liked Bullitt for his early defense of them, but of course did not place him in the category of John Reed.

The tour closed at Odessa, where the travelers boarded an Italian liner that looked elegant because it was clean. Russia had created a vast enthusiasm for fresh linen and for plumbing that worked. On the leisurely passage to Marseilles, Margaret's histrionic gifts flared up in a skit that she wrote and directed for the usual gala evening. To judge by a surviving verse, Margaret Sanger was no longer the woman rebel:

It's a long way to Communism; it's a hard row to hoe;
It's a big jump from Capitalism and the sweetest things we know.

You can have your Marx and Engels and work your five year plan;
But we'll take our bourgeois culture and good old Uncle Sam.

At Marienbad there was a cable from Grant, who had left earlier
to return to medical school. In New York, he had found his brother
sick again. During the last years Stuart had undergone nine operations for mastoiditis and for his sinuses, badly hurt when a squash
racket smashed the bone over one eye. The doctors were now considering a tenth operation. To thwart that possibility, Margaret gave
up her plans with Noah and started home. In New York, she accepted the alternative of a warm dry climate; so together she and
Stuart set out for Tucson, Arizona. Riding with him in his little
Ford coupe, Margaret at long last gave her elder son her full attention. Beside his health, he had several problems.

As a boy, Stuart had found his satisfactions in sports, in which
he excelled, but he was slower than Grant in finding his profession.
He had stuck out the early part of the depression as a broker on
Wall Street, but had learned that he too wanted to be a doctor. He
had been taking courses in chemistry and biology so that he could
enter medical school in the fall. Now once more he had to revise
his plans.

Tucson's climate was so obviously right for Stuart that eventually
he settled there as a physician. His mother also came to love the
place and having been drawn closer to this son than she had ever
been before, she persuaded Noah that they too must have a western
home, although for some years it was mostly a stopping-off place
between trips.

Early in 1935 Margaret received the kind of invitation that she
could never refuse. The All-India Women's Conference had endorsed
birth control and wanted her at their next meeting to perfect their
plans. An old friend, Edith How-Martyn, proposed to make the long
journey worthwhile by booking her for a three-month tour. Mrs.
How-Martyn, now director of the International Information Center,
an outgrowth of the Geneva conference, would do the advance
work. Here was a chance to reach the second largest population in
the world, a population second to none in poverty and growth rate.

The tour opened that November with two memorable days with Gandhi. His note, in answer to her own, greeted her on landing. "Do, by all means, come whenever you can. And you shall stay with me, if you would not mind what must appear to be our extreme simplicity; we have no masters and no servants here."

Although he lived in egalitarian simplicity, Margaret found it hard in caste-ridden India to travel without a retinue. Friends told her that she must have someone to care for her bedding, which had to be taken everywhere with her, make train reservations, and buy food en route. So for the first time she traveled with not only a secretary, but a servant, who needed an extra coolie for his luggage.

A two-wheel cart met her at Warha, the village nearest to Gandhi's settlement. It was Monday, his day of silence, so she was merely presented in the large room where he sat in meditation, cross-legged on the floor. Rising at once, he beamed in wordless greeting. His appearance, says her *Autobiography,* was perhaps even more exaggerated than his pictures: "His ears stuck out more prominently; his shaved head was more shaved; his toothless mouth grinned more broadly, leaving a great void between his lips. But around him, and a part of him was a luminous aura. And once you had seen this, the ugliness faded and you glimpsed the something in the essence of his being which people have followed and which had made them call him the Mahatma."

She accepted him as a saint, never wanting anyone's support more than his, and yet even that first day was disappointed. Everything was so crudely inefficient from the primitive irrigation system and cotton-growing to the paper-making and oil press. "It seemed so pitiable an effort, like going backward instead of forward and trying to keep millions laboring on petty hand processes merely to give them work to do by which they might exist."

Mrs. Gandhi, who had been a child bride, marrying a child husband, both twelve years old, still supervised the meals, where everyone sat on the floor, helping himself with his fingers to the large array of fruits and vegetables served on shining trays. Hot milk, soups, and porridge rounded out the menus.

Writing on a slate, Gandhi invited Margaret to join him next day on his early morning walk. A few others came also, while along the way, men, women, and children waited near their homes to see him pass. Some prostrated themselves as before a holy man. Skirting the refuse of the narrow alleys, the walkers came at last to the open fields, studded with occasional huts, enlivened with babies, goats, and dogs. Some people were out bathing themselves or preparing for the day.

In their two long talks Gandhi and Margaret agreed completely on the need for family limitation, but they could not agree on how. Total abstinence was for him the only moral way. He argued that wives should resist their husbands and if need be, separate from them to avoid sexual relations. To Margaret this was not only unrealistic, but disastrous. He was courteously silent when she spoke, but when he resumed his argument, he seemed not to have heard her. There was no dialogue.

To Gandhi, sexual union was merely lust. He deplored the fact that in his youth he had desired his wife, and he now included celibacy as a cardinal virtue, along with truth, nonviolence, fearlessness, and self-control. Margaret felt that he had no rational view of married love, but had reverted to the Eastern asceticism so like the priestly view of Christianity.

Perhaps by way of consolation Gandhi finally assured her that her efforts had not been wasted. He was infinitely kind, but she knew that he would never help her. Saintly though he was and possessed of such spiritual force that he could win a bloodless war of independence for his people, he seemed to Margaret to have odd gaps in his judgment. To expect illiterate girls, married as children, many living in purdah, to exert such moral suasion on their husbands as to limit sexual relations to three or four times in a life, was incredible. It was more naive than hoping to turn back the Industrial Revolution with hand spinning.

More congenial were the views of the poet Rabindranath Tagore. Although the first to hail Gandhi as "Mahatma!" years previously he had written Margaret the best answer to the Gandhian view.

Santiniketan,
September 30, 1925

DEAR MARGARET SANGER,

I am of the opinion that the Birth Control Movement is a great movement not only because it will save women from enforced and undesirable maternity, but because it will help the cause of peace by lessening the number of surplus population of a country, scrambling for food and space outside its own rightful limits. In a hunger-striken country like India it is a cruel crime thoughtlessly to bring more children to existence than could be taken care of, causing endless suffering to them and imposing a degrading upon the whole family. It is evident that the utter helplessness of a growing poverty very rarely acts as a check controlling the burden of over-population. It proves that in this case nature's urging gets the better of the severe warning that comes from the providence of civilized social life. Therefore, I believe, that to wait till the moral sense of man becomes a great deal more powerful than it is now and till then to allow countless generations of children to suffer privations and untimely death for no fault of their own is a great social injustice which should not be tolerated. I feel grateful for the cause you have made your own and for which you have suffered.

. . . .

Sincerely yours,
RABINDRANATH TAGORE

Almost at the other end of the continent from Wahra, beyond Calcutta, Tagore lived in the House of Peace on an estate used in part for agricultural experiments. With his wide-ranging, humanistic concerns, his long white hair and beard, his handsome head with meditative eyes, he seemed an Eastern version of Havelock Ellis. In spite of wealth, he lived in monastic simplicity, his room filled with books and papers. Like the ancients, he taught his students in a mango grove or under banyan trees.

Among India's intellectuals, another leader who gave Margaret both practical aid and hope was Mme. Pandit, the future ambassador to the United Nations and later the president of the United Nations General Assembly. Sister of Jawaharlal Nehru, who was then in England and was already considered Gandhi's heir, her active sympathy suggested future cooperation.

As Margaret made her trek around India, she came to know the country as have few visitors. Occasionally she was entertained in the palace of a maharaja, but she also spent hours in the worst slums of Bombay. With an interpreter, she talked to the lean women with their children, weak-limbed and sunken-eyed. Her *Autobiography* stresses the omnipresent contrasts: "The loveliest architecture in the world was set against nauseating squalor. Wealth beyond calculation existed alongside poverty that was living death, dazzling mental attainments beside an ignorance utterly abysmal." After the Women's Conference, she might have added that the will of the majority was commonly ignored at the whim of the mighty.

Toward the end of December Margaret reached the tip of the continent, the state of Travancore. There a remarkable Parsi, Mrs. Rustomiji Feridoonji, was the guiding spirit of the Women's Conference and hoped to add birth control to the public health program. Already some municipalities supported a form of socialized medicine, sending out midwives and doctors to the poorest areas. Mrs. Feridoonji insisted that wherever vaccination went, birth control should go too. Margaret helped to draw up plans and prepared to speak for them.

But if Mrs. Feridoonji was the mind and spirit of the conference, its titular head was the maharani of Travancore. Entertaining at a lavish garden party the day before the opening, she asked Margaret to return the next morning for a further word in private. Since the birth control resolution was to come up at nine, Margaret agreed with some misgivings and appeared at the palace well in advance of that time.

While Margaret nervously saw her watch tick off the precious minutes, the maharani inquired solicitously about every member of her guest's family. Finally her hostess came to the point, which she admitted was a delicate one. She would like the American guest to abstain from the debate and to shift her own talk to some other subject—brothels, for instance. True, there were none in Travancore, but it was a subject on which all women agreed.

With as much patience as she could manage, Margaret reminded the great lady that she had come all the way from New York to support birth control. The maharani sighed. A group of Catholics, including her own social secretary, had threatened to walk out if the resolution passed. Once again, in far-off India, Margaret was confronting a Catholic cabal! Surely, she insisted, the needs of millions of people outweighed the feelings of a few foreigners. Reluctantly, the maharani yielded, but to placate the opposition, she allowed them two speeches for every one in favor of the resolution.

The maharani's ruling produced a tedious day, like a rerun of all the arguments that Margaret had heard for twenty years. At the end, three-fourths of the delegates voted for birth control. No Indian opposed it, only Eurasians. No married woman opposed it, only spinsters. Because of their stand that day, the All-India Women's Association emerged as a meaningful force.

On this first trip to India, Margaret's chief impact was on the medical profession. She addressed the All-India Obstetrical and Gynecological Congress at its initial meeting; she spoke to the All-India Nursing and Medical Association at Hyderabad and to many district and local associations. Usually she showed two films, *The Biology of Human Reproduction* and a training lesson for doctors on contraception. Everywhere she left gyneplacques, models of the female reproductive organs, which were unknown in India. Although the phallus had played a part in traditional Hindu worship, the female organs were shrouded in mystery. Among Moslems, where purdah existed, this was natural, since a doctor might not see, much less examine, a woman patient. Instead, he used a medicine doll on which the midwife marked the area of pain. From this he made his diagnosis. At best, few Indians ever saw a doctor, but the enforcement of such standards of female modesty raised the toll of maternal and infant deaths to what Indians called Himalayan heights.

Because most of the population lived on one poor meal a day, they could not dream of buying any contraceptives. Margaret had brought along a new kind; harmless, usually effective, easily available, and a year's supply cost only twenty cents. It was a foam powder made from rice and supplemented by a rubber sponge.

Most doctors doubted that Indian women would use any contraceptive, but wherever Margaret had the chance to question them, they showed the universal and desperate desire to be free from constant pregnancy. But there was a stumbling block. Although parents were hungry because of their large families, their children were their only social security. Men wanted at least two sons, preferably a dozen, to care for them in old age.

Margaret's talks persuaded forty-five local medical societies to launch their first birth control programs, while fifty hospitals and clinics set up information centers. This was a drop in the Indian sea of need, but it was a start.

In her ten-thousand-mile tour of India, Margaret gave sixty-four lectures along with uncounted informal talks and interviews. She endured intense heat, perpetual motion, and fatigue. As if indestructible, she let Mrs. How-Martyn book her for the return trip and met her schedule in Rangoon and Malaya. However, in Hong Kong, she was seized with acute pains. Good trouper that she was, she dosed herself with codeine so that she might finish her lectures before seeing a doctor. He diagnosed a gall bladder attack and rushed her to a hospital where she was trapped for two weeks. Ignominiously, she had to cancel her China schedule, which she always regretted. This halted her last chance to return to the world's largest nation.

Delaying the gall bladder operation until she reached home, she managed to fulfill her Hawaiian lectures. They went so well that she complacently kept on postponing the operation in order to meet her lecture requests. The most challenging of these looked like a reprieve for her China failure. The Chinese Medical Association, prompted by Mme. Chiang Kai-shek, asked her to return as their guest. The press welcomed the news of Margaret Sanger's sailing to the Orient armed with contraceptives to halt China's teeming millions. But from the start the trip was disastrous. During a rough sea, she slipped on deck, breaking her arm. The ship's doctor set it so badly that it had to be rebroken and reset in Tokyo. Nevertheless, nothing but a war would stop her this time, but war did. While under surgery, Japan bombed China and the invasion of the mainland commenced. Margaret, accepting her fate, returned home.

The totalitarian states were demanding lebensraum for their respective and unrestricted numbers of yellow-skinned, black-haired, and blond babies. Japan had first shown that the League of Nations was only a "paper league" when it seized Manchuria. Mussolini had confirmed it when he bombed the Abyssinians. Hitler then seized and fortified the Rhineland and was even now taking Austria. Soon he would welcome Chamberlain to Munich and take the Sudetenland.

For a second time Margaret saw the world plunging toward Armageddon. It was not just the slaughter that she dreaded, but that war turned the clock back on all progress. During the Tokyo stopover, Shidzue Ishimoto had described her country's internal events. To defeat their opponents, the militarists had resorted to murder. They had revived the "Dangerous Thought" law, which was creating widespread terror and repression. Dr. Majima was in prison, and all of the birth control clinics were closed. Shidzue herself was under surveillance, although her husband had joined the empire-builders and was in Manchuria exploiting the mineral resources.

Elsewhere the tide ran the same, with repression destroying Margaret's work. The Nazis, who had long since closed the clinics, were now exhorting every soldier to leave the Fatherland children, or at least prospective ones. Himmler encouraged German women to beget the offspring of soldiers, "even outside wedlock." As war spread, so did these attitudes. When France fell, Marshal Pétain declared that in the future girls would be trained only for the traditional role of raising brave men. Blaming defeat on Conscious Generation (the old Syndicalist Slogan), he said that it had "eaten away French virility and was threatening race suicide." Race suicide became the world's new bogy.

In spite of the One-Package Victory of 1937, not all legal points had been settled. Two years later, a district court upheld the closing of the mothers' clinic in Pittsfield, Massachusetts. Another court supported the Connecticut ban on the use of contraceptives. Margaret's New England friends begged her to come and defend her cause. When she did so, she found an emotional climate like that of twenty years before. In the largest Boston parish, Father Connor read Pétain's words, adding that birth control was "unpatriotic and disgraceful." This was repeated at every mass. "God will not be mocked," warned the priest. "Nations preaching birth control will disappear from the stage of life, as have ancient Rome and France."

His words echoed across the nation, some priests elaborating the point. "Better a baptized idiot than a child unborn," declaimed Father Joseph Vaughn on radio KFAC, Los Angeles.

The Worcester and Springfield, Massachusetts, papers printed anonymous letters, signed "Patriot," attacking the "chief proponent of the subversive doctrine undermining American virility." Catholic pressure against Margaret Sanger was so great that "in the interest of harmony," the New Haven Board of Education canceled her meeting in the high school and Holyoke's Congregational Church did the same. In this case, there was a heartwarming twist to the episode, when Catholic labor leaders offered their hall "in the interest of free speech and fair play." With only two hours to notify the public, handbills attracted an overflow crowd.

Personal losses darkened these years. At the age of eighty and with a fatal growth in his throat, Havelock Ellis died in the summer of 1939. In her sparsely written journal, Margaret noted: "It seemed for days that something deeply vital had ceased to function. The security of his friendship was one of the delights of my life. But to see him last year . . . to realize his frailty. . . . It was no kindness to wish it otherwise. A great man, a beautiful spirit, a world's work done. What more can one ask of life? Finis."

More poignant was the loss of Dr. Hannah Stone because she was only forty-seven and still doing the world's work. "God should be petitioned and questioned on why this should be done to us," was Margaret's stern reaction. Little publicized, Dr. Stone was one of whom friends spoke only in superlatives. Because the clinic could not afford her, she had worked there without pay, building an outstanding institution. At her death, she left a file of 100,000 case histories, which impressed the medical profession far more than any argument. Furthermore, her file offered invaluable aid for future innovators in contraception. She herself had become the nation's chief authority in her field, and with her husband, a noted urologist, she had written *A Marriage Manual*. Eventually, Dr. Abraham Stone took her place as director of the enlarged clinic.

Early in 1941 came a letter from Shidzue Ishimoto, prescient not only for its grasp of her nation's policy, but of her own remarkable future. She feared that this would be her last communication until peace came to the Pacific. No individual could stop the tide that was sweeping their shore.

"I feel now," she wrote, "that I am actually reviewing the panorama of revolution here in this country. We are losing all of the charms of life in discarding the old order, yet we do not know what is coming. . . . We have read in history the story of revolution with thrills, but it is trying, disagreeable to stand through.

"After long mental sufferings, disappointments and rethinking I have come to the conclusion that . . . we must have an infinite faith in the future. So I try to keep my courage in an attempt to build a new future program for our women through studying the history of women of the world. . . ."

On December 7, 1941, Margaret Sanger, still the unswerving pacifist that she had been in 1917, wrote bitterly in her journal: "So it has come to pass, as many pro-British Americans have wished and prayed it would. Now all promises not to send our boys to fight on foreign soil are off." In another vein, she added, "Stuart and Barb have named the baby Margaret. . . . Blue eyes, delicate features and going to be lovely I know." Thus she greeted her new joy, Margaret Sanger II.

At this time the Slees were living in the Catalina foothills near Tucson. Before the depression, Noah had sold his Three-in-One Company and had gone through the bad years with better luck than most people. Although his fortune dwindled, there was nothing material that he lacked. On the other hand, there was nothing now to which he looked forward. Eighty-two years old and often ailing, his interests had shrunk while Margaret's had taken on a global scale. In Tucson there was no outlet for his practical skills, which had once made him his wife's partner and added purpose to his life.

Not long after Pearl Harbor, Noah had two falls in one evening. Since the doctor found no damage, they blamed his unsteadiness on a refill of an Old Fashioned cocktail. But Margaret thought her husband greatly changed. She took no trip away from him that year and tried to adapt to his desires. Because it annoyed him when she concentrated on writing, she took up painting, like Grandma Moses, and she too was a grandmother. Hers also were bright, decorative pieces, although in Mexican instead of New England tradition. This new vocation was more sociable than writing, and she never minded Noah's interruptions. Cut off from her work by the war, as well as by Noah's illness, she found pleasure in her hobby and to perfect herself, took a correspondence course in painting.

In her starkly frank journal, she had written harshly of Noah's petty tyrannies. Perhaps now she saw that marriage had not been easy for him either. With few activities of his own, it had been hard to have a wife so famous and self-sufficient. As his own confidence diminished, he had tried to keep her home with querulous complaints, but at the call of her work, she had always left him. Later she had returned to his loneliness, full of her own pressing responsibilities. Once she asked him if his years of marriage with her had been happy. He could not say that they had all been happy, but he pleased her by adding that they were never dull.

The Slees went back to Willow Lake in the spring of 1943, but in the early summer Noah had another fall. Half paralyzed, he later wanted to return to the sunshine of the West. This time they lived in a house near the center of Tucson, within easy call of doctors. Noah's chief pleasure was an electric buzzer on his chair, by which he could summon Margaret wherever she was. At last he had a full-time wife, but the jovial country squire had long since departed. "He wants to die," Margaret wrote to her friend Dorothy Gordon, "but his heart is too strong and regular. So he lingers helpless and depressed. It is so sad that I weep and weep my eyes out . . ." "I am totally decrepit," he dictated in a note to his niece, Carol. "Really I do not understand why I am kept here. . . . There is no joy in being aged."

A week later, on the first day of summer 1943, he was dead. In her journal his wife wrote, "I was close to him this whole year. The household revolved around his every wish, his food, his comforts. He never failed to tell the world how wonderful, how intelligent I am, but never told me. It might spoil me . . . go to my head. (True too)," she added ruefully. "So as one looks back on those years from 1921 to 1943, all the petty irritations and annoyances are wiped out. Death removes them all. It was not the memories of the unreal, only the goodness, kindness and loving things remain in my thoughts of J. Noah. I'm glad of that."

Belonging to the World

29

After cataclysm comes rebuilding. Whole cities and nations lay in ruins and along with them, the international movement to which Margaret Sanger was committed. To start all over took courage and this time something harder—courage restrained by everlasting patience. Feeding the hungry, sorting out displaced people, and putting up essential structures were the European priorities. Not since the First World War was Margaret so long diverted from her work.

Of course she had her own involvements in World War II, for her sons, both doctors and now both married, had served overseas. Stuart was wounded in the Battle of the Bulge while Grant in the navy, was out in the Pacific. Their mother had never again hoped to enjoy such a Christmas as that of 1945 with her dear ones safely home in Tucson. Writing of the great joy in her journal, she noted that "they were all here this morning for the tree." "All" meant Grant with his wife and young sons, as well as Stuart's family, now enriched with a second little girl.

Grant soon went east to settle his future, which eventually was as a surgeon attached to New York's Presbyterian Hospital. Stuart built an excellent practice as an internist in Tucson, where his daughters became his mother's abiding delight. The small namesake had at once crept into the bleak spot in her heart, which had never recovered from the loss of Peggy. Instead of talking to Margaret II as to a child, she had bridged the generations by making her a friend and confidante. Whatever her maternal failures, Margaret was an in-

spired grandmother. This role, with unspecified functions, not including routine domesticity, suited a person belonging chiefly to the
world.

Grounded in Arizona at this period, she lived to some extent like
other women, although the many facets of her nature began to
amaze even her friends. She, who had often been called single-
minded, was now likened by an admirer to a lovely fountain that
was never turned off.

Two of the new facets had been activated by Dorothy Gordon,
singer, painter and later founder of the radio and television Youth
Forum. Their friendship, as Margaret once wrote, ripened into "a
sort of kinship different from anything else." They had met as
travelers, not personages, and indeed had established some intimacy
before the Gordons learned that their new acquaintance was the
famous Margaret Sanger. In July, 1923, they had unsuspectingly accompanied the Slees on their deferred honeymoon, a cruise to Alaska.
Later Mr. Gordon had become Noah's lawyer and their sons enjoyed
Stuart and Grant. The families often visited in each other's homes,
at which times the younger woman was of course drawn into the
birth control movement; more unusual, she, in turn, affected Margaret's life.

Dorothy Gordon brought with her the world of music. With her
help, Margaret built a library of fine records and to further her education, even took piano lessons. As an opera enthusiast, she brightened her days with music. It was also Dorothy Gordon who encouraged her hobby. On a visit to Tucson, Mrs. Gordon had equipped
herself with an easel and paints, which, after brief use, she left with
her hostess. Margaret's delight in her new venture helped her to endure Noah's long illness; more than that, it gave her resilience over
the years. Instead of desiccating as a frustrated reformer, she kept
young with creative, widening concerns.

During the forties Margaret Sanger was not only Tucson's most
distinguished citizen, but the favorite to enliven dinner parties. Furthermore, she was not above working for her cause at the local level,
for she organized a mothers' clinic, which she supported with an
annual fund-raising lecture.

Since she did not approve of living in the past, she sold her two homes. Willow Lake had served its purpose and the midtown Tucson house had been convenient during Noah's illness, but not congenial. Stuart easily persuaded her that the ideal spot on which to build was alongside his swimming pool. There the granddaughters might run in to say good morning after their early dip.

Her first hope was that Frank Lloyd Wright of Phoenix would draft her plans, but he would not do so for that site. Later the press quoted him as saying that the house was essentially her own design, which was true, although she had professional help. Her years with Bill Sanger had given her some know-how, and she had courage to build what she wanted, a home as modern and unusual as herself. Topped by a studio, most of the structure was on the ground floor, the rooms widening, fan-shaped, with a forty-foot glass frontage onto the Catalina foothills.

While the building rose, its owner took a correspondence course in interior decorating, although again she did not try to meet conventional standards. Essentially, her house was a showcase for her treasures. There were "the ancestors," two majestic portraits, given by the mayor of Shanghai. Nearby were French tapestries, Korean chests, Persian rugs, Japanese scrolls, and a smiling Buddha. A museum house, some thought it, but indubitably the setting of a planetary personage.

It was also the setting for international delicacies. Although she had seldom had time for domestic arts, she had always enjoyed them and on her travels had gathered foreign recipes and costumes. With a flair for cooking, she now earned a reputation for her chicken curries and exotic dishes. The Stuart Sangers, dining with her Thursday evenings, enjoyed a gourmet's tour of the world. Each menu of a foreign land was enhanced by appropriate ceremonies, as well as the costumes worn by both hostess and granddaughters. Sometimes she staged large, gala, international parties. Increasingly fastidious, she trained the White Russian couple who for many years had cared for the Slees, to make what they served unique as well as delicious.

While she marked time in this agreeable fashion, the first stirrings from the old European movement finally came in 1946 from unbombed, neutral Sweden. Mrs. Ottesen-Jensen, who would be a steady force for reconstruction, called a conference on sex education, with the broader hope of reactivating international concern. This was the signal for which Margaret was waiting; she was ready to give the balance of her life to rebuilding her cause. Well along in her sixties and in frail health, the comforts of her personal life were as nothing compared to her commitment.

On her way to Stockholm, Margaret stopped off to see the ailing H. G. Wells. When he had spoken in Phoenix at the start of the war, she had written sadly in her journal that he had become "a typical propagandist." In the First World War he and Shaw had courageously remained internationalists. Perhaps during the Battle of Britain, she realized that it was easier to stay philosophically aloof in Arizona than in London. In any case, after the Armistice, she had plied him with food packages, as she had all of her English friends. Recently he had cabled cheerful messages, such as, "Come on over. Won't last long" and "Last big chance. Really dying." So she came to say good-by to the final flicker of that lusty, exploring spirit who had completely understood her work. A few weeks later, he was gone.

In Stockholm, where she was the featured speaker, she cooperated on a plan for a British conference in 1948. Sanguinely, an English doctor took on the double duty of setting up an organization committee and of locating accommodations. After six months with no report, she crossed the ocean again. At her age, she could not afford postponement of the plans; that would have been the ultimate betrayal of her cause. Beneath her fragile exterior was a steel-like resolve to do whatever had to be done, if need be by herself. With no mandate, she simply took matters into her own hands, which luckily, were not empty. Mrs. Stanley McCormick, now her close friend, had given her a check "for her dreams."

Most of Margaret's former advisers in England, that brilliant group of friends and writers, were gone. But Julian Huxley remained, and so did Clinton Chance. The latter's discriminating hospitality brought together a new set of experts and officials. No doubt one of them mentioned Cheltenham, for Margaret inspected and then acclaimed this spa town in Gloucestershire, as a charming substitute for crowded, battered London.

The chief roadblock to a conference was the morale of the trustees of the old movement, more badly wrecked than their bombed-out mothers' clinic. They protested that with a shortage of funds and manpower, they could not assume the burden of an international meeting. Mrs. McCormick's check transformed the burden into an opportunity for re-establishing themselves.

The Cheltenham Conference on Population and World Resources in Relation to the Family—another mouth-filling name chosen by the heirs of the Neo-Malthusians—went off as scheduled. With a new look, featuring Sir John Boyd Orr of the United Nations Food and Agriculture Organization, it ensured a permanent future. At the last session, the delegates voted that in 1952 they would launch an international association.

After more than a decade of death and stagnation, the movement was reviving. Aware that her own time was running out, Margaret Sanger planned boldly. Since the population crisis was centered in the Far East, that should be the launching pad. India was the ideal site. Not only was world attention on the new nation, but it was the first large country to give at least verbal endorsement to family planning.

In high excitement Margaret wrote of the opportunity to Lady Rama Rau, head of India's association. The latter's reaction was the same as the British had been and for the same reason. Their Himalayan domestic needs made it impractical to take on international responsibilities. The fact that the proposed host country shied away from the honor was not important to Margaret Sanger. Again she simply bought support by underwriting the expenses. At this point in history, lack of local funds and even whispers of "a one-woman movement" would not stop her. Somehow, she would find the money and after success, everyone would be reconciled.

Meanwhile, the one nation that was urgently begging for her help was denied it. Defeat had ended the hope of Japanese expansion and paved the way for birth control. A new political leader was campaigning on this issue, a familiar figure with another name,

Shidzue Kato, the former Baroness Ishimoto. The extraordinary career of this "Japanese Margaret Sanger" had arisen from the tragedy of her marriage.

As a young man, the Baron had embraced socialism with fanatic zeal. Later, as he began to doubt that it was the wave of the future, he dropped it. After fumbling a political career, he consoled himself with the geishas and then, reverting completely to his class interests, joined the empire-builders, deserted his family, and settled in Manchuria.

When the government closed the birth control clinics and imprisoned Dr. Majimi, Shidzue herself was suspect for her pacifism, as well as her connection with the clinics. She was briefly imprisoned and then kept under house arrest. Nevertheless, she managed during the war to divorce her husband. He had taught his young bride to honor labor leaders and now she married an important one, Kanjo Kato, whom she described as "a man's man, not sweet like candy." At the age of forty-eight, in the midst of an air raid, this remarkable woman gave birth to a daughter. When the Emperor announced peace, she wept with thanksgiving.

In 1946, with 13 million women voting for the first time, both Katos ran for seats in the Diet. Mark Gayn, author of *A Japanese Diary,* was on hand at a street rally for Shidzue's political debut. Opponents were attacking her variously as an "unreformed patrician," a radical, and an unprincipled female supporting birth control. He found her poised, charming, and bilingually witty. Raising her Samurai voice to "metallic" audibility, she gathered an amazed crowd, remaining calm and courteous during the later question period.

Both Katos, Social Democrats, were elected and she, being the best known of the women legislators, spoke for them all when they were received by General MacArthur. "We Japanese women," she pledged, "will never vote for militarists." Peace was their foremost concern; second, the ending of the feudal family system. When she was assigned to the committee which wrote the constitution, she was prepared to draft the sections outlawing discrimination on account of sex.

Meanwhile, rice riots and unemployment kept the spotlight on Japan's excess population. After defeat, whole families from China, Manchuria, and other occupied lands had hurried back to their crowded islands. In spite of war losses, the census recorded 80 million and each year added another million. With army sanitation, the death rate had dropped; with peace and the returning soldiers, marriage and birth rates had soared. The one hopeful fact was that by now a consensus favored population curbs. Dr. Majimi had not only reopened his clinics, but multiplied their numbers. More sensational and dubious was the effect of a eugenics law legalizing abortion.

To the uninformed man it seemed easier to have a foetus cut out of his wife's body than to practice birth control. In the first year there had been a million operations—more potential life lost than by the atomic bombs. That was why Shidzue, head of the Family Planning Association, wanted Margaret Sanger to dramatize the issue.

There was no place that Margaret desired more to be than Japan, but history was curiously repeating itself. Her attempt to go there in the twenties had been vetoed by native militarists. A quarter of a century later the commander of the occupation forces did the same. There was no mystery. As Tokyo's largest paper put it: "In view of the pressure of the Catholic Church groups, it was believed impossible for General MacArthur to allow her [Mrs. Sanger] to lecture to Japanese audiences without appearing to subscribe to her views." There were 130,000 Catholics in a population of 80,-000,000.

Arguing that mass protests would again overcome the ban, Shidzue collected thousands of petition signatures. The press on both sides of the Pacific also entered the controversy. Wrote Eleanor Roosevelt in her column: "There is a problem in Japan with its tremendous yearly increase in population and its limited resources. . . . Mrs. Sanger was the obvious person to consult, and why our occupying forces should interfere with the wishes of the Japanese people in this respect is a little difficult to understand."

For seven months cables and letters shuttled to and from General Headquarters and spokesmen for the Sanger tour. Finally Florence

Stephenson Mahoney, a long-time friend and a resident of Washington, took over the negotiations. General Sams, chief of public health and welfare for the occupation forces, told her that he had personally stopped the visa because they "did not need Margaret Sanger barnstorming in Japan." Furthermore, as he solemnly explained, "birth control has nothing to do with population problems." The latter depended on business enterprise. This rationale had been developed sometime earlier when a Scripps Foundation study had warned that only birth control could correct the imbalance caused by Japan's mounting population and dwindling resources. The report had caused such a storm among Catholics that it had been suppressed.

General MacArthur himself finally tried to close the incident with a lofty reminder that he was swayed by neither the advocates for nor opponents of birth control. His policy was based "purely on a matter of principle." More than a year later, when the visa was suddenly available, it was not because irresistible force had crashed through the immovable object, but because the object had been catapulted out of the way. General MacArthur had been relieved of his command on April 11, 1951.

Margaret could not leave at once because of a new obstacle, more maddening than the general's interference. While vacationing with the Stuart Sangers, she had suffered a coronary thrombosis, hospitalizing her for six weeks. She then agreed to postpone Japan until the fall of 1952, combining it with her trip to India.

From this time on she suffered recurrent and severe angina pains, making her dependent on various drugs. Seldom again was she free from physical ailments, sufficient to keep anyone else at home. Dorothy Brush, now Mrs. Alexander C. Dick, wrote in *Our Margaret Sanger,* "The human limitations which apply to most of us, just never apply to her at all. She treats her body like a Victorian child . . . it must be seen and not heard; if it aches, it must ache in silence." She offered an extraordinary example.

In 1949, Smith College had awarded Margaret the honorary degree of LL.D., which pleased her greatly, perhaps the more so since she had missed the chance of a college education. On leaving the campus, Mrs. Dick accidentally slammed the car door on Margaret's hand. For a moment she slumped over with the pain. Then, since no bones were broken, she refused to see a doctor and asked her friend to drive on, but just not talk for a while. After a period she announced that she was all right. Dismissing the blood blisters on her hand, Margaret insisted that she felt only "a great white light of burning joy" over the day. To Mrs. Dick this was something of a miracle, but it was not unique. In the same book of memoirs, a doctor tells of listening for two hours as Margaret first spoke and then answered questions, while all the time he knew that she was suffering "piercing pains" from a sacroiliac strain. Like a good trouper, Margaret Sanger ignored infirmities by concentrating on her main concern.

The summer before her grand tour she kept four secretaries busy with her global mail. At the age of seventy-three, although not even her sons guessed it, she faced two major undertakings. The success of the Indian conference depended on her advance preparations. She alone was responsible for the site, which most people thought recklessly remote from the source of potential delegates. To assure a representative gathering, she ran a double-pronged campaign, wheedling Near Eastern doctors to come to Bombay and at the same time cajoling American donors to pay the travel cost. For moral authority, as well as publicity, she lined up prestigious sponsors, with the American group headed by Eleanor Roosevelt, Albert Einstein, and other Nobel Prize winners.

Whenever able, she shared her conference plans with one of these local groups, where she was always in demand. Sitting among her friends—whether or not she had met them, they took a corporate pride in their celebrity—she confided her hopes. A small figure, with bright, arresting eyes, she was always perfectly turned out these days with beguilingly tinted copper hair. She played adeptly on their heart strings as she described India's sunken-eyed, spindle-legged children and their gaunt mothers doomed to an annual pregnancy. Suddenly and quite spontaneously, one of the audience would announce that she was collecting money for Margaret's needs. What neighbor could resist? The guest of honor, with head tilted in her listening way, would then relax as substantial contributions poured in.

Not everyone helped; those closest opposed her. Stuart wanted her to abandon the whole trip, and four doctors agreed. If she went, warned one, he did not expect her return. She just laughed. Why did they think she was there? Most of her friends and relatives were dead, and she lingered only so that she might reactivate the movement. For more than a decade she had marked time and now was ready to pour out her life in this commitment.

The Sangers were reassured to know that Dr. Abraham Stone and Dorothy Dick would accompany her. For them it was a heavy and frustrating responsibility. At the start, after excessive hospitality on their Hawaiian stopover, Margaret suffered a slight attack. Rallying, she not only squelched plans to protect her from over-exertion, but suddenly improvised a large thank-you dinner for her hosts.

Perhaps Juliet Rublee was still her best interpreter. Trying to explain to Mrs. Dick how their friend functioned, she wrote that of course Margaret had "realized that she was in danger of possibly sudden death. . . . Her only hope was to be left alone and untrammeled." Then she could follow truth and God's guidance. Naturally her guardians were hurt when she withdrew from them, but sometimes she "had to be alone, absolutely quiet," as when the car door slammed on her. Then she received help from "cosmic forces."

In Japan, Margaret needed all possible help, as well as her trouper's art of conveying youthful delight. Her welcome surpassed the sensational one of the twenties. When she walked down the gangplank, it was like stepping into *The Mikado*. Fifty young women in ceremonial kimonos were bowing and smiling in a receiving line. She was crowned with a golden wreath of chrysanthemums, while a hundred and forty news and camera men swarmed about her.

Soon she was rushed off for interviews, a broadcast, a reception, and then dinner. With her picture daily on the front page, everyone recognized her. Treating her like a movie star, people crowded close to touch or kiss her hand. By the end of the week she wrote that she was "tired enough to die." Yet, outwardly, she remained serene and smiling.

In her unscheduled hours, she visited Dr. Majimi's clinics, consulted on the extension of work through the Health Ministry, and suggested setting up a teaching clinic, an educational program, and research into maternal health statistics.

The great innovation was Shidzue's sound trucks. A fleet of them covered the working class districts, announcing, "Sanger is here. Sanger says no abortions." Where there were crowds, "Sanger" mounted the platform to explain the superiority of birth control right to the people. Shaken by defeat, Japan was looking for new solutions and hailed her as a prophet. Her message would free people not only from excess children, but from future wars. With Shidzue's skill and the coverage by the powerful Mainichi press, which sponsored her tour, in ten days the issue of birth control permeated Japan as it never had the United States.

India was different. Since most people lived in villages scattered over the vast continent, divided by every barrier, including caste, language, and illiteracy, mass media offered no short cuts. The new administration had endorsed birth control, but Margaret wanted to learn what they were doing.

The ceremonial welcome was exhilarating. For the first time a large nation sent a top official to greet them, Vice President Radhakrishnan, a leader of UNESCO. The mayor of Bombay also welcomed the group and entertained them at his palace. A year's efforts at rounding up delegates had paid off with representatives from sixteen countries, several of them from the Near East who had never before attended such meetings.

The government already had a record of deeds with two hundred functioning clinics and a promise of a hundred more on army posts. Furthermore, the new Five-Year Plan listed family planning as a major goal. Paltry of course was the $1.3 million allotted to the work, but the partition of the continent, followed by riots and vast refugee problems, had drained its resources. Margaret saw that with the best of good will, the new administration could not rapidly change the habits of villagers who believed that children were God's gifts and that two sons were needed to care for a couple in their old age.

Between conference sessions, in the hot hours meant for rest, Margaret visited Bombay's clinics or consulted with physicians and nurses, many of whom had heard her lecture on her first visit. Some had walked miles to attend, with no money for their keep. As his only sustenance for the day, one doctor gratefully devoured a gift of fruit in her room.

At the final session, the conference fulfilled its purpose by organizing the International Planned Parenthood Federation. Whatever happened to her, Margaret Sanger knew that now there would be a force to carry on. Remote, impoverished nations would not have to pioneer in isolation. In the future a permanent organization would encourage the work, pool experience and to some extent, resources. She had said, "We can," when others had said, "Impossible!" She had said, "We must," when others had wanted to relax. If she had been arbitrary, nevertheless, it was her vision, her persistence, her financing that had achieved the organization.

Sailing for home, Margaret Sanger enjoyed a personal satisfaction. In spite of her erratic physical self, she had fulfilled her schedule. In the next eight years she would continue her global travels, but with mounting difficulties. Friends thought her foolish to take such risks, but their cautious advice may have been basically wrong. She lived longer and more strenuously than most women, including her three sisters, none of whom had started with the handicap of tuberculosis.

In the last fourth of her life she was hospitalized for gall bladder, appendicitis, coronary thrombosis, and twice for pneumonia, once with a double virus and pleurisy. She suffered from recurrent pleurisy, lumbago, bursitis, sacroiliac strain and insomnia. And yet during this period her achievements were monumental. Throughout her life she did much that was bad for her health, but by focusing on her work, she not only subdued her bodily pains, but continued to keep her commitment, which was the source of her vitality.

The paramount concern of Margaret Sanger's last years was the development of a physiological contraceptive. On her return from the Soviet Union in 1934 she had hoped for an American spermatoxin, similar to the suppressed Russian one. She had even secured a grant from a foundation for a few experiments on laboratory animals at the University of Pennsylvania, but soon afterward other approaches seemed superior.

In 1936 Carl C. Hartman, known for his classic study of the reproductive system of the opossum, published *The Time of Ovulation in Women.* This established the role of the hormones and endocrine system in human reproduction. In his last working years Dr. Hartman tested oral contraception on animals. After the war, younger men began to study progesterone, a female hormone secretion triggered by ovulation.

As research inched along, Margaret Sanger nearly burst with impatience. The historian Toynbee rightly pointed out that man was "godlike in planned breeding of plants and animals, but rabbitlike in unplanned breeding of ourselves." The United States government not only poured out millions annually for farm research, but had recently spent two billion on a crash program to produce the atomic bomb for mass destruction. Not one cent would it give to research in human fertility control.

Not being a scientist, Margaret never presumed to say that an oral contraceptive was the answer to rabbitlike breeding. Actually, she thought in terms of a vaccine or hypodermic given under medical supervision with an immunization lasting months instead of hours. But in her major concern she recognized that her only part was to channel funds to those equipped to make the decisions.

During the twenties, Noah's fortune had underwritten many important innovations, but in her old age, when her interests had become global, as well as scientifically revolutionary, she had to depend on others for finances. She became the propulsive force that brought together funds and the needed skills. The wealthy women whom she had drawn into her movement sustained her venturesome ideas. Two of her closest friends even carried some of her own heavy expenses for extended travel and secretarial aid. Dorothy Dick and Ellen Watumull of Hawaii both controlled the grants of small foundations, set up in the names of their respective and late husbands.

Most of the large funds for special projects originated in the Santa Barbara home of Mrs. Stanley McCormick. Increasingly Margaret spent her summers in her friend's guest house. The climate suited her, but more important, Mrs. McCormick's drawing room was a meeting place of generous donors, including Amy Du Pont and Mrs. John Rockefeller. However, the sum of their contributions was a pittance compared to that of their hostess.

Kate Dexter McCormick was no ordinary rich widow, nor was she interested in ordinary philanthropy. Daughter of a well-known Chicago lawyer, she had earned a B.S. degree in biology in 1904 from the Massachusetts Institute of Technology. She was the second woman to graduate there. That same year she married the youngest son of Cyrus McCormick, founder of the International Harvester Company. Her dazzling prospects were shattered almost at once when her husband developed schizophrenia. For the rest of her long life Kate McCormick lived half recluse and eccentric, dressed in the old-fashioned styles of her youth, but dispensing funds with the utmost discrimination to a few "unpopular" projects, such as research into the causes of schizophrenia. That study revealed an imbalance of adrenal hormones in those afflicted. Mrs. McCormick's one continuing concern was birth control, to the importance of which Margaret's imprisonment in 1917 had "awakened" her.

Soon after World War II, Stanley McCormick died and the key scientists involved in his wife's research program joined a new institution, the Worcester Foundation for Experimental Biology. There, Gregory Pincus, a world authority on mammalian reproduction, began studies on the role of the internal chemical messengers called steroid hormones. Margaret Sanger came to believe that no living scientist was better equipped than he to make the break for which she waited. In an interview, she found him eager to start the work, if assured sufficient funds. But the continuing cost, after a first outlay for a suitable laboratory and animal house, would be incalculable. Margaret sounded out some of the large foundations, but when she was rebuffed, she turned again to Mrs. McCormick.

Besides her interest in the subject, there were two persuasive factors. Mrs. McCormick already respected the scientists at Worcester and her early academic training gave her the unique vision to invest in biochemical research. Still, she was not impulsive. Since the proposal would take capital funds for an indefinite period, she asked her lawyer, W. H. Bemis, to sit in with her during a week's conference at Santa Barbara in 1952, while Margaret Sanger presented the case for a crash program.

In a letter of April 15, 1969, Hudson Hoagland, the first director of the Worcester Foundation, states that in the early fifties Dr. Pincus was not working on anything corresponding to the pill, but on basic research. "The government would give us nothing for work on antifertility compounds nor would philanthropic foundations, both for the same political reason—fear of the Catholics." "Had not Mrs. McCormick come to our rescue financially," he stated unequivocably, " 'the pill' would not have been developed. It was a direct growth of her financial aid."

The object of the proposed research was to develop an agent that would stop the production of mature egg cells, just as natural hormones block ovulation during pregnancy. Dr. Pincus directed the work, but two others are linked with him as "fathers" of the pill. Dr. M. C. Chang made the laboratory observations of the effects of various man-made steroids on animals. Dr. John Rock then tried out the more promising steroids on volunteers at the Free Hospital for Women in Brookline. Dr. Rock, a noted obstetrician and gynecologist, was also a devout Catholic, but believing that the pill was "an adjunct of nature," conformed to Catholic theology.

A letter from Dr. Rock gives a tantalizing glimpse of those who might be called the "mothers" of the pill. Before he started his Brookline experiments, Dr. Rock was one day expecting a call from Mrs. McCormick, whom he understood might pay the costs for his work. For a wealthy patroness, he thought her "dowdy" in her antique style. Doubtless she was also intense, as Dr. Hoagland described her, but she let her "livelier" companion do most of the talking. It was some time before he realized that the second lady was Margaret Sanger.

In the ensuing years, according to Dr. Pincus, the pill was more widely tested than any drug in history. After the Brookline tests, it was used on thousands of volunteers in Puerto Rico, Haiti and Los Angeles. It would be some years before the pill was on the market.

At a Stockholm meeting in 1953, Margaret was elected president of the International Federation, entailing much travel, with three more trips to Japan. Shidzue, now Senator Kato at the top of what she called the "political seesaw," arranged for her mentor to be the first foreigner to address the Japanese Senate. Margaret urged that the government subsidize the 53,000 native midwives to teach birth control, a policy which was soon adopted. On this visit an admirer described her at a garden party as "pretty as a picture with a cartwheel hat on a head of soft curls and the most sincere and dear face one could imagine." At that time Margaret Sanger was seventy-five years old.

In the midst of her round of activities, she had time to consider the second generation of Katos, and invited Sumiko, Mr. Kato's daughter, to spend a season in her home, following her stepmother's precedent of learning spoken English in secretarial courses. Sumiko, a bright and charming girl, accepted, and she later used her new skills to translate her hostess's *Autobiography* for a Japanese edition. She also returned the American hospitality by taking the Sanger girls into her home when they once crossed the Pacific with their busy grandmother.

The tour of all tours came in 1959. Like Sarah Bernhardt, Margaret Sanger had returned repeatedly to Japan with undiminished luster and escalating honors. The real farewell was highlighted by news surpassing any contrived ceremonies. It was the record of the nation. In less than a decade, Japan had cut its birth rate by more than 50 per cent. The crowded islands had become the world's proof that family planning worked. Furthermore, the practice of contraception was gaining over that of abortion.

The goal of her last trip was New Delhi, which offered Margaret a supreme moment. As usual, she had been filled with apprehension. "I have been planning and hoping," she wrote to Margaret Sanger II, "to be well enough to come on the long air trip to attend the Sixth International Family Planning Conference in this city." Without the constant attention of her companion, she conceded that it might have been impossible. Instead, it was "an historical event in my life and joyous." Prime Minister Nehru made it so.

Often brusque with Anglo-Saxons, he had neither the saintliness nor the eccentricities of Gandhi. A man of the twentieth century, his commonsense grasp of India's needs was the same as Margaret's. They also shared the bond of those who had set their lives in jeopardy for their commitments.

"He bent over me," she wrote her granddaughters, "and said, 'It is wonderful that you come to us from so far away.' Then he offered me his arm and together we walked into the great auditorium, facing hundreds of camera shots and newsmen."

It was a picture, Nehru with patrician air and features escorting a frail figure with eager eyes and unrepentant copper-tinted hair. She was eighty, ten years his senior—but no one guessed it.

"I had to speak from the platform," her letter went on, "and I said that Mr. Nehru was the greatest living statesman in all the world. So it is a great victory for our cause and I am happy that I came." She enclosed three snapshots of the two "talking and talking. . . . Be sure to hold these forever," she admonished.

Two years earlier she had tried to resign as international president, and now she insisted on doing so. She accepted the title of founder and president emeritus. At the last session the assembly passed a resolution that said in part, "Through her indomitable courage, her steadfast dedication and her great vision for nearly half a century, Margaret Sanger has seen her mission come to fruition in the development of national organizations united in the International Federation and the governmental acceptance of family planning in several countries. The 750 delegates and observers from twenty-seven countries assembled at this conference offer to Margaret Sanger their deep admiration, affection and gratitude."

They also presented *Our Margaret Sanger,* two volumes of reminiscences, impressive for the depth of feeling of most of the eighty contributors. She had "reoriented the lives" of men and women from New York to Texas, from Hawaii to Hong Kong, Singapore, India, Germany, and England. Some talked of love at first sight and of their astonishment to find a great leader so small, winsome, and unassuming. They stressed her delight in all that added "to the joy and laughter of life" and noted her "elasticity" of thought and open-mindedness toward any rational opinion. Others, including members of her family, told of her many-faceted kindnesses.

There was a young brother, for whom she had "opened up the

world," there was Ethel Byrnes's daughter, Olive Richard, who found in her aunt the empathy she sorely needed and there was "Old Faithful," whose happiness for nearly forty years rested on her relationship with Margaret Sanger and her sons.

Above all, the volumes memorialized a great soul. Because she lived the truth as she saw it, she had continued to grow. Not only did she bring out the best in others, but she had the capacity to lift people above their "narrow, personal concerns to a universal, expanded view." To experience her friendship was life-enhancing, even exciting.

As a public figure, she was not quite through. Before the close of 1959, she challenged the nation's executive to a debate. President Eisenhower had requested a study of the military assistance program to be made by General William H. Draper, Jr. Because the latter found that the economic gains of many impoverished countries were canceled by their population growth, he recommended that the United States, on request, should help other nations to curb their growth. After first agreeing, the President was flooded by so many Catholic protests that he backed away, suppressing the report on the ground that such aid was "not our business."

Octogenarian Margaret Sanger announced that the President's views should be "straightened out" and she would be glad to straighten them. Nothing came of her challenge, except that experts corroborated her views. India's ambassador to the United States explained that although the United States had given his country $3 billion since independence, it could not help much because of the rise in the birth rate. The world had recognized "the danger of atomic explosion; now let it recognize the other explosion."

In 1960 Margaret Sanger's alarm erupted a final time. Although a Protestant President had vetoed the Draper Report, a Catholic President might veto the progress of the last half century. She was suffused with bitter memories—the Town Hall raid, the raids on her two clinics, the ban on the St. Louis theater, and all of the other bans, including her story on the Mike Wallace show recently canceled on the pressure of two priests.

One day she announced that if the Democratic candidate won, she would leave the country. This time she backtracked. Soon after John

F. Kennedy became President, he rescued the Draper Report from the trash can. If nations asked for help in curbing their growth, he said that his administration would give it.

Within three years a Sponsors Council for the Planned Parenthood-World Federation was headed by two former presidents, Harry Truman and Dwight Eisenhower. The latter had the grace to announce that "Once as President, I thought and said that birth control was not the business of our federal government. The facts changed my mind. . . . I have come to believe that the population explosion is the world's most critical problem. In some areas it is smothering economic growth; it can threaten world peace. Millions of parents in our country—hundreds of millions abroad—are still denied the clear human right of choosing the number of children they will have. Governments must act and private citizens must cooperate urgently through voluntary means to secure this right for all peoples. Failure would limit the expectations of future generations to abject poverty and suffering and bring down upon us history's condemnation."

Thanks to "the pill," released for general use in 1960, the spread of birth control was greatly accelerated. From some thousands of volunteers, the numbers using it had quickly jumped to more than 6,500,000 American women—one out of every five in the childbearing years—and to 5,000,000 women in other parts of the world. Here at last seemed complete assurance against pregnancy and in a form easy to take and acceptable. Some medical and lay journals pronounced it the "perfect contraception," but from the start there were dissenters, including Dr. Pincus and Dr. Chang. Better than others, they knew that their product could be improved. It was burdensome to take daily and too expensive for the poor. Before the pill was on the market, they were starting tests to perfect it. Before reports came in of bad side effects on some women, they were working on a new approach, the "morning after" pill. Here the goal was to expel the fertilized egg before it became implanted in the uterus. Among its many assets was the fact that using fewer hormones and aiming at a single target, it would be less likely to upset any bodily functions.

In all the floods of publicity about the famous pills, one story was never told, that of the two old ladies, both well along in their seventies, who conceived and financed the Worcester project. In turn, this launched what has been called a worldwide sociomedical revolution. Mrs. McCormick had a passion for anonymity, but Dr. Hoagland states that her gifts to the Worcester Foundation alone, were around two million dollars. There was another $160,000 for Dr. Rock's experiments.

A few weeks before Mrs. McCormick died, at ninety-two in 1967, she reversed the usual procedures to thank Dr. Hoagland for accepting her help. It had been a great privilege, she said, to use her money for a successful cause in which she deeply believed. Along with five million for Planned Parenthood, she left another million to the Worcester Foundation, although Dr. Pincus's death had preceded hers by several months.

Early in the sixties, Margaret Sanger grew very old and feeble. Sometimes crowds still came to see her, as did a national convention. Informed that the archaeologists meeting in Tucson had received no official welcome, she, who had arranged so many conferences, invited the 150 delegates to cocktails. Enthroned on a small settee, regal in a hostess gown, crowned with her copper-colored curls, she enthralled her guests as she chatted with them in groups of twenty.

In 1961 Julian Huxley, now Sir Julian, headed a New York lunch, publicized as A World Tribute to Margaret Sanger. She was presented with a princely gift of $100,000 for the expansion of her work. But there uniquely, her life-long terror of public speaking conquered the once invincible trouper. Grant had to make the response.

In 1966 a thousand gathered in her adopted Tucson to hail "The Woman of the Century." Having learned her lesson, she let Stuart represent her, while she stayed home. Home? Well, with her bad heart and arteriosclerosis, her son had moved her to a nursing establishment. She had resisted, as an aging queen would resist exile from the autonomy of her own palace for confinement in a dismal, alien cell. Her bereavement was partly assuaged by a second move to a better nursing home where she was surrounded by her own furniture and endowed with a kitchenette, in which Daiquiris or tea might be provided for her guests.

Visitors came from all parts of the country, for she had seldom broken with a friend. Former staff members and volunteers in her cause kept the rare loyalty of comrades in arms. Together they had once faced danger and won through to victory. Often they found her alert, even gay and ready for a party. Sometimes while they reminisced, the familiar inner flame again illumined her crumpled face.

The incandescent news of her last years was the ruling of the United States Supreme Court on the Connecticut law which made the use of contraceptives a crime. Four decades earlier Margaret Sanger and Kate Hepburn had opened war on this police-under-the-bed statute, as it was known. It had not interfered with the rich, but it had stopped the spread of information to the poor. Twice the Connecticut Court of Errors had upheld the law in sensational cases, one involving the mother of three deformed children, the other a half-paralyzed invalid for whom further pregnancies would be fatal.

Second only in significance to the ruling was the source from which it came, a brief filed as *amicus curiae*. For the third time in mid-twentieth century, distinguished Catholics took the lead in advancing the birth control movement. Dr. Rock, collaborating with Dr. Pincus, had developed the first biochemical contraceptive, "the pill." John F. Kennedy had been the first American President to accept government responsibility in dealing with population problems. Now Catholic lawyers, cooperating with the Catholic Council on Civil Liberties, produced the winning argument. Their brief said that the Connecticut statute unjustifiably invaded the privacy of married couples, depriving them unreasonably of their liberty in violation of the due process clause of the Fourteenth Amendment.

In *Griswold v. Connecticut*, June, 1965, there was unanimous condemnation of the law, although two justices wrote a minority dissent. Seven joined in striking down the law on the grounds that it infringed upon the ancient "right to privacy." The right to privacy! That was what Margaret Sanger had been talking about all the time. The right of women to protect themselves without state interference. Birth control was a personal, not a legal matter. This victory assured a basic freedom by which mankind might rear a better race.

. . . . .

Margaret Sanger died on September 14, 1966, a few days before her birthday. The obituaries said that she was eighty-three years old, but as usual they were wrong about her age. She was nearly eighty-seven.

Paraphrasing what she had written thirty years earlier for Havelock Ellis, gives a fitting epitaph: "A great woman, a beautiful spirit, a world's work done. What more can one ask of life? Finis."

Bibliography

Most of the printed material and correspondence of the early birth control movement are stored in 272 large containers in the Manuscript Division of the Library of Congress. Here, too, are Margaret Sanger's scrapbooks of clippings, personal letters, and bits of an erratically kept journal. The vast amount of later documents, along with more scrapbooks, letters, and jottings from all periods, as well as the files of *The Women Rebel* and *The Birth Control Review,* 1917–1928, are in the Sophia Smith Collection at Smith College.

Paramount to an understanding of Margaret Sanger's life are her own books, after which I list a few others.

By Margaret Sanger

The Practice of Contraception, An Introductory Symposium and Survey, Sanger, Margaret, and Hannah M. Stone (eds.). Williams and Wilkins, 1930.

My Fight for Birth Control. Farrar and Rinehart, 1931.

Margaret Sanger, An Autobiography. W. W. Norton, 1938.

Woman and the New Race. Truth Publishing Co., 1920.

Pivot of Civilization. Brentano, 1922.

Married Happiness. Cromwell Press, 1926.

Motherhood in Bondage. Brentano, 1928.

Other Books

BEARD, MARY, *The Force of Women in Japanese History.* Public Affairs Press, 1953.

BROUN, HAYWOOD, AND MARGARET LEACH, *Anthony Comstock, Roundsman of the Lord.* Albert and Charles Boni, 1927.

BRYANT, KEITH, *The Passionate Paradox* (Life of Marie Stopes). Norton, 1962.

CALDER-MARSHALL, ARTHUR, *The Sage of Sex, A Life of Havelock Ellis.* Putnam, 1959.

COLLIS, JOHN STEWART, *Havelock Ellis, Artist of Life* (A Study of His Life and Work). Sloane Associates, 1959.

DELISLE, FRANÇOISE, *Friendship's Odyssey.* Heinemann, 1946.

DENNETT, MARY WARE, *Birth Control Laws.* F. H. Hitchcock, 1926.

DUVALL, ELIZABETH S., *Hear Me For My Cause,* Selected Letters of Margaret Sanger. The Sophia Smith Collection, Smith College, 1967.

ELLIS, HAVELOCK, *My Life; Autobiography of Havelock Ellis.* Houghton Mifflin, 1939.

GAYN, MARK, *Japan Diary.* William Sloane, 1948.

GOLDBERG, ISAAC, *Havelock Ellis; Biographical and Critical Survey.* Simon and Schuster, 1926.

HERSEY, HAROLD BRAINERD, *Margaret Sanger, Biography of the Birth Control Pioneer.* Pulp Publishing Co., 1938.

ISHIMOTO, SHIDZUE, *Facing Two Ways: The Story of My Life.* Farrar and Rinehart, 1935.

KNOWLTON, CHARLES, *The Fruits of Philosophy; or The Private Companion of Young Married People* (1832).

LADER, LAWRENCE, *The Margaret Sanger Story.* Doubleday, 1955.

LUHAN, MABEL DODGE, *Movers and Shakers.* Harcourt, Brace & World, 1936.

MAUDE, AYLMER, *Life of Marie Stopes.* London: Williams and Norgate, 1924.

MALTHUS, THOMAS R., *Essay on the Principle of Population.* First edition, 1798; revised second edition, 1803.

Our Margaret Sanger. Watumull Foundation, 1959.

PETERSON, HOUSTON, *Havelock Ellis, Philosopher of Love.* Houghton Mifflin, 1928.

STOPES, MARIE, *Contraception.* Putnam, 1931.

———, *Married Love.* Putnam, 1918.

TRUMBULL, C. G., *Anthony Comstock, Fighter.* Revell, 1913.

WEBB, BEATRICE, *Our Partnership.* Longmans, Green, 1948.

WELLS, H. G., *The Passionate Friends.* Harper & Row, 1913.

———, *Socialism and the Family.* Fabian Club Lecture, 1906.

Index

Wise Parentage (Stopes), 152
Wobblies. *See* International
    Workers of the World
Women and the New Race
    (Sanger), 118, 136, 138–139
Woman Rebel, The, 41, 49–56, 59,
    61, 88, 128, 133
Women's Marquette League, 192
Women's Peace Conference, 82
Worcester Foundation for

Experimental Biology,
    254–255, 260
World Population Conference, 2,
    215

Yarros, Dr. Rachel, 186
Y.M.C.A., New York, 45
Young Reconstruction League, 163